GHANA—THE ROAD TO INDEPENDENCE

GHANA

THE ROAD TO INDEPENDENCE
1919–1957

F. M. BOURRET

University of the Sacred Heart
Tokyo, Japan

STANFORD UNIVERSITY PRESS
STANFORD, CALIFORNIA
LONDON: OXFORD UNIVERSITY PRESS

This is a revised edition of The Gold Coast, *which was first published by the Stanford University Press in 1949. A previous revised edition was published in 1952 as Publication No. 23 of the Hoover Library on War, Revolution, and Peace*

PREFACE

On 6 March 1957 the former Gold Coast colony came to the end of its road to independence and celebrated its entry into the family of autonomous nations as the state of Ghana. The world, which is showing an ever-increasing consciousness of African affairs, has evinced much interest in this new state, the first British colony in tropical Africa to become a self-governing nation. Such interest is all to the good for both exact knowledge and sympathetic understanding are essential if the older nations are to assist these new states in a peaceful sharing of the full life of the free world. The recognition of this situation supports the need for the careful study of both the African continent as a whole and of each separate division with its complexity of individual characteristics and problems. A case study of one of these emergent states where a step by step working out of policy can be seen in detail is often more helpful than theoretical discussions and avoids the dangers of sweeping generalizations. This book is an attempt to provide such a survey of Ghana. The new nation is a comparatively small area with only about four and a half million inhabitants, but the Ghanaians are an intelligent people who are facing with vigour the basic problem of adjustment to modern conditions. Their territory is one of the richest and most promising of West Africa, and it is already evident that they will exercise much influence in the future destiny of the continent.

If world opinion has found much to praise in the conduct of the new state of Ghana, it has also found matter for blame—although it must be acknowledged that it has not always done so with an understanding of the issues at stake. A study of the pre-independence history of Ghana, while throwing light on the difficulties of the present situation can at the same time, reveal something of the country's culture and basic traditions. It can make clear the policies followed by the British colonial authorities and the challenging problems which the people of Ghana had to meet as they forged ahead on their journey to independent statehood. The new edition of this book, after giving a rapid survey of the historical background covers in more detail the twentieth-century story of the old Dependency and that most interesting phase from 1948 to 1957 when the Gold Coast, under the leadership of Dr. Kwame Nkrumah, greatly speeded its political advance. Thus the reader is able to follow, step by step, one of the most important and interesting developments of our century, the gradual emergence of an African colony into the full responsibility of autonomous existence.

The earlier years of Gold Coast history are of special importance in explaining the regional tensions which the Ghana government has had to face. A nation which comes to existence in an area which was previously divided into numerous sections and tribes—many of which had conflicting though often admirable traditions—must undoubtedly suffer from such tensions. The former Dependency was divided into four administrative sections: the coastal area, which was the first to come into contact with European traders and therefore developed a certain sophistication and ease with the ways of the world; Ashanti, with its highly organized kingdom and its memory of military victories over the coastal tribes; Togoland, a former German colony, and finally the Northern Territories, far in the hinterland and the most primitive of all in social and economic development. Only when the reader sees the full implication of these area differences can he realize the greatness of the problem. The early chapters of this study discuss these differences and describe in great detail how, by means of indirect rule, the British tried to preserve the native and traditional institutions from disintegrating influences. Their support of native administrations may have tended to preserve tribal divisions and therefore was, to some extent, responsible for Ghana's present concern for political unity. Looked at from another point of view, however, it can be seen that British policy, through its creation of certain common administrative and economic institutions, did much to develop in the Gold Coast something of a national viewpoint.

In addition to this problem of sectional tensions Ghana faces other difficulties which are also connected with her earlier history. Though the colonial systems of central and local government gave valuable political opportunities to those who took part in them, this group was a limited one and the people as a whole had no opportunity to grow in that degree of civic maturity which seems necessary for the success of a full parliamentary régime. No one knows yet what type of government Ghana may eventually develop, but it seems likely that it will have certain characteristics which are peculiarly African. Owing to the strong position of the Convention People's Party and to the weakness of the opposition group it is possible that some sort of 'limited or directed democracy' may keep control in Ghana for a number of years to come. It is therefore important to understand the nature of these varying interests and of the traditional usages which Ghana has inherited from the past. In their haste to develop economic resources, underdeveloped countries can easily be led to sacrifice democratic processes in order to attain modern prosperity and security. But such a policy would tend to stifle the normal activity and growth which are the very life of the nation. The foundations of true nationality lie in such living forces as language, culture, religious and spiritual ties which tend to show certain local variations at the very time that they mingle and coalesce to form that new thing which is a national consciousness. It is a very challenging assignment for young states to build up a strong and clearly recognized central authority, and at the same time to preserve a respect for individuality, for minority views, and an appreciation for the spiritual as well as the material values of life. Intermediate groups having their foundation in the varying interests of family, school, labour and religious institutions, &c., should be encouraged because they can make a valuable contribution to national life and can be barriers against the possible development of authoritarianism. From the exuberance of a true people, bound together in both local and national concerns, an abundant life will be diffused into the state and all its organs, making it conscious of its own responsibility and giving it a true instinct for the common good.

If the history of Ghana is important for an understanding of that country, it is also helpful for the other sections of the continent which often have similar problems. It seems clear, moreover, that Ghana's influence and example will be important factors in the future development of Africa. As the continent's pace of advance quickens it is becoming more and more evident that a correct understanding of both background problems and current situations is essential if the maturer states of the world are to give the right kind of sympathy, support, and material aid to the emerging states of the new Africa.

The primary sources on which this work is based are the publications of the Gold Coast and British governments and debates of the Gold Coast Legislative bodies. Use has also been made of Gold Coast newspapers, publications and propaganda material of the political parties and reports of various African societies dedicated to the further development of the country. I was fortunate in having the manuscript read by several authorities who have had long experience in Gold Coast affairs, either in official capacity or in African political groups. I am most grateful for their criticism and suggestions and regret that I cannot express my appreciation in a more specific manner. Throughout the planning and writing of this survey I have had the encouraging help of Professor Carl Fremont Brand of Stanford University and of Professor Harold Fisher, former chairman of the Hoover Institute and Library.

The Hoover Library has an excellent collection of Gold Coast documents and with few exceptions, the materials quoted are from this source. It is a pleasure to acknowledge the courtesy and devotedness of the Hoover and Stanford library staffs, and especially of Miss Nina Almond, Mr. Philip McLean, Miss Minna Stillman and the late Mrs. Ruth R. Perry. I wish also to express my great indebtedness to Mr. Patrick Hulede, formerly of the Achimota Training College and the Kumasi College of Technology, whose untiring interest in searching for manuscript material and in collecting African publications has been invaluable to me.

I am grateful to Professor Fage of London University, late of the University College, Ghana, for his help in revising the early chapters of this book and to Mr. David Kimble of the Department of Extra-Mural Studies, to Mr. Emil Rado of the University College, Ghana, and to Professor David Apter of the University of Chicago for their advice on Chapters X and XI.

F.M.B.

Tokyo
   12 April 1960

FOREWORD TO FIRST EDITION

The Gold Coast has been in contact with Europe since the beginning of modern times, but modern times in the Gold Coast began only a few generations ago.

A decade before his discovery of America Columbus visited the rocky surf-swept Gold Coast. He helped adventurous Portuguese who built the grim fortress of São Gorge. Other fortresses rose along the Guinea Coast to give shelter to traders of half a dozen nations who came to these shores for gold, ivory, and pepper. Later the need for labour in the West Indian and American colonies made trade in human beings more profitable than the luxury goods of the earlier days. For two centuries the slave trade flourished until, in the nineteenth century, the conscience of the Western world decisively aided by changing economic interests first condemned, then outlawed, and finally ended this shameful traffic.

The Gold Coast did not lose contact with the outside world, for it possessed natural resources suited to the requirements of the new industries and the expanded trade of the power age. The demand for palm-oil, for example, greatly increased, and the Gold Coast could produce it in large quantities. The most spectacular growth was in the cocoa industry. In 1891 the Gold Coast exported 80 pounds of cocoa; forty years later the export was 300,000 tons.

There has always been a market for gold, which, as its name suggests, the Gold Coast possesses. New industrial processes have created a market for industrial diamonds, manganese, and bauxite, which are also found in this territory.

From the first trading ventures down to the beginning of the nineteenth century, Europeans treated the Gold Coast as they treated so many other outlandish places, as a region where profits could be made by exchanging European manufactured goods for more valuable human and natural materials. Traders of several nations engaged in this trade without fighting about sovereignty over the area. Gradually, however, the British established their ascendancy and assumed responsibility for regulating relations between Europeans and Africans.

Since 1874, when Great Britain formally annexed the Gold Coast as a colony, educational and political institutions have developed in the rhythm of such developments in the empire. In recent years, and especially in the period covered by this monograph, the tempo of development has been tremendously increased.

The Gold Coast has become, first economically, and later politically a part of the world community. The economic well-being of its people has been linked to the world market, and their prosperity depends on the economic health of Western Europe and America. The security of the Gold Coast people is no longer a hazard of war between the Ashanti and Fanti tribes or between Africans and British. The security of the Gold Coast depends, as World War II demonstrated, on peace between Germans and British, Russians and Americans, Japanese and Chinese.

With the dependence on the world community for well-being and security, there has also developed a demand for the right of participation in that community, not as a second-class member or, as the current usage has it, as a non-self-governing territory, but as a self-governing, full-fledged member of the community of nations.

The transition of regions like the Gold Coast—and there are many—from colonial status to independence and self-government, at a time when the security of all regions depends more and more on the recognition of inter-dependence and the surrender of full sovereignty, is one of the most important and interesting problems of these times.

Dr. Bourret has told with great clarity and sympathy the story of how one non-self-governing territory has moved from dependency towards self-government under the tutelage of the government that has had the most experience in guiding this historical process. The problems and the achievements of British imperial policy since World War I are reflected in the story of one of the smaller but most interesting members of the empire. This story is a contribution to our understanding of one of the most significant and complex issues of our generation.

HAROLD H. FISHER

STANFORD UNIVERSITY, CALIFORNIA
February 1949

CONTENTS

MAP

GHANA—THE ROAD TO INDEPENDENCE

CHAPTER I

THE LAND AND THE PEOPLE

The state of Ghana, until 1957 known as the Gold Coast, lies midway on the Guinea littoral of West Africa. The usually accepted limits of West Africa are the Senegal River on the west and the Cameroons on the east, while the Sahara forms a convenient boundary to the north. From the geographical point of view the divisions of this vast territory are latitudinal: first, a band of humid tropical forest which is interrupted near the coast by areas of mangrove and savannah; second, a wooded savannah to the north; and third, a dry, treeless savannah stretching far into the interior where it eventually merges into the Sahara.

In spite of these horizontal zones, the political divisions, along the Guinea Coast, cut directly across them. They have been likened 'to a terrace of narrow houses some closely walled-in at the rear, others—the French colonies—opening on to a vast court, the well-nigh limitless hinterland of the Western Sudan'.[1] The Gold Coast was one of these 'walled-in' colonies, situated between 3° 15' W. longitude and 1° 12' E. longitude, with the French Ivory Coast to the west, the French Mandate of Togoland to the east, the Upper Volta district of the French Sudan to the north, and the Atlantic Ocean to the south. This type of political division, ignoring as it does both economic and tribal areas, created many difficulties for both the French and British administrations and led, at one time, to some discussion of a possible federation of existing units.[2]

The term 'Gold Coast', probably first applied to this area in the seventeenth century by the Dutch, came later to include more than just the strip of coast line. The name was given to the entire dependency which included the colony of Ashanti directly to the north and, beyond that, the protectorate of the Northern Territories. Throughout these

[1] Walter Fitzgerald, *Africa, a Social, Economic and Political Geography of Its Major Regions* (New York, 1939), p. 323 (hereafter cited as Fitzgerald, *Africa, a Geography*). Gold Coast Survey Department, *The Atlas of the Gold Coast* (Accra, 1945). D. A. Chapman, *The Natural Resources of the Gold Coast* (Achimota, 1940).
[2] *Parliamentary Debates*, 5th ser., Commons, vol. CCCXCI, cols. 142–3.

1

pages the term 'Gold Coast Dependency'[1] will be used to refer to all three divisions while 'Gold Coast Colony' will be reserved for the section on the littoral only. After World War I a fourth unit, the mandated area of British Togoland, was placed under the administrative control of the governor of the Gold Coast Dependency. The area of the Colony was 23,490 square miles, of Ashanti 24,560, of the Northern Territories 30,600, and of Togoland 13,040—a total of 91,690 square miles.[2]

The population of the Dependency was unevenly distributed, as will be seen in the tabulation given[3] below, which gives population figures according to the 1948 census.

Gold Coast Colony	2,050,235
Ashanti	818,944
Northern Territories	866,503
Togoland	382,768
Total	4,118,450

The geographical and economic characteristics of the several divisions of the Dependency were largely responsible for this unequal distribution of population. Physically the entire territory can be divided into four easily recognized areas—the coastal lands, the Ashanti plateau, the plains of the Volta and its tributaries, and the northern plateau grass-lands.

The coastal lands, averaging from 20 to 40 miles in width and including the greater part of the original colony, contain over half the population of the entire country. This is because most of the important urban centres—Sekondi, Takoradi, Cape Coast, and Accra, the capital —lie within this area.

It is rolling country covered with scrub and grass. The agricultural products include such foodstuffs as cassava, corn, and vegetables. There is also growing interest in citrus fruits and bananas for local use and export. Coco-nut palms—useful for both copra (dry coco-nut) and coco-nut

[1] On 6 March 1957 the Gold Coast Dependency changed its name to 'Ghana'. The term 'Gold Coast' has been retained throughout this narrative, however, since it is concerned with the period prior to independence. Ghana is now divided into five regions: Northern Ghana, Ashanti, Trans-Volta Togoland, Eastern Region, and Western Region. The old divisions have, however, been retained in this narrative.

[2] *Annual Report on the Gold Coast for the Year 1946*, p. 83 (hereafter cited as *G.C. An. Report*). The French and British mandates over Togoland were changed to trusteeships in 1946.

[3] *G.C. An. Report, 1949*, p. 10. In 1957 the estimated population was 4,763,000.

The GOLD COAST

Principal roads
Railways
Cocoa areas
Gold mines

IVORY COAST

Tumu

MAMPRUSSI

Gambaga

UNDER FRENCH TRUSTEESHIP

WA

NORTHERN

Wa

White Volta

DAGOMBA

TERRITORIES

Tamale

UNITED KINGDOM

Yendi

UNITED TRUSTEESHIP

Bole

GONJA

Black Volta

Salaga

KRACHI

Yeji

Kete Krachu

Kintampo

Wenchi

ASHANTI

Sunyani

Mampong

R. Volta

Goaso

Kumasi

Ho

Wiawso

Obuasi

Koforidua

Enchi

Oda

Keta

Dunkwa

Nsawam

GOLD

COAST

Ada

Prestea

Accra

Tarkwa

Winneba

Axim

Cape Coast

Gulf of Guinea

Sekondi

Takoradi

J.F.H.

0   50   100   200   miles   300

[Adapted with permission from Rita Hinden, *Plan for Africa*.
London: George Allen & Unwin.]

oil—grow well on the more level tracts of the coastal zone, especially in the western and eastern parts. Fishing in the Atlantic, in the coastal lagoons, and in the rivers is another occupation of the peoples of this district. That portion of the coast to the west, beyond Cape Three Points, has a far heavier precipitation (up to 100 inches) than the rest of the littoral, and rain forest is dominant. As a result, the population of this western section is less dense, and its economic and social development has been slower than the eastern part.

The Ashanti plateau, as a geographical division, should not be confused with the political section of the same name. They are not coterminous. The plateau contains most of the rain forest of the country which is to be found not only in Ashanti but in the Gold Coast Colony as well. It averages 500 to 1,500 feet above sea-level and has a high rainfall, usually exceeding 50 inches. The forest itself consists of tall, massive trees, often 200 feet in height, whose thickly entangled branches form a green roof overhead, impenetrable by the sun. A network of vines provides so close a vegetation that the heavy rains cannot cause erosion, and thus the rich soil is preserved. The moist, twilight atmosphere within the forest is ideal for the growth of cacao, which requires great humidity and shade. The preservation of the forest is therefore essential to the economic prosperity of the people. Devastation caused by railway building, mining activities, and wasteful agricultural and timber-cutting methods has already made serious inroads on this precious natural heritage. There is evidence, moreover, that the Sudan type of vegetation—which is infinitely less valuable—is gradually moving southward. The creation of forest reserves and systematic reforestation is, then, one of the most serious problems of the country. The Gold Coast Government's attempted solution will be the subject of a later discussion.

The third physical division includes the plains of the Volta River and its tributary, the Black Volta. This stream takes its rise in the French Sudan to the north and runs the full length of the country, emptying into the Gulf of Guinea near Ada, some 60 miles from the eastern frontier. The Black Volta forms the north-western boundary line of the Northern Territories; turning eastward it meets the main stream just north of Ashanti. These plains, then, extend north and north-east of the Ashanti plateau. Their supply of rainfall is low, precarious, and confined to a short season. Population density is under ten on the average, while large areas are completely deserted. There is little agriculture, and cattle raising is prevented by the widespread prevalence of the tsetse fly.

Modern irrigation methods and tsetse clearance could greatly raise the economic value of this poorest section of the country.

The last geographical division, that of the northern plateau grass-lands (500–1,500 feet), has a more dependable rainfall than that of the Volta plains. Its light soil, suitable for agricultural purposes, and its tsetse-free cattle lands make possible some economic prosperity and hence a higher density of population which is as great as 170 per square mile in some parts.

The climate and vegetation of the country are determined by these same physical divisions. The coastal and rain-forest areas have constant heat throughout the year, accompanied, as has been said, by a high degree of humidity except during the winter when the *harmattan*, a dry north-easter from the Sudan, may bring some relief.

The vegetation of the forest belt is, of course, tropical. Besides cocoa, the oil palm, the kola tree, wild rubber, mahogany, and other valuable timber trees provide exportable products. For local consumption yams, plantains, sweet potatoes, beans, and peanuts are also grown. As it is not possible to keep cattle in the forest area, there is an insufficient meat supply. Fishing and hunting only partially remedy this deficiency, and lack of protein is a recognized source of much of the malnutrition found among the inhabitants of the country.

Both the Volta plains and the northern plateau belong to the savannah belt of West Africa and therefore have a Sudan rather than a forest type of climate and vegetation. While there is a high level of temperature throughout the year, the atmosphere is dry instead of moist. In these sections the *harmattan*, with its load of fine sand particles, is dreaded, while it is the moisture-laden monsoon of the summer months which brings the inhabitants the bulk of their rainfall. Whatever precipitation there is is quickly absorbed, however, and the growing season is a very short one. In the most northern parts millet, guinea corn, peanuts, and beans do well. Farther south yams and rice can be added to the local diet. The trees of the savannah grow in open forests or are sometimes widely scattered. Among them the shea tree is highly valued. Its nut, containing a rich fat called shea butter, is used for cooking purposes by the inhabitants.

As for the mountainous areas of the Gold Coast the main features are: (*a*) a range of hills running south-west to north-east from near Accra to Togoland, and (*b*) the steep scarp face of the Ashanti plateau which runs from south-east to north-west.

Of the Volta River and its principal tributary, the Black Volta, something has already been said. The smaller tributaries, the Red Volta and the White Volta, flow from the Sudan into the north-eastern corner of the country. The other rivers are smaller and of less importance than the Volta. Among them it is sufficient to mention the Tano and the Ankobra, in the far western section of Ashanti and the Gold Coast Colony, and the Pra River which forms a portion of the boundary line between these two areas until it turns southward and flows into the Gulf of Guinea near Sekondi. None of the rivers of the Gold Coast are navigable except the Volta, the Tano, and the Ankobra, and even these can only be used by steam launch or lighter in their lower reaches though there is also a certain amount of canoe traffic. The inhabitants, therefore, must depend almost entirely upon railway and motor roads for transportation.

The coast line provides no natural harbours, and, until the 1920's, surf boats and lighters carried all cargo out to the ocean-going vessels, which added to expense and often resulted in salt-water damage to the cocoa and other perishable goods. Since then, harbour facilities have been provided at Takoradi and more recently at Tema. In this need for more extensive communications lies the explanation of the considerable debt which burdened the country for many years.

The natural resources of the Gold Coast can be considered under four heads: agriculture, forestry, livestock, and mining.[1] Among the agricultural exports cocoa holds first place. The Gold Coast produces over one-third of the world's supply. Although no accurate survey has been made, it is estimated that one million acres, or 1,563 square miles, with 400 or more trees to an acre, are devoted to this crop. There is economic danger, however, for a one-crop country; and efforts are being made to stimulate the cultivation of other exports, especially since the cocoa industry has been seriously threatened by the development of 'swollen shoot', a plant disease.

From the magnificent forests of the Gold Coast mahogany and other valuable timbers are cut for both local and foreign use. Rubber is also exported whenever the price in the world market is high enough to make the tapping of the trees profitable.

Cattle raising is successful only in the tsetse-free districts of the north and in a small section on the eastern extremity of the coast. As this does not provide a sufficient meat supply, much importation is necessary. There would be great possibilities for the development of this industry

---

[1] *G.C. An. Report, 1946*, pp. 34–46. Each year the Annual Report contained a full account of the progress in the development of natural resources as well as a survey of the political and social situation in the colony.

if sufficient revenue were available for further cattle breeding and clearance of the tsetse-ridden areas.

Among the mineral resources gold, which gave its name to the Dependency, has been exported to Europe since the arrival of the Portuguese in the fifteenth century. Though accurate statistics are not available it has been very conservatively estimated that between 1483 and 1903 over £21,000,000 worth of gold reached Europe.[1] Since that time the industry has grown considerably and in some years the value of the annual export has reached nearly three-quarters of a million ounces. Its purity gained for it a premium of one shilling to the pound as early as the reign of Charles II and its use for English money was responsible for the name 'guinea' being given to the old 21-shilling piece.

In 1915 large manganese deposits were first discovered. Because of the war, mining was immediately begun, and today Ghana is recognized as possessing one of the world's greatest supplies of this mineral as well as the largest single manganese mine. By the 1950's production had reached over 600,000 tons a year.

The diamond-mining industry, begun in the early 1920's, has now developed to such an extent that Ghana takes third place after the Belgian Congo and South Africa in its supply to the world market. Diamond production in 1956, for example, amounted to 2,539,000 carats.

Large bauxite deposits were discovered in 1921 in the regions south and north-east of Obuasi—a town in southern Ashanti. Further deposits were later found in the western sections of the Northern Territories. The entire supply is now estimated to be over 200,000,000 tons. Prior to World War II lack of suitable transportation had prevented exploitation, but with the outbreak of the conflict the government built a spur line to one of the bauxite deposits and started mining operations. In 1953 thorough investigations were begun to ascertain the possibility of hydro-electric development and aluminium production in the Volta area.

Smaller deposits of other minerals add to the potential wealth of the country. Tin has been located near Winneba, and there are evidences of oil in the area between Axim and Half-Assini on the western littoral.

---

[1] A. W. Cardinall, *The Gold Coast, 1931. A Review of the Conditions in the Gold Coast in 1931, as compared with those of 1921, based on Figures and Facts collected by the Chief Census Officer of 1931 together with a Historical, Ethnographical and Sociological Survey of the People of that Country* (Accra, 1931), p. 76 (hereafter cited as Cardinall, *The Gold Coast, 1931*).

Deposits of limestone and granite and of a high-grade clay suitable for pottery and tile manufacturing also exist.

The native people of this land so rich in natural resources belong, for the most part, to that pure type of Negro which is found in the forest areas of West Africa. Anthropologists believe the peoples of Africa to have been derived from three principal stocks—Bushman, Hamite, and Negro.[1] Due to the wandering of the tribes throughout the centuries, these groups are now somewhat mixed. The Negroes of the southern portion of West Africa, in the area stretching from the Senegal River to the eastern frontier of Nigeria, have been protected by their forests, however, from the invasions of other peoples and have retained, therefore, a purer form of their natural characteristics. Among these characteristics are a dark-brown skin (popularly called black), curly hair, broad nose and wide nostrils, thick lips often everted, and, in the male, a height averaging sixty-eight inches. In West Africa, the Negro usually lives in walled compounds often containing several family groups under the authority of a senior member. They are agricultural, not pastoral, and the hoe rather than the plough is their farming implement. They have achieved a high development of arts and crafts. Politically, every degree of centralization or lack of it is found among them, as will be seen in a later discussion.

In contrast to the pure Negro of the forest belt is the Negroid type of the Sudan. There the open character of the savannah vegetation made possible the southward movement of the Hamites of the Sahara and of North Africa. As a result of the mingling of Negro and Hamitic peoples a less pure type has resulted. Members of this group are taller and have lighter skins, more aquiline noses, and narrower nostrils than the forest Negro. These characteristics become even more pronouncedly Hamitic in the northern parts towards the Sudan. When living in tsetse-free areas, these people sometimes turn to pastoralism, although they often keep their agricultural habits as well. In some sections the influence of Islam has been very strong, while other groups have resisted any Muslim encroachment.

The population of West Africa, then, can be divided roughly into two great groups—the pure Negro of the forest area and the Negroid type of the Sudan. In the Gold Coast we find this same division—the Akan-, Ewe-, and Gã-speaking peoples of the south are Negroes, whereas the

---

[1] Lord Hailey, *African Survey: A Study of Problems arising in Africa South of the Sahara* (London, 1938), p. 18. C. G. Seligman, *Races of Africa* (London, 1930), p. 19.

peoples of the Mossi-Dagomba states in the Northern Territories are Negroid. There are, of course, areas where the two types have intermingled and characteristics are less clear-cut.[1]

It is probable that, in most cases, the present peoples of the country were not the original inhabitants. Tradition, which can in many cases be substantiated by what we know of the early history of West African kingdoms, holds that the Akans were the first group to migrate into the Gold Coast. Driven southward by the pressure of Hamitic tribes to the rear, they came down from the north-west. During the period between the fourteenth and seventeenth centuries, three successive waves of Akans entered the forest area of Ashanti and the plains of the Volta with some tribal groups penetrating to parts of the coast itself. Originally they may have been a nomadic, pastoral people but the character of the land they settled in determined a shift to agricultural pursuits. These Akans fall into two great groups, the Twi-Fanti group which is found principally on the coast and in the forest area, and the Twi-Guang group which settled on the plains of the Volta and the Black Volta. Many Akan tribes developed centralized yet democratic forms of government in which a paramount chief with his council rules over large areas of land. Outstanding among these was the Ashanti confederacy, a highly organized group of states which dominated much of the Gold Coast Dependency during the eighteenth and nineteenth centuries until its power was broken by the British. The Akans, moreover, often possess marked trading ability, and many of the Fanti on the coast served as middlemen between the European merchants and tribes of the hinterland, and were later to be largely responsible for the remarkable development of the cocoa industry of the twentieth century.

The second set of invaders probably belonged to a group which came originally from the north-east and which eventually organized the Mossi-Dagomba states of the upper Volta area. By conquest and peaceful penetration they established themselves as rulers over the original inhabitants of this region which included parts of the north and eastern sections of the present Northern Territories and Togoland. The

[1] There are many small tribal divisions in the Gold Coast and over fifty languages or dialects. The treatment given in this section follows the work that has been done in recent years by various anthropologists and ethnologists. Their study is far from complete, however, and further research may reveal other classifications. Moreover, this discussion considers only the outstanding linguistic groups, as it is believed sufficient for the purpose of a general historical survey. Further details can be found in the excellent articles which appear from time to time in *Africa, Journal of the International Institute of African Languages and Cultures,* as well as in separate monographs. See, for example, R. S. Rattray, *The Tribes of the Ashanti Hinterland* (Oxford, 1932), 2 vols.; *Gold Coast Atlas,* 1945.

Mamprussi and Dagomba states of today both share in the common origin of the Mossi-Dagomba group. During the invasions most of the original chiefs were killed, but in some areas—where the invaders were not so strong—their rightful heirs were allowed to assume positions of religious authority, while the foreign conquerors kept political control. Thus a double set of rulers was established. The holder of the sacerdotal office, known as the *tendana*, was priest of the earth-god and as such retained some power and control over the land. These people have successfully resisted all Muslim invasions and have preserved their original animistic belief, which they share, in its principal tenets, with the other tribes to the south. Though the 1931 census recorded 54,662 Muslims for the entire Gold Coast, the majority were so in name only.

South of the rain forest and to the east, the Gã- and Ewe-speaking peoples are found. These tribes appear to have migrated thither from the east during the seventeenth and later centuries, coming from various parts of what is now Nigeria, and by a series of stages moving westwards to their present home.

The British mandate of Togoland presents, in almost every case, the same ethnic classifications as does the Gold Coast proper, for the international boundary along the Volta and Daka rivers is merely an arbitrary one drawn with no reference to tribal groupings. Thus we find representatives of the Mamprussi, Dagomba, Gonja, Akan, and Ewe peoples on both sides of the frontier. The union of the two territories under a single administration has, in many instances, reunited tribes which had been split by the former Anglo-German divisions. There are other instances, however, where the problem is still unsolved, and portions of some Gold Coast tribes are to be found in the French territories of Dahomey, Togoland, the Upper Volta, and the Ivory Coast.

Besides the languages of the Kwa unit (Akan, Gã, Ewe, &c.) and the Gur unit (Mole and Dagbane—linguistic equivalent of Mossi-Dagomba-Mampelle, &c.) there are a number of smaller language groups, some of whose languages, especially in eastern Togoland, appear to be quite distinct from those of the major groupings.

Negroes of Hausa and Fulani stock, usually Muslim in name at least, are found scattered throughout the towns and along the trade routes of the country, and are almost invariably engaged in commercial undertakings.

It can be seen there was only some degree of correspondence between political and linguistic divisions. Thus all the Mossi-Dagomba peoples were found in the Northern Territories, or in the northern province of Togo, which areas had been united under one administration.

On the other hand, the Twi-Fanti groups were divided between the Gold Coast Colony and Ashanti, and the Twi-Guang between Ashanti and the Northern Territories. In both cases, however, the frontiers respected the integrity of the lesser tribal divisions. These were so numerous that the Gold Coast Colony contained sixty-three different native states, Ashanti twenty-five, and the Northern Territories twenty-one. Thus it is evident that though several groups may have spoken the same or closely allied languages, they were often politically autonomous.

For administrative purposes each of the four sections of the country was subdivided into provinces.[1] The Gold Coast Colony had three—the Western, Central, and Eastern Provinces; Ashanti had two—the Western and Eastern; and the Northern Territories also had two—the Northern and Southern Provinces. Togoland was likewise divided, but its Southern Province was joined as an administrative unit with the Eastern Province of the Gold Coast Colony, while its northern sections were linked with the two provinces of the Northern Territories. The boundaries of the various provinces were so drawn as not to cut across the frontiers of any native state.

There was great similarity in the political institutions of these various native states. Each Akan tribe owed allegiance to a paramount chief elected or enstooled from a definite group of families by a council made up of elders who were heads of important families or the natural aristocrats of the group. The paramount chief was aided in government by divisional chiefs, chiefs, and village headmen and, in theory at least, was not expected to interfere in the internal affairs of these subdivisions. Any Akan chief could be destooled[2] by the people who elected him—a peaceful and democratic method but one which, in practice, led to a certain instability in political affairs. While the institutions of some of the other peoples of the Gold Coast were less compact and less democratic than those of the Akans, they were influenced by their political and military customs. Some of them adopted the idea of a paramount chief and the custom of enstoolment and destoolment.[3]

[1] In 1957, after the Gold Coast became independent, some of these terms and divisions were changed.

[2] The stool embodies the spirit of the tribal ancestors. To be made a chief is to occupy the stool. Hence enstoolment refers to the election of a chief, and destoolment to his removal from office.

[3] For a full discussion of the social and political institutions of the Gold Coast see: R. S. Rattray, *Ashanti Law and Constitution* (London, 1929); K. A. Busia, *The Position of the Chief in the Modern Political System of Ashanti* (London, 1951); M. J. Field, *Akim-Kotoku, An Oman of the Gold Coast* (Accra, 1948); M. Fortes and E. E. Evans-Pritchard, *African Political Systems* (London, 1950); Madeleine Manoukian, *Akan and Ga-Adangme Peoples of the Gold Coast* (London, 1950).

CHAPTER II

THE GOLD COAST BEFORE 1919

Sailors and traders of the ancient world had some slight contact with the Gold Coast, but it was the Portuguese who first made it known to Christian Europe.[1] Early in the fifteenth century these hardy seamen, with the inspiration and support of Prince Henry the Navigator, had courageously dared the unknown and ventured down the West African Coast. By 1434 the dreaded waters of Cape Bojador had been passed and exploration begun in earnest. When Henry died twenty-six years later, much of the Guinea littoral was known, and fortifications and trading posts already marked it as a Portuguese monopoly. In 1471 men in the pay of Fernando Gomes, a merchant with a government monopoly for the trade of the coast south of Sierra Leone, landed on the Gold Coast and obtained from the inhabitants a supply of that precious metal for which the country was later to be named. They called it 'Mina', the mine, so great was the quantity of gold that could be purchased. During the next decade the export of gold-dust and nuggets to the homeland continued. The fame of the place spread and with it came danger of rivals. In 1482 King John II of Portugal sent an expedition under Diego d'Azambuja who was accompanied by Bartholomew Diaz and perhaps by Christopher Columbus, to build a fort—at a place which later came to be called Elmina[2]—as a fortified warehouse and protection against possible interlopers. São Jorge da Mina, St. George of the Mine, was soon completed—the first of that long line of forts which were eventually to be built by European traders, and some of which still dominate the coast line today. In the beginning the merchants from Castille were the principal rivals of the Portuguese, but by the early sixteenth century the French and then the English were venturing down the Guinea Coast. In 1530 William Hawkins traded in Upper Guinea, but in 1553 Thomas

[1] For the early history of the Gold Coast see W. E. F. Ward, *A History of the Gold Coast* (London, 1948); J. W. Blake, *Europeans in West Africa, 1450–1560* (London, 1942) and *European Beginnings in West Africa, 1455–1578* (London, 1937). See J. D. Fage, *An Introduction to the History of West Africa* (Cambridge, 1955) for the relationship of the Gold Coast to West Africa.

[2] See Ralph M. Wiltgen, *Gold Coast Mission History, 1471–1880* (Techny, Illinois, 1956), p. 53, for a discussion of the name 'Elmina'.

Windham ventured farther and was probably the first Englishman to reach the Gold Coast itself. News of commercial profit spread rapidly in Elizabethan England, and before the reign was over Hawkins's son, Sir John, had carried off a shipload of slaves from Sierra Leone to the West Indies, and two chartered companies had obtained monopolies for the trade on the Guinea Coast.

Dutch, Swedes, Danes, and Brandenburgers followed the French and English example, so that eventually forts of half a dozen nations marked their trading posts to east and west of São Jorge. The Dutch, most aggressive of all, succeeded in driving out the Portuguese in 1642 and setting up their own headquarters at Elmina. Though rivalry led to many quarrels among the various European groups—as when the Dutch burnt the English forts in 1664 and 1665—the competition was of a commercial nature and there was not yet any question of opposing territorial or political rights. The unhealthy climate that was later to give the Guinea Coast the name 'white man's grave' had already taken a heavy toll of lives. Traders, as a consequence, came seeking spices, gold, and 'black ivory', but without a view to colonization. This same treacherous climate accounts, to a great extent, for the fact that the men who entered the service of the trading companies were not usually of a type to give good example to the Africans. In the absence of adequate medical knowledge the tropical fevers worked havoc with their constitutions. Heavy drinking and lax morality aggravated the situation. It is not surprising that most men who went to the Gold Coast did so with the conviction that they were never to return.

Across the Atlantic, however, permanent colonies were now being established and the demand for slave labour grew year by year. The early slaving ventures—largely Portuguese[1]—had only been a start. It was not until about 1650 that the English began the annual transport of thousands of Africans to the new world. For a time chartered companies held royal monopolies and built forts wherever commercial need or international rivalries made it necessary. After the Glorious Revolution, however, monopolies became increasingly unpopular, so that the Royal African Company lost its privileges, and the government opened the slave trade to all British citizens alike. During the eighteenth century this trade in 'human raw material' increased yet more. While the merchants of many nations took part, the English had the lead and in some years transported as many as 50,000 slaves.

[1] Papal decrees which forbade slave trading to Catholics were largely ignored. See Wiltgen, *Gold Coast Mission History*, ch. 4.

Though the Royal African Company lost its monopoly, it was still expected, with some government aid, to keep up the English forts as a protection for British citizens. It found difficulty in meeting expenses and was therefore replaced in 1750 by the African Company of Merchants.[1] This new venture was open to any merchant who paid a 40-shilling fee, and resembled the regulated companies of early modern times in that each member traded as an individual, rather than as a part of a corporation. A government subsidy supplied the upkeep of the forts, and the organization remained in control until the early years of the nineteenth century.

By the eve of the French Revolution, only the British, Dutch, and Danes held posts on the Gold Coast proper. The other nations had either confined themselves to other parts of the Guinea littoral or had left the area altogether. Slave trading continued but was beginning to arouse criticism in Europe. On the Continent, philosophers of the eighteenth century preached a doctrine of human equality. In England opposition arose from another quarter. The Quakers, and later the Methodists and Evangelicals, objected to the nefarious traffic for humanitarian and religious reasons. In the 1780's some of these anti-slavery agitators succeeded in getting the British government to consent to a settlement at Sierra Leone for freed slaves. The movement grew. Though delayed by the wars following the French Revolution, parliament, in 1807, finally abolished the slave trade in all British possessions.

This change in the attitude towards slavery was not without its effects on the fortunes of the Gold Coast. The local tribes had co-operated with the Europeans by acting as middlemen in the transfer of slaves from the hinterland. Principal among them were the Fanti. There was a bitter enmity between this tribe and the powerful Ashanti federation to the north. As the British used the Fanti as collaborators, they were to adopt the policy of protecting them against their more warlike northern neighbours. This dependence on a foreign power had weakened the loose alliance which bound the Fanti tribes together, and had lessened their military skill and initiative. They had, moreover, by this time acquired much experience as traders and, relying on English support, were determined to monopolize the southern traffic and force the Ashantis to work through them in all their dealings with the British. In contrast to these coastal peoples, split up into dozens of small native

[1] K. G. Davies, *Royal African Company* (London 1957); E. C. Martin, *British West African Settlements, 1750–1821* (London, 1927).

states, the Ashantis were members of a highly organized military confederacy. During the eighteenth century they succeeded in conquering
some of the surrounding states, from which they henceforth collected
a regular tribute. Their wealth came from this tribute, from the plunder
of war, and from the substantial profits of the slave trade. The Ashanti
merchants could also buy European goods on the coast (firearms, spirits,
textiles, &c.) and sell them at a profit in the protected market of their
own states. The Ashanti expansion, however, was not without its danger
for many of the conquered states resented their defeat and would
remain loyal only as long as the confederacy was powerful. Any stoppage
of the slave trade could lessen Ashanti wealth and seriously endanger
her military position.

The abolition of the slave trade then was not well received by the
Ashanti, nor indeed by any Gold Coast middlemen. In order to earn
a livelihood some of these men were now forced to turn to agriculture
or other occupations. In the following years the value of legitimate
exports somewhat increased, but not sufficiently to make up entirely for
the lost profits of the slave trade, so that the quantity of European
imports soon showed a resultant drop. They declined, for example, from
over £1,500,000 in 1806 to less than £600,000 in 1810.[1] The temptation
to evade the British naval patrol soon suggested itself. American and
even English slavers, built for speed, and flying the Spanish flag, could
sometimes slip past the slower British cruisers. It was only the abolition
of slavery in the Americas (Lincoln's proclamation, 1862; victory of the
North, 1865; Cuba, 1880-6; Brazil, 1883-8) that finally ended the slave
trade across the Atlantic.

On the Gold Coast the African middlemen kept up, as far as possible,
an illicit slave trade, although they would find themselves, as time went
on, forced to rely more heavily on legitimate commerce. At the same
time, the Ashanti invasions of the coastal areas, after 1807, endangered
whatever legitimate trade there was, and also the very existence of the
European forts, which were not in a position to repulse an Ashanti
attack. As a result the British, Danes, Dutch—the only Europeans now
left on the Gold Coast—had to acknowledge Ashanti control over the
Fanti states and in some cases to pay rental for the land on which the
forts stood. But friction continued and under the circumstances conflicts
were bound to result. In the wars which followed—marking the course
of the greater part of the nineteenth century—the Ashantis could easily

[1] W. Walton Claridge, *A History of the Gold Coast and Ashanti* (London, 1915),
vol. 1, p. 283,

have defeated the Fanti had not the British lent their aid to the latter. Once peace was re-established the British returned to the inexpensive policy of non-interference in native affairs. As will be seen later, the British statesmen of the time were influenced in their policy, on the one hand, by a desire to keep expenses as low as possible in maintaining the West African settlements; and on the other hand, by the arguments of the traders, missionaries, and leaders of anti-slavery movement, who claimed that government support was necessary for the protection of their activities. These conflicting aims had a marked effect on British policy towards the Gold Coast, and it was only in the last quarter of the nineteenth century that the government finally decided to take a definite stand and to annex the territory to the Crown. It will now be necessary to trace briefly the story of this development.

In 1821 the government in London, dissatisfied with the British Company of Merchants' inability to prevent the slave trade, withdrew its charter and united the Gold Coast settlements to the colony of Sierra Leone. For the first time these forts came under British government control. The governor of Sierra Leone, Sir Charles Macarthy, presently visited his new territory and rashly decided, though supported by insufficient forces, to plunge into another war with the Ashanti. The British were disastrously defeated, and Macarthy himself lost his life. Though they eventually reversed the situation and defeated the enemy at the battle of Dodowah, they had fallen so low in the esteem of the Africans that they were little nearer the establishment of peace with the Ashanti. The expense and disasters of the campaign led to another change in policy, whereby in 1828 parliament decided to abandon the Gold Coast. But the merchants, who found it of some commercial value, now asked for a return to merchant control. A 'Committee of London Merchants' was therefore authorized to form a new organization which would control the trade and, with the aid of a government subsidy, keep up the forts. Under the remarkable guidance of George Maclean,[1] a British army officer who was president of the local merchants' council from 1830 to 1844, the Gold Coast for the first time knew real peace and prosperity. Maclean so gained the confidence of the Africans that he was able to extend British influence over the entire coastal area up to the Pra River, the southern boundary of Ashanti. To him belongs the

[1] For a discussion of the period of Maclean's influence and the following years see, J. D. Fage, 'The Administration of George Maclean on the Gold Coast, 1830–44', *Transactions of the Gold Coast and Togoland Historical Society*, vol. I, part 4, 1955; and G. E. Metcalfe, 'After Maclean, Some Aspects of British Gold Coast Policy in the mid-nineteenth Century', ibid., vol. I, part 5, 1955.

credit of laying the foundation of the Dependency, which he accomplished with the paltry subsidy of £3,000 to £4,000 a year. He assisted at trials in the chiefs' courts and helped secure a more humane type of justice. In 1831 he negotiated a series of peace treaties in which the Ashantis renounced their claims of suzerainty over the coastal states and promised to keep the peace.

In spite of Maclean's success some slave trade still existed among the inhabitants, which led to public criticism in England and in 1842 to a parliamentary investigation. While the select committee appointed for the purpose reported very favourably to the House of Commons on Maclean's work, it recommended that control of the Gold Coast forts should be resumed by the Crown and that the informal method of jurisdiction which had grown up should be more accurately defined.[1] As a consequence, in 1844 the British government once again assumed authority. In the same year, in an effort to somewhat clarify the relations between the English and the Fanti, declarations known collectively as 'the Bond' were drawn up.[2] They contained a rather vague acknowledgement on the part of the chiefs of the 'power and jurisdiction' of the British government and stated:

. . . murders and robberies and other crimes and offences will be tried and enquired of before the Queen's judicial officers and the chiefs of the district, moulding the customs of the country to the general principles of British law.

No protectorate, however, was proclaimed nor was there any mention of a territorial cession. This treaty is of importance in Gold Coast history as it was to have some influence on the subsequent relations of the British and the Africans. Since the chiefs were not conquered, but had voluntarily submitted to British power, they continued during later years to speak of their inherent rights and to maintain an attitude of independence towards unpopular British legislation.

With Maclean's death in 1847, the administration fell into less efficient hands. Though attempts were made in 1854 to set up a legislative council representative of the chiefs and to collect a poll tax, these measures were not permanent. In 1863 following a British refusal to surrender certain fugitives from Ashanti the fifth Ashanti war broke out. The available British forces failed to repel the consequent invasion, and

[1] *Parliamentary Papers, Commons, 1842*, vol. XI, 'Report of the House of Commons Select Committee on the West Coast of Africa.'
[2] ibid., *1865*, vol. v, p. 419; J. B. Danquah, 'Historical Significance of the Bond of 1844', *Transactions of the Historical Society of Ghana*, vol. III (1957).

the prestige and prosperity gained during Maclean's time were lost. At home, 'Little Englandism' was exerting an influence and there was much clamour for complete and final withdrawal from so troublesome an area. The Colonial Office therefore sent out a special commissioner (Colonel Ord) in 1864 to report on the four West Africa settlements and in the following year a parliamentary select committee was appointed to study the West African problem. It drew up a long report covering every angle of the situation on the West Coast and recommended that, while it was not possible for the British government to withdraw wholly or immediately, nevertheless 'all further extension of territory or assumption of government' would be 'inexpedient', and that the object of British policy 'should be to encourage in the natives the exercise of those qualities which may render it possible for us more and more to transfer to them the administration of all the governments, with a view to our ultimate withdrawal from all, except, probably, Sierra Leone'.[1]

As a result of this report the governor of Sierra Leone once again assumed control of the Gold Coast, but the recommendation for eventual withdrawal was never carried out. The reasons for this are varied, because at different times during the nineteenth century political, commercial, humanitarian, and religious groups all exercised influence on British colonial policy.

Not many years after the select committee of 1865 drew up its report, the era of 'Little Englandism' was to draw to a close, and the slogan of 'Peace, Retrenchment, and Reform' was to give way before a renewed imperialism. Increased nationalism, industrial competition, the need for new markets, for raw materials, and for opportunities of profitable investment were all forces which led many of the nations of Europe to a new interest in colonial expansion in the last decades of the nineteenth century.

Political and economic forces, however, were not the only ones at work. The influence exercised by the humanitarian and religious bodies was also a powerful one. Even in the eighteenth and early nineteenth centuries, such societies as the Wesleyans, the Anti-Slavery and Aborigines' Protection Society, and various missionary bodies had begun to work for the betterment of backward peoples.[2] They had

[1] *Parliamentary Papers, Commons, 1865*, vol. v, p. iii, 'Report of the Committee appointed to inquire into the Condition of the British Settlements on the West Coast of Africa.'
[2] Klaus Knorr, *British Colonial Theories, 1570–1850* (Toronto, 1944), contains a full account of the various pressure groups which influenced British colonial policy.

succeeded in obtaining the abolition of the slave trade and of slavery, in founding Sierra Leone as a colony for both freed Negroes and white emigrants, and in beginning the work of spreading Christianity and education among the natives of the different parts of the British Empire. In the Gold Coast itself, the earliest missionaries were Portuguese priests. They were followed in the seventeenth and eighteenth centuries by an occasional representative of the churches of the various European nations which had settlements on the coast, but no attempt at organized missionary and educational work throughout the territory was made until the nineteenth century. In 1827, Swiss missionaries of the Basel Society came to the eastern section of the Gold Coast and eventually built up flourishing establishments. They were followed in 1835 by the Wesleyans, in 1847 by the North German Missionary Society, and in 1880 by the Catholics. No further groups came until the twentieth century.

The members of these various bodies as well as those who supported them at home, were usually animated by the highest ideals. They desired to spread the blessings of Christianity among the pagan tribes; also, to repair the harm done through the slave trade by helping to develop legitimate commerce. Some have cynically described this alliance of humanitarian and commercial interests in the terms of Cecil Rhodes's well-known phrase, 'philanthropy plus 5 per cent'.[1] It is quite true that many of the early traders to the Gold Coast were not exemplary characters and that some of them gave the Africans models of the worst rather than of the best of the European manner of living. It is also true that some of the missionaries had commercial as well as religious interests. This does not change the fact, however, that hundreds of men volunteered for work in a land best known in England as the 'white man's grave', and left behind them a record of what was often heroic devotion and zeal in their work of evangelization.[2]

The fact that the British decided to remain in the Gold Coast and eventually annexed it as a colony, after so many years of vacillating policy, can be explained, then, by the pressure of various groups in England. Commercial and political influences were probably the strongest, but to these must be added the idealism of those who wished to give the Africans the best of Christian civilization.

[1] Quoted by Leonard Barnes, *The Duty of Empire* (London, 1935), p. 140.
[2] The Methodists and the Basel Society, for example, had to make repeated starts to establish themselves, because the men first sent out died within a few months of their arrival. The African Society of Lyons, a Catholic body, lost 280 men in less than sixty years in their West African missions alone.

The years that immediately followed the report of the select committee of 1865 were filled with events which brought great changes on the Gold Coast. In 1850 the Danes turned over their forts to the British and in 1872 the Dutch, discouraged at the lessened commercial profits which resulted from the almost continual warfare between the Fanti and the Ashantis, decided to do likewise. This left the British as the sole representatives of the various groups of Europeans who had, from time to time, held trading posts on this section of the Guinea Coast. The transfer of Elmina and the other Dutch forts to the British angered the Ashantis, however, and in 1873 led to the outbreak of a sixth war. This time the British determined to settle the quarrel once and for all. They brought troops from England and, cutting a road through the forest advanced to Kumasi ,the capital of the Ashanti Confederacy, defeated the enemy, and left their town in smoking ruins. By the Treaty of Fomena which ended the war the Asantehene, king of the Ashantis, was forced to renounce his suzerainty over those states which the Ashantis had recognized as independent in Maclean's treaty of 1831. He was to keep the road open to Kumasi for trade and he was further required to do all in his power to abolish human sacrifice, and to pay a large indemnity to the British.

In the same year (1874) the British government decided to assume full control over the coastal areas by annexing them as the Gold Coast Colony.[1] Legislative and executive councils were set up to aid the governor, and provision was made for the beginnings of roads, sanitation, and other elementary needs.

If order and prosperity once more returned to the Gold Coast, it was not so in Ashanti. The British had broken up the existing government, and had made no provision to replace it. The now independent tribes began quarrelling among themselves, and almost constant civil war resulted. The young Asantehene, King Prempeh, begged the British to send a resident to Kumasi and to assist him in restoring order. For a time the British refused, going back to their old policy of non-interference. This further embittered the Ashantis, and conditions grew worse from year to year. In the 1890's, however, a new development led the British to change their attitude. The French in the Ivory Coast and the Germans in Togoland were beginning to seek treaties of friendship with the various tribes on the western, eastern, and northern boundaries of Ashanti. If the British did not definitely establish themselves in the hinterland, there was danger that the Colony might be shut in on

[1] *British and Foreign State Papers,* 1874, vol. LXVI, p. 957.

all sides. Urged on by this international rivalry, the British, in 1895, demanded that Prempeh accept British protection and fulfil the unkept terms of the Treaty of Fomena. When he refused, troops entered Kumasi and the governor demanded his submission and the immediate payment of the long-overdue indemnity of 50,000 ounces of gold. King Prempeh, a mere youth, was now thoroughly disheartened by the poverty and disorder of his kingdom and the superior strength of the British. Therefore he, with the Queen Mother and other notables, in a dramatic scene before his chiefs and people and the British soldiers, made his complete submission to the governor by removing his crown and embracing the governor's feet. He then claimed the protection of Queen Victoria. When he insisted that he was unable to pay so great a sum as 50,000 ounces of gold, however, the governor refused to believe him and arrested him then and there. The Ashantis—stunned by what appeared to them an act of treachery—made no move to retaliate, and the king, his mother, and his chief supporters were eventually deported to the island of Seychelles off the east coast of Africa, where they remained until 1924.

For a time there was apparent peace between the Ashantis and the British. A small garrison was stationed in Kumasi, and the inhabitants seemed resigned to accept the situation. They still had possession of the golden stool, however, for the British had never been able to locate its hiding-place. To the Ashantis this stool was a symbol of their nation-hood; it contained the *sunsum* or soul of the people and, according to an ancient tradition, as long as they kept its possession their spirit could never be broken.[1] The governor, Sir Frederic Hodgson, who had some vague notion of the importance which the Ashantis attached to this symbol, believed that the British could never completely establish their authority until they had secured it. In 1901, consequently, he decided to visit Kumasi and demand the stool. Accompanied by only a small detachment of troops, he made his way through the forest from Accra to Kumasi, where he called together an assembly of the principal chiefs. In a speech that was highly offensive to the recently humbled African leaders, he ordered the Ashantis to agree to payments on the indemnity and to give up the golden stool. Incensed at his tactless demand and eager to regain their independence, they besieged Hodgson in the fort and mobilized their forces for war. It was only after bitter fighting that the rebellion was eventually quelled and peace restored. This time the British realized the inadequacy of compromise, and in January 1902 a

[1] Rattray, *Ashanti*, p. 292; *Ashanti Annual Report, 1921*, pp. 21–29.

Royal Order in Council annexed Ashanti outright and determined its boundaries. At the same time, the so-called Northern Territories, the very primitive section which lies between Ashanti and the Sudan, was formally declared a protectorate.

Treaties with France in 1889, 1893, and 1898 had already defined the frontier between the Ivory Coast and the Gold Coast, and had set the eleventh parallel, with a few deviations, as the extreme north boundary. In the Heliogoland Treaty of 1890 and again in 1899, a dividing-line between the British and the Germans in Togoland was agreed upon. The opening of the twentieth century, consequently, found the Gold Coast divided into three main divisions—two colonies and one protectorate—with German neighbours to the east and the French on the north and west.

In the meantime, while Ashanti wars were being fought and international boundaries delimited, the Gold Coast Colony itself had been making some progress. This was more marked in the economic field than in the political. An ordinance providing for native government was enacted in 1883.[1] Its main purpose was to safeguard the traditional position of the chiefs; but it had not been conspicuously successful and their authority was steadily diminishing, especially in regard to the educated classes in the coastal towns. The strengthening and modernizing of tribal government and its co-ordination with the functions of the central government remained as one of the major problems of the British authorities in the Gold Coast. It was not until the 1920's that any successful solution was found.

In economic matters more promising conditions obtained. A remarkable increase in prosperity came during the first and second decades of the twentieth century due, in large part, to the sudden development of the cocoa industry. Cacao seedlings were first brought to the Gold Coast in 1857 by the Basel missionaries; but it was a native labourer, returning from work in a plantation in Fernando Po, who really introduced the industry. In 1879 he brought in some cocoa pods. The seeds grew successfully and in a few years the first small consignment of cocoa, 121 pounds of beans valued at £6 1s., was exported to Europe. The Africans seemed to have realized the possibilities of such a crop, and cocoa farms spread rather rapidly. With absolutely no European capital and very little government help, the farmers near the coast, and later those in the interior, went ahead with their planting of cocoa trees.

[1] *British and Foreign State Papers, 1882–1883*, LXXIV, pp. 605–16.

The following figures[1] tell the story of the rapid development of the Gold Coast's chief item of export. The tabulation gives the quinquennial average of the cocoa export.

Years						Five-Year Average by Tons
1891–1895	.	.	.	.	.	5
1896–1900	.	.	.	.	.	230
1901–1905	.	.	.	.	.	3,172
1906–1910	.	.	.	.	.	14,784
1911–1915	.	.	.	.	.	51,819
1916–1920	.	.	.	.	.	106,072
1921–1925	.	.	.	.	.	186,329
1926–1930	.	.	.	.	.	218,895

After cocoa, it was usually gold which held the second place in the list of the Gold Coast exports. The traders obtained much of this precious metal from the natives in the early days of the European settlements. Until the 1880's there was not any attempt at regular mining, and even then lack of suitable means of transportation hampered development. In 1901 a short railway, the first in the Gold Coast, was completed from Sekondi on the coast to Tarkwa, the centre of an auriferous area. This brought about something of a boom, and hundreds of concessions were granted by the chiefs. Though many of the ventures proved unwise, some valuable properties were leased and large-scale operations begun. By 1912 gold accounted for more than £1,500,000 in the list of annual exports.

As a result of the Ashanti revolt of 1900 further railway development was believed to be imperative, so that three years later the Sekondi–Tarkwa line had been continued on to Kumasi, the capital of Ashanti. This made rapid communication with the interior possible in the event of further local outbreaks. Once the cocoa farms had spread to Ashanti, the railway was of great value, too, for transport purposes. A second line was begun in 1911 to connect Accra, the capital of the Gold Coast Colony, with Kumasi, but completion was delayed until after the war. Gradually better roads were also built and some motor transportation was introduced.[2] By 1919 the Dependency had some 1,200 miles of

[1] *Gold Coast Handbook, 1937* (London, 1937), p. 38.

[2] Sir Hugh Clifford, governor of the Gold Coast during these pre-war years, states that it was the Ford truck which was most responsible for the opening up of the forest areas to motor transportation. Lighter than the English lorries, it could be used on native-built roads, and its standard parts made repairs possible even in the primitive conditions of the hinterland. See 'The Gold Coast', *Blackwoods*, vol. cciii (1918), p. 57.

motor roads, but the old system of native head carriers was still used in less developed areas.

There were other commercial products to be transported to the coast or to local markets, for the government early realized the danger of a one-crop economy. It made some limited attempts to stimulate the output of timber, rubber, coco-nuts, palm-oil, palm-kernels, cotton, and other tropical products. It also encouraged cattle raising in the Northern Territories, fishing on the coast and in the rivers, and truck farming to add to the food supply of the Dependency. Here was a field in which there were immense opportunities for improvement, provided that technical aid, capital, and increased transportation facilities could be made available. Later government efforts in this matter will be discussed in a further chapter.

A vast field for social work, too, lay at hand. In the *laissez-faire* atmosphere of the nineteenth century, such little education as existed was largely in the hands of the missionaries, but towards the end of the century the government undertook a policy of increased aid to mission schools and even of opening establishments of its own. In 1919 there were 19 government schools and 204 mission schools which were assisted by government funds, and probably about 250 unassisted schools.[1] Some progress in technical, agricultural, and teacher training had also been made. The Accra Technical School and the Accra Government Training College were both opened in 1909.

The first two decades of the twentieth century, then, were marked by a very rapid economic progress which had far outstripped that in the political field. There was also a territorial addition, for Togoland, the German colony to the east, was conquered by the French and British in the first month of World War I and was temporarily divided between them until the peace conference should determine its final status.

To the north the people of Ashanti, under the able and sympathetic administration of the chief commissioner, Sir Francis Fuller, had begun to appreciate British rule and had found in cocoa farming a legitimate and profitable outlet for energies that had formerly been only too often expended on slave trading or warfare.

In the Northern Territories, too, some progress was made after 1902 when that section had been declared a British protectorate. Slave raiding and tribal wars were prevented, roads built, trade encouraged, and a few beginnings of missionary and educational work undertaken.

During the First World War the population of all three sections, the

[1] *Report on the Education Department, 1919*, pp. 6, 18.

Gold Coast Colony, Ashanti, and the Northern Territories, loyally supported the British cause and made generous offerings towards the war expenses. It was evident that the Ashantis had, to a great extent, laid aside their resentment against the British and that peace was firmly established throughout the Dependency. But there was need for many political, economic, and social improvements, and Sir Hugh Clifford, the far-seeing and energetic administrator who was governor from 1912 to 1919, made plans for widespread changes. Many of his plans, however, were impeded by the war and in 1919 the people of the Gold Coast looked forward eagerly to the return of peace and to the possibility of a new era of development for their country.

CHAPTER III

THE GOVERNORSHIP OF
SIR GORDON GUGGISBERG, 1919–27

At the end of World War I a new governor, Sir Gordon Guggisberg, was appointed for the Gold Coast. He arrived in Accra in October 1919, full of interest and enthusiasm for the work he was about to undertake. Early in the century he had spent some time in the Dependency and in Nigeria as head of the Survey Department; and for a few months in 1914 he was director of the Gold Coast public works, until he was recalled to the army for active duty in Europe, commanding the Royal Engineers. He was not, therefore, unacquainted with the problems of the colony he was to govern so successfully for the next eight years. The situation he found on his arrival was an unusual one in several ways, for the war had not only cut down the official staff to the absolute minimum and prevented much development that was pressingly needed, but had also stirred up unrest among some of the educated population.

Guggisberg was well aware of these difficulties, but even more so of the fundamental soundness of the relations between the government and the Africans, and of the great promise which the Gold Coast held out for rapid economic and social progress. During his years of surveying in West Africa, his work had given him much opportunity for close daily contact with the African, and he was convinced that it was only lack of opportunity which had prevented him from reaching an intellectual development comparable to that of the European.[1] A spirit of idealism seems to have guided him in his attitude towards the African. At the end of the war he had made a vow to dedicate the rest of his life to the welfare of his fellow men, and therefore welcomed the offer made by Lord Milner, Secretary of State for the Colonies, of the governorship of the Gold Coast. A man of energy, foresight, and administrative ability, he carefully outlined in a 'Ten Year Development Plan' what

---

[1] Baron Sydney Olivier, 'Sir Frederick Gordon Guggisberg', *Dictionary of National Biography, 1922–1930* (London, 1937). 'Governor's Address', 9 October 1919, *Gold Coast Gazette* (13 October 1919), p. 1103.

he hoped to accomplish during the 1919–29 decade. In each address to the legislative council, and on other appropriate occasions, he explained his policy to the Africans, reviewed what had already been accomplished, and outlined what was still to be done in the future.

His main object was 'the general progress of the people of the Gold Coast towards a higher state of civilization, and the keystone of the progress is education'.[1] Since schools and other necessary social services were very costly and brought in no financial returns, it would be necessary to greatly increase the revenue of the Dependency. This, he believed, could be best accomplished by an improved and extended transportation system which would open up new areas to the world market, and reduce freight rates on both exported and imported goods. The plan called for an expenditure of £24,000,000 to be obtained from the existing surplus of £1,250,000, from loans, and from the augmented revenue which he expected would soon result from such progress.[2] Though the 1920–3 depression and other unexpected developments made it necessary to reduce the total expenditure to £16,645,848, the bulk of the scheme was carried out as planned, and when Guggisberg left the governorship in 1927, the greater part of the work was already completed.

The fact that boom conditions characterized the cocoa market in 1919 and in the early months of 1920 helped the new governor to gain the support of his officials and of public opinion for what appeared to many as a daring undertaking. The price of cocoa soared to £80 a ton and even, in some cases, to £120.[3] The Gold Coast farmers and middlemen enjoyed conditions of a pleasant if unstable prosperity, but they were not to last. By the middle of the year 1920 a depression had forced down world prices, with a resultant sharp decline—not only in the incomes of the Africans but also in the general revenue of the colony which was so largely dependent on export and import taxes. The government officials had always realized the danger of a one-crop economy,[4] but the farmers,

---

[1] 'Governor's Address to the Legislative Council', 1 March 1923, *Gold Coast Gazette* (17 March 1923), p. 349.

[2] Frederick Gordon Guggisberg, *The Gold Coast: A Review of the Events of 1920–1926 and the Prospects of 1927–1928* (Accra, 1927), p. 72 (hereafter cited as *Events, 1920–1926*). This volume contains Guggisberg's final address and report to the legislative council and gives a very complete summary of the progress of these years.

[3] The normal price of cocoa in the 1920's was about £50 a ton, but it dropped to £20 to £30 a ton in the early years of the 1930 decade.

[4] Cocoa exports accounted for from 70 to 80 per cent of total exports during the period 1919–32, but they have since dropped to from 50 to 60 per cent and mineral products have increased. S. Herbert Frankel, *Capital Investment in Africa* (London, 1938), Table 78. See also *G.C. An. Report, 1949*, p. 16.

ignorant of economic laws and often blissfully improvident, had a painful object lesson—one which, unfortunately, was soon forgotten by the greater number of them.

The depression conditions lasted from the summer of 1920 until the early months of 1923. The government reduced the official staff and some of the estimated expenditures of the Ten Year Plan, but refused to cancel the export tax on cocoa or to make any changes in projected railways and harbour developments. The tax on cocoa, first levied in 1916 as a war measure to replace the revenue ordinarily obtained from import duties, aroused much criticism among the Africans, who believed that they bore the burden of the tariff, which amounted to 12 to 28 per cent of the value of the cocoa. The governor, on the other hand, was convinced that it did not harm the farmer, and that the resultant revenue was essential. He went even further and levied new export duties on kola and on timber.

The whole question of taxation had always been a difficult one on the Gold Coast, for the Africans held that it was one of their rights to be free of direct levies. During these years, in spite of the criticism against customs duties, the total of all rates amounted to only 16 shillings per head in comparison to £23 in the United Kingdom. Because of the uneven distribution of wealth a graduated income tax would have been the most just form, but Guggisberg was of the opinion that the cost of collection, under existing conditions, would be out of proportion to the amount of revenue obtained. Even if such a type of levy had been practical, it is doubtful if it could have been enforced in face of the deep-rooted opposition of the Africans.

But customs duties could not provide sufficient revenue for the ambitious aims of the Ten Year Plan, and loans were therefore made in London—one for £4,000,000 at 6 per cent in 1920, and another for £4,628,000 at $4\frac{1}{2}$ per cent in 1925. The capital thus obtained was used for waterworks and for railway and harbour development. In order to provide a sound financial position for the Dependency, in the face of an increasing debt, Guggisberg set down definite principles by which all future estimate committees could be guided. The most important of the rules he summarized as follows: '. . . that the annual revenue should cover both Recurrent and Extraordinary Expenditure and a contribution to the Railway Renewals Fund, after which there should be a small annual surplus for contingencies'.[1] In a lean year the government would first reduce extraordinary expenditure and then recurrent ones. In a

---

[1] 'Governor's Address', *Gold Coast Gazette* (17 March 1923), pp. 60–71.

flush year it would consider lowering taxes and railway rates. He provided, moreover, for the nucleus of a General Reserve Fund of £500,000 'which should be built up annually by its own interest until it reached an amount proportional to our capital value as a country'. This fund was not to be used without the permission of the colonial secretary, and then only in the wholly exceptional case of a complete failure of trade and after every possible economy had been made. He set the final amount at £2,000,000, and thereafter all interest would go into the general revenue. His plan has since been followed, and during the great depression of the 1930's the Gold Coast was able, by stringent economies, to weather the storm without touching the Reserve Fund.[1] Provision was also made by Guggisberg for definite annual contributions to sums for the renewals of railway and harbour facilities. Though the Colony debt was over £11,000,000 in 1927, nevertheless the financial position of the Dependency was sound.[2]

The greater part of the Ten Year Plan was, as has been seen, concerned with transportation. In 1919 the Gold Coast possessed a completed railway from Sekondi, on the western littoral, to Kumasi, the capital of Ashanti; a branch of this line from Tarkwa to Prestea in the heart of the gold-mining district; and an uncompleted section of track which was eventually to link Accra, the capital of the Colony, with Kumasi. By 1923 this latter part was finished. Between 1923 and 1927 the Central Province Railway, from Huni Valley to Kade, was built in order to open up cocoa and mahogany areas and to increase shipments to the new harbour at Takoradi. In addition surveys were made for possible extensions into the Northern Territories, for Guggisberg believed that this section of the Dependency would never be fully developed until it had railway connexions with the coast. Later governors disagreed with this opinion, however, as it was found that motor roads and a good truck service were sufficient and less costly, and that a railway would probably never pay for itself.

In all, 233 miles of new railway were built between 1919 and 1927 and 250 miles of prospective lines surveyed, at a total cost of £5,948,000.[3]

These new means of transportation made possible the further spread

[1] In 1946 the General Reserve Fund was £1,500,000.
[2] The ratio of debt charges to domestic exports has never exceeded 10 per cent. Frankel, *Capital Investment in Africa*, Table 37.
[3] Legislative Council, *Debates* (1930), 'Governor's Address', pp. 139–40. No further railway building was done until the Second World War, when the urgent need of aluminium led to the construction of a 50-mile spur from Dunkwa to Awaso, in the heart of the bauxite area. *Labour Department Report, 1943–1944*, p. 3.

of cocoa farms, and freed hundreds of head carriers to augment the insufficient labour supply in both agricultural and mining fields. Nevertheless, there has been much recent criticism of what are now held to be overbuilt or unwisely financed railway systems.[1] Good motor roads would have provided sufficient transportation in most cases. The work was paid for, moreover, by private loans at high fixed interest rates when equity capital or, better still, government subsidies or low interest rate loans would have done away with the heavy drain that the public debt service made upon the colony's resources. Though it is unfortunate that Guggisberg was not successful in borrowing at a lower rate, there is perhaps some excuse for the charge of overbuilding. Motor transport was not as developed in the early 1920's as it is now, and lorry rates per ton mile were 2s. 9d. in contrast to the 4d. to 7½d. of the freight charge by rail. The governor can scarcely be blamed for not foreseeing that truck charges were to fall as low as 3d. per mile within the next ten years.

In spite of Guggisberg's lack of appreciation of the full possibilities of automobile development, he saw the necessity of good roads as feeders for the railways and for short hauls. At the close of World War I there were some 1,200 miles of roads in the Dependency—many of them built by the chiefs in their desire to transport cocoa to the market —and suitable for only light Ford trucks. In the 1919–27 period, 3,388 miles of new roads were built and 1,310 reconditioned, thus bringing the total to 4,688 motor miles. Some of them were tarred macadam, the best in British tropical Africa. Transportation methods have changed in the Gold Coast from the days when cocoa was borne along narrow jungle paths by head porters, and palm-oil was rolled in eighty-four-gallon casks from the forest to the coast, where surf-boats carried all cargoes out to ocean-going freighters.

It was the inefficiency of these loading methods and the crowded conditions on the beaches of the various ports—where thousands of tons of perishable cocoa were sometimes piled during the height of the season—that led the governor to make plans for better shipping facilities. The Gold Coast has no natural harbour, but Takoradi on the western littoral was chosen by consulting engineers as the most suitable location at which to develop one. Preparations were begun in 1921, and, in spite of the business slump and much adverse criticism, the work was

---

[1] Frankel, *Capital Investment in Africa*, pp. 405–6 and 418–20. Hailey, *African Survey*, pp. 1603–10. Rita Hinden, *Plan for Africa: A Report prepared for the Colonial Bureau of the Fabian Society* (New York, 1942), pp. 149–55.

continued. It was not opened for commerce until 1928 and further extensions were added later, bringing the total cost up to £3,230,912.[1] The harbour was formed by two great breakwaters enclosing an area of 220 acres and containing wharves for cocoa, timber, and manganese export, sufficient storage and loading space, and a petroleum berth equipped with pipe-lines from ships to tanks two and a half miles inland. During most of the 1930's the harbour operated at a loss because of the burden of its heavy debt charges and the competition of the cheaper surf-boat ports at Accra and other coastal towns. While this method of financing the undertaking has been subjected to the same type of criticism as that levelled at the railways, the harbour has since proved itself invaluable in the economic development of the country.

The Ten Year Plan called for extended communication facilities, and both telephone and telegraph services were substantially increased. The estimates for further water supply and hydro-electric developments, on the other hand, had to be greatly reduced as it was later seen that certain medical and educational requirements were even more essential.

As Guggisberg had foreseen, new means of transportation brought with them an augmented commerce. The average annual value of the total trade (exports and imports) for the seven-year period 1920–6 was over twice as much as that of 1913–19. The colony's revenue also showed well over a 100 per cent increase.[2] Guggisberg felt that he had been justified in undertaking the Ten Year Development Plan.

The foundation of all this prosperity was, in large part, the export of cocoa; and it was necessary, therefore, to make every effort to safeguard the industry. The protection of the forests, an absolute essential to its well-being, was becoming year by year a more serious problem. Originally a belt of dense rain forests had covered the entire southern portion of the Gold Coast, but by the early twentieth century the entire Ho district of Togo, three-fourths of the Eastern Province, and one-third of the Central Province had given way to a savannah type of vegetation. Experts found that deforestation was going on at the rate of 300 square miles a year, and informed the government that it would be necessary to set aside some 40 per cent of the remaining area as reserves, if further

[1] *G.C. An. Report, 1928–29*, p. 21.
[2] *Events, 1920–1926*, p. 174. Average annual revenue, 1913–19, £1,635,650; 1920–6, £3,829,705.

damage was to be prevented.[1] Because of African opposition to any official action, Guggisberg urged the chiefs to establish reserves themselves, according to the by-law power given them in the Native Jurisdiction Ordinance of 1883. As nothing was done in 1924 to carry out his request, he warned them again that he would give them but two years more. At the end of this period only six native reserves totalling 240 square miles had been established, whereas the Forestry Department had declared that 6,000 square miles were necessary. The failure of the chiefs was due to a number of reasons: ignorance of the danger involved in further deforestation, fear that the reserves would become Crown lands, unsettled boundary disputes between stools, and the fact that the chiefs of the Central and Eastern Provinces had already alienated lands available for reserves.

Forced on by the grave necessity of the situation, Guggisberg again conferred with the chiefs in order to obtain suggestions which might prevent a repetition of the deadlock of 1911. Though his Forestry Bill met with local opposition in 1927, it became a law. It provided for the establishment of Forestry Department reserves whenever the chiefs failed to do so, but it did not deprive the Africans of ownership, as only the forest rights and not the land itself were bought by the government.

From the very beginning of Guggisberg's term of office he had insisted that if a higher state of civilization was his aim for the people of the Gold Coast, the keystone of that progress was education. In this field above all was he an enthusiast, and it is for his changes in educational policy and for the building of Achimota College that he is remembered, as well as for the Ten Year Plan and for the inauguration of a new constitution and Native Administration Ordinance. While many still believe that some of his decisions as to primary schools were unwise, most are agreed that Achimota has proved itself a very worthwhile institution.

[1] In 1910 a British expert made a thorough study of the forest situation for the British government. See H. Thompson, *Reports of Gold Coast Forests*, Cd. 4993, 1910. This led the Gold Coast government to pass a law in 1911 authorizing the establishment of reserves. Some of the Africans, however, raised strenuous objections on the grounds that such reserves would be the beginning of official seizure of tribal land. A delegation was sent to London to protest against the legislation and in reply the secretary of state for the colonies appointed a special commissioner, Sir H. C. Belfield, to determine whether there was actual danger to native rights. See *Report on the Legislation governing the Alienation of Native Lands in the Gold Coast*, Cd. 6278, 1912, and Casely Hayford, *The Truth about the West African Land Question* (London, 1913).

Though Belfield reported that African rights were sufficiently safeguarded by the Ordinance, the government decided, in view of the opposition that had been aroused, not to apply the law.

One of his first acts on arrival in the Gold Coast was to appoint a committee to study the educational situation. Their report was identical, in large part, with that published by the Phelps-Stokes Commission which visited West and South Africa in 1920, in an attempt to suggest methods by which African education could be improved in line with those which had been successfully worked out at the Tuskegee and other institutes in the United States.[1] Guggisberg was encouraged by the fact that the two reports agreed to such a great extent with his own theories. He soon prepared, in conjunction with the Education Department and the heads of the missions, a very definite plan for the guidance of those responsible for the schools of the Dependency. It was based on sixteen principles,[2] among which were the necessity of improved teacher training, well-staffed and equipped secondary schools, equal opportunities for boys and girls, more stress on trade schools and training in agriculture and handicrafts rather than exclusive attention to literary subjects, the value of games and Scout methods, and, above all, the absolute necessity of character training if the African was to develop personal worth and the power of leadership. To implement this policy a new education ordinance was introduced in 1925 to the legislative council, and put in effect two years later. Because the new law required a higher standard, which many were unable to meet, by 1930 some one hundred and fifty bush schools had been closed. There was much criticism at the time,[3] especially because only about 10 per cent of the children of the Dependency attended school of any kind.

If inefficient establishments were closed, through the lack of properly trained teachers, the government and the various missions made every effort to fill the need by opening normal schools for both men and women. Outstanding among these was the Prince of Wales College at Achimota. The story of the inception and development of this remarkable experiment in African education is a fascinating one. The foundation-stone was laid in 1924; it was dedicated by the Prince of Wales the following year, and on 28 January 1927 it was formally opened by

---

[1] This commission was financed, in very large part, by the Phelps-Stokes Fund. In her will Miss Caroline Phelps-Stokes had bequeathed her fortune to trustees with the instruction that the income be used, *inter alia*, 'for the education of Negroes, both in Africa and the United States, North American Indians and needy and deserving white students'. See *Education in Africa: A Study of West, South, and Equatorial Africa by the African Education Commission: Report prepared by Thomas Jesse Jones* (New York, 1922); Edwin Smith, *Aggrey of Africa* (London, 1929), Chapter X.

[2] 'Governor's Address', *Gold Coast Gazette* (3 February 1925); ibid. (25 April 1925), pp. 580–615.

[3] Legislative Council, *Debates* (1929–30), pp. 168, 218.

Sir Gordon Guggisberg.[1] Planned on a large scale and equipped in the most up-to-date manner, it was finally completed in 1931 at a cost of £617,000. Though it was freed from government control by the creation of an Achimota Council in 1930, it received a grant of £48,000 a year from the general revenue of the Dependency. The staff was composed of both Europeans and Africans and every effort was made to provide on native soil for the best in English education, but at the same time to adapt it to African requirements and to preserve all that was worth while in the indigenous culture of the past. Among the members of the original staff was James Kwegyir Aggrey, the African deputy vice-principal. A native of the Gold Coast, he went to America as a young man where he attended a college for Negroes, and later worked for his doctorate at Columbia University. His deep appreciation of the need for co-operation between the white and the black races, and his own personal gifts and charm, gained for him so much admiration from educational leaders that he was chosen in 1920 as a member of the Phelps-Stokes Commission. While the group was in the Gold Coast, Guggisberg met Aggrey for the first time, and, impressed with his ability and personality, he later readily acquiesced in his appointment as the deputy vice-principal of Achimota, and eventually a real friendship developed between the two men. As a native of the Colony and yet with wide experience of racial problems in the rest of Africa and in the United States, Aggrey was able not only to break down the misunderstanding and opposition that grew up in connexion with the new college, but also to further, to a remarkable degree, a mutual understanding between the two races. After his sudden death in the summer of 1927 Guggisberg wrote of him that 'Africa had lost one of her greatest sons' and by his passing 'a blow had been dealt to the progress of the African races . . . Aggrey, indeed, was the finest interpreter which the present century has produced of the black man to the white.'[2]

During his lifetime Aggrey had often referred to the fact that it was necessary to use both the black and the white keys of the piano to produce beautiful music, and he used this simple figure as an example of the co-operation which should unite the two races. After his death Principal Fraser of Achimota had several artists on the staff design a shield for the college which would embody this idea. Black and white bars form the body of the shield, while beneath is the motto, *Ut omnes unum sint*.

[1] *Report on the Achimota College, 1926–27. G.C. An. Report, 1926–27*, p. 39. Smith, *Aggrey of Africa*, pp. 225–45 and *passim*. A fuller account of Achimota College will be given in a later chapter.
[2] Smith, *Aggrey of Africa*, pp. 286–7.

Besides Achimota these same years saw the opening of several trade schools throughout the Dependency. They were all boarding-schools with European headmasters who used Baden-Powell Scout methods for maintaining discipline and building up school spirit, with the hope that not only technical training but character development would result.

The improvement of health and sanitation services were also included in the Ten Year Plan, and a large modern hospital near Accra, eighteen smaller hospitals, and twenty dispensaries were completed before 1927. A start was made in infant welfare work, and the Medical Research Institute was enlarged. Important as these additions were, they were entirely insufficient for the size of the population, and in view of the widespread incidence of malnutrition, and of malaria, tuberculosis, sleeping sickness, yaws, nephritis, leprosy, venereal, and other serious diseases. The problem was a grave one which would require greatly increased governmental attention and financial aid, if it were to be satisfactorily solved.

CHAPTER IV

POLITICAL DEVELOPMENT, 1919-27

In the preceding chapter a survey was made of the material advancement of the Colony during the years 1919–27. A far more difficult problem faced Sir Gordon Guggisberg in the matter of political development and native administration. Before discussing his policy in these fields, it would be helpful, perhaps, to give a general picture of the method of government which existed in the Gold Coast at the opening of his period of office. An attempt will then be made to trace the improvements which he brought about through the new constitution of 1925, and through a completely revised native administration ordinance.

Shortly after the new ordinance was promulgated Guggisberg's extended term of office came to an end. The actual working out of the new laws and their results will therefore be left to a subsequent chapter.

The system of government of the Gold Coast has been described in official reports as a mixture of direct rule by the central government and of indirect rule through the indigenous African institutions. There was a steady bias towards the latter.[1] The direct government, as in the majority of British Crown Colonies, was administered by a governor assisted by an executive and a legislative council and a staff of political and technical officials. Local government was largely in the hands of African chiefs and their councils of elders who were, generally speaking, representative of the various sections of the community. Native administration was regulated by the 1883 ordinance until 1927, when it was replaced by a new code.

The governor was the chief executive authority for the entire Dependency, but was responsible to the secretary of state for the colonies and had to refer all important matters to him. He made appointments for all positions whose salary was £400 a year or less, while those with higher

---

[1] *G.C. An. Report, 1931–1932*, p. 4. A detailed description of Crown colony government is given by Sir Frederick Lugard, *Dual Mandate in British Tropical Africa* (London, 1922), Chapters V–IX; Lord Hailey, *African Survey*, pp. 160–73, 224–35; Martin Wight, *The Gold Coast Legislative Council* (London, 1947), is a detailed and valuable study of constitutional development, 1925–45.

remunerations were under the control of the Colonial Office. When the Africans disagreed with the governor on any point, they did, on occasion, send petitions or delegations to the secretary of state for the colonies.

The executive council, during the period under consideration, consisted of the following British officials: the colonial secretary, the chief commissioners of Ashanti and of the Northern Territories, the attorney-general, the financial secretary, the director of medical services, and the secretary for native affairs. It was an advisory body to whom the governor had to submit all Bills before proposing them to the legislative council. The governor had the final word in case of disagreement, but the members could always report their views to the Colonial Office. The advantages of an executive council lay in the fact that the representatives of various departments could thus give their advice and criticism, while their viewpoint was usually broader than that of separate committees.

The administrative branch was made up of political and technical services. The former included, during this period, the colonial secretary, the secretary of native affairs, and the division of the political officers who resided in the various provinces and districts. For administrative purposes the Gold Coast Colony was divided into the Western Province with six districts; the Central Province with four; and the Eastern Province with eight. At the head of each province was a provincial commissioner, while in each district, a district or assistant district commissioner resided.[1]

Ashanti was divided into an Eastern and a Western Province, each with four districts, while the Northern Territories had a Northern Province with four districts and a Southern Province with five.

The number of political officers varied from time to time, depending to some extent upon the financial condition of the Dependency. In 1922, for example, there were eighty-eight officers, of whom forty-four were assigned to the Colony, twenty-three to Ashanti, and twenty-one to the Northern Territories—a comparatively large staff. This number was somewhat reduced during the depression of the 1930's.

Lugard speaks of the political officer as 'the backbone of the colony',[2] for on him depended, in large part, the character of the relations between the central government and the African authorities. He had to help to

[1] Some of these arrangements were changed when the 1946 constitution went into effect.
[2] Lugard, *Dual Mandate*, p. 128.

guide local rulers, administer justice, enforce ordinances, settle disputes, compile endless routine reports, and—in some of the smaller districts —supervise such technical work as road-building and sanitation. His aim was to foster co-operation between the British and the Africans and to promote progress and civilization. For this, much sympathy, firmness of will, initiative, and a sense of fair play were considered necessary, and students from the English public schools who had later been to Oxford or Cambridge were often appointed by the Colonial Office.

The technical service included such departments as the medical, agricultural, public works, and survey. With the ever-increasing activity of their staffs and the growing power of African authorities in local government, the problem of co-ordination between these two groups became more acute. It was possible, however, for the political officer to act as a link between them, representing the interests of the local authorities without prejudicing the necessary independence of the various departments in technical matters.

The legislative council formed another part of the central government of the Gold Coast Colony. First inaugurated in the nineteenth century, in 1916 it was given new form and in 1920 included eleven official members—the executive council and heads of several other departments—and nine unofficial members. Among the latter there were usually three chiefs, three educated Africans from the coastal towns of Accra, Cape Coast, and Sekondi, and three Europeans representing commercial interests, but all were appointed by the governor. So constituted, the council was not representative of the entire colony and had no real power, as the government kept control through its official majority, but it did allow for public discussion of projected laws and provided a means for adapting them more fully to local needs. In actual practice, the Gold Coast council had greater influence than in most African colonies, and more than once legislation was abandoned because of opposition by the council.[1]

A study of the history of the various colonies and dominions in the British Commonwealth will provide examples of the normal development of a legislative council. The unofficial members are eventually elected in whole, or in part, instead of being appointed by the governor. The next step towards self-government is the exchange of an official for an unofficial majority, but with the governor still retaining some

[1] See, for example, Legislative Council, *Debates* (1931), for opposition to the proposed income tax. The law was not passed until 1943. J. W. de Graft Johnson, *Towards Nationhood in West Africa* (London, 1928), Chapter XI has a discussion of Crown colony government in the Gold Coast from the African's point of view.

control either through a body of reserved subjects on which the council may not legislate or through the veto power. In the final stage the governor's power is progressively held in abeyance until ultimately withdrawn. This process marks the course by which a dependency gradually advances towards responsible government, the essence of which is the accountability of the executive to the legislative body.

Many of the educated class on the Gold Coast were keenly conscious of the fact that other British colonies had advanced through these various stages to eventual self-government, and they looked forward to the day when they too could claim the same right. This desire expressed itself from time to time under various forms. There were movements which were nationalistic in character, appeals for increased African participation in the European administration, protests against legislation which was considered inimical to native rights, as well as outright demands for increased self-government.

One of the earliest manifestations of this spirit of self-determination was in 1871, when a number of chiefs and educated people met together and drew up an elaborate constitution creating a Fanti Confederation. They were influenced in part by the House of Commons resolution of 1865, which had recommended that the English encourage the Africans to prepare for eventual self-government; and in part by the desire to meet their Ashanti enemies with the strength of a united front. In spite of the British government's official statement, however, the plan was regarded with disapproval by the local authorities and, as a result, came to nothing.[1] Three years later the British finally decided to take over full control of their Gold Coast settlements, and these were annexed as a Crown colony. This move ended, for a time, any clamour for independence.

The nationalist spirit which had given birth to the Fanti Confederation did not entirely die out. Some thirty years later it flared up afresh in another form—in the opposition to the Public Lands Bill of that year. Ever since the 1860's the chiefs had been selling land to foreigners. As the government did not want the country to come under the control of European mining interests, it passed an ordinance placing any transfer of public lands to private persons under the supervision of an official concessions court. The Africans believed that such a step would have the effect of converting native holdings into Crown lands, and that

[1] *Parliamentary Papers, Commons, 1873*, vol. XLIX, 'Correspondence Relative to the Fanti Confederation'. The constitution of the Confederation is printed pp. 3–9. For African opinion on the affair, see Johnson. *Towards Nationhood in West Africa*, Chapter VI.

eventually the British government would be the owner of all the un-occupied areas of the Gold Coast. In an effort to organize the opposition to this new law, the Aborigines' Rights Protection Society was formed by many of the chiefs and educated Africans of the Central Province. It sent a deputation to London to protest against the Bill, which, as a result, was withdrawn and replaced in 1900 by the Concessions Ordinance. This second law gave the British courts some supervision over the validity of concessions, but made it quite clear that the Africans retained possession of their land.

The Aborigines' Rights Protection Society continued, after its victory of 1897, to lead the opposition to any government policies which it considered contrary to African rights. It was recognized by the governor as a correct channel of local opinion until 1925, when the inauguration of the provincial councils provided what the government considered a more representative body.

During World War I an official policy once again aroused local criticism. In 1916 an export duty was imposed in all West African colonies on cocoa, palm products, groundnuts, hides, and skins. The Gold Coast legislative council unofficial members voted solidly against these measures, but they were passed by the official majority. After the war, the Africans asked that the tax be discontinued, but they were again refused. At the same time the world-wide agitation for self-determination was affecting the Africans as well as other dependent peoples.[1] One result of these post-war conditions was a quickening of the political ambitions of the peoples of West Africa. In March 1920 a conference of representatives of the four British colonies, Sierra Leone, Gambia, Gold Coast, and Nigeria, met in Accra where the National Congress of British West Africa was organized. At its first general meeting a number of resolutions were passed, the most important of which asked for fuller

[1] In New York, for example, Marcus Garvey headed a convention of Negroes which drew up, in 1920, the *Declaration of Rights of the Negro Peoples of the World*, demanding, in colourful and flamboyant language, full political, civil, and social rights and declaring that Africa belongs to the Negro. For the full text, see R. Buell, *The Native Problem in Africa* (New York, 1921), vol. II, Appendix XLIX.

In Paris, a Pan-African Congress met during the Peace Conference under the presidency of M. Diagne, an African deputy from Senegal, and prepared resolutions of a more reasonable character, asking for an increased share in the government rather than for immediate control of Africa as had done Garvey. See Lugard, *Dual Mandate*, p. 83. For the comment of the missionaries on the post-war unrest, see *International Review of Missions*, vol. XII (1923), p. 161; vol. XIII (1925), pp. 3–24. The missionaries believed that some of the trouble was due to returned soldiers who had lost much of their respect for Europeans during their war contacts. Communistic propaganda, and echoes of the Pan-African movement all helped to feed the new spirit of dissatisfaction.

African elected representation and for control of the purse.[1] In October 1920 the Congress authorized a delegation of African students in London to petition for these reforms. Though its resolutions were not made in any spirit of disloyalty,[2] the secretary of state for the colonies replied that West Africa was not yet ready for elected councillors. Shortly afterwards, however, he reversed his opinion and granted the principle of election to the Nigerian council, while in the Gold Coast, Sir Gordon Guggisberg, convinced that the 'time had come for giving Africans greater and better representation',[3] began preparations for a new type of town council for the coastal cities, for a constitution which would provide for elected members to the legislative council, and for a reorganization of the Native Administration Ordinance. In 1924 the first of these changes, the Municipal Corporations Bill, was introduced into the council. It was to replace the former ordinance of 1894 which had applied to Accra, Cape Coast, and Sekondi, providing for town councils with an official majority and with the power to impose local rates and perform certain administrative functions. This law had not been successful, however, as the Africans felt they had no real responsibility, and in many elections few, and sometimes none, took the trouble to stand for office or to vote.

Guggisberg believed that a new type of council with an elected majority would teach the Africans valuable lessons of local self-government and prepare them for positions of wider responsibility. The Municipal Corporations Bill of 1924 accordingly provided for a majority of elected councillors, gave them power to levy new rates and draw up the estimates—subject, however, to government approval—and opened the franchise to all who owned or occupied a house of a £5 rateable value. The municipal members of the legislative council approved of this new ordinance, but when it was published there was an outburst of

---

[1] The story of the Congress by a native of the Gold Coast is to be found in M. Sampson, *Gold Coast Men of Affairs* (London, 1937), pp. 27–31, 168 ff. See also Buell, op. cit., pp. 832–3; George Padmore, *How Britain rules Africa* (London, 1936), p. 371. This book was written by a native of Trinidad who was, at the time, bitterly opposed to British rule, and who was sometimes inaccurate in statements. He presented the viewpoint of the radical Negro, however, and often drew attention to facts worthy of consideration. Chapter XIV deals with the history of the African nationalist movement, especially in the Gold Coast.

[2] The congress declared that its fundamental policy was: 'To maintain strictly and inviolate the connection of the British West African dependencies with the British Empire and to maintain unreservedly all and every right of free citizenship of the Empire and the fundamental principle that taxation goes with effective representation.' Quoted by M. A. Ribeiro, 'The Political History of the Gold Coast', Achimota Discussion Group, *Quo Vadimus or Gold Coast Future* (Achimota, 1940), p. 14.

[3] *Events, 1920–1926*, p. 238; Buell, op. cit., vol. I, p. 833.

opposition centring in Accra, where the poorer classes feared the imposition of increased rates, while others held that African institutions would be undermined by the power of an elected mayor.[1] In view of sustained disapproval, Guggisberg eventually withdrew the ordinance, but he made no attempt to hide his disappointment. He believed that municipal government was the finest training field for wider responsibility and told the legislative council:

. . . it is the acid test of fitness of the citizens of our urban areas to take a greater share in the government of the country. I use the word 'acid' advisedly after the experience of the past few years, for municipal government in this country requires far greater resolution than it does in the more advanced countries of the world.

And again he told them that he found this refusal:

. . . the only real disappointment which I have had as your Governor. . . . Perhaps the time is not yet ripe. Anyway, seeing that the citizens of our seaports think as they do, it would not be right at the present moment to force the responsibility of local municipal self-government on them. Until they feel they can resist the popular outcry . . . until, in fact, they feel themselves better fitted to bear the responsibility of municipal self-government, the application of the Ordinance should be deferred.[2]

Since the 1924 Bill had failed, the government in 1927 finally amended the former Town Council Ordinance so that there were then five official and five unofficial members, including one European, appointed by the governor and four elected Africans.

It may seem somewhat contradictory that the Africans, after demanding increased self-government, should have opposed the Municipal Corporations Bill. It is necessary to distinguish, however, between various groups of public opinion. The educated Africans in the coastal towns, having almost no opportunity to share in tribal administration, were constantly agitating for greater representation in the municipal and central government, while most of the chiefs and the bulk of the people, on the other hand, were far more interested in their own institutions or in avoiding the burden of increased rates.

During these years Guggisberg made efforts to satisfy the demands of the intellectual classes in another direction, by promising them an

---

[1] Ribeiro, op. cit., pp. 14–16.
[2] *Events, 1920–1926*, p. 13; Hailey, *African Survey*, p. 523.

increased share of the administrative positions usually held by Europeans. The economic development of the Gold Coast had not broken up tribal life to the same extent as in most African colonies, so that greater social and educational progress had therefore been possible. This had resulted in a fairly large group of literate persons in Accra, Sekondi, Cape Coast, and other towns, among whom were clerks, teachers, clergymen, merchants, and even doctors and lawyers.

The government was not adverse to giving Africans positions of responsibility whenever candidates with the necessary force of character and educational requirements were available. As the Gold Coast possessed no institution of higher learning prior to 1927, suitable training could only be obtained in England. To satisfy this fundamental need for African leaders had been one of Guggisberg's primary aims in establishing Achimota. Graduates from this institution would not be available for some years, but in the meantime the governor promised to make as many appointments as possible, and in the years 1919–27 there was an increase from three to thirty-eight in the number of Africans holding positions usually occupied by Europeans.[1] On the ground that Africans were living in their own country and had not, therefore, two establishments to provide for as had the Europeans, they received one-sixth less salary and shorter periods of leave.

Among the various political problems of the Gold Coast one of the most important—that of the local administration—yet remains to be discussed.

As has already been pointed out, one of the aims of the British government was to rule, as far as possible, through the agency of indigenous institutions. Such a policy is usually defined as 'indirect rule'. It is not a new practice—parts of the Roman Empire were thus governed, for example—but it is one which has been the subject of much comment and study since it was initiated by Lord Lugard in Northern Nigeria, and developed, with striking results, by Sir Donald

---

[1] *Events, 1920–1926*, p. 254. Guggisberg refused to consider appointing Africans as provincial or district commissioners, giving as his reason that the chiefs would not co-operate with educated Africans or those of other tribes; that there were sufficient opportunities for political positions in their own local government; and that there were, at the time, no suitable candidates. The Africans, however, believed that this was an unjust policy. See, for example, Legislative Council, *Debates* (1929–1939), pp. 153–6, 184, 232.

The governors who followed Guggisberg, as a result of changed conditions, were able to declare themselves willing to appoint Africans as political officers whenever those with the proper qualifications applied. See, for example, Governor Slater's statement, Legislative Council, *Debates* (1929–1930), p. 232. No actual appointments were made, however, until 1943.

Cameron in Tanganyika.[1] Indirect rule did, in fact, become the foundation of a new school of colonial administration, and was adopted by the British as a pattern for the rule of many of their colonies.[2] It was in line with the trend towards a more enlightened and progressive treatment of dependent peoples which became increasingly evident after the end of World War I. Lugard pointed out in 1922 that while it was generally conceded that the Africans would eventually be sufficiently advanced for self-government, nevertheless they were not yet ready to stand alone, and still needed the guidance of controlling powers. The advocates of indirect rule asserted that this method provided the best means of preparing them for this future goal.

The essential aim of this policy was 'the development of an African society able to participate in the life of the modern world as a community in its own right';[3] or, again, it has been defined as 'a system by which the tutelary power recognizes existing African societies and assists them to adapt themselves to the functions of local Government'.[4] Such a policy required the conservation of what is best in African culture and the utilization, to the fullest extent, of the indigenous institutions in administering the colony. It is this last aspect of indirect rule which has met with most imitation and with most criticism, for it has been assumed that the whole system consists in this alone, and has therefore

---

[1] Lugard, *Dual Mandate*. Lugard, *Revision of Instructions to Political Officers* (Lagos, 1918), gives his explanation of the theory and practice of indirect rule. Sir Donald Cameron, *My Tanganyika Service and Some Nigeria* (London, 1939).

[2] Governor Slater, for example, told the legislative council in 1930 that '. . . government's declared policy . . . is so to guide the development of native institutions in this country that they will become more and more an integral part of the machinery of government'. Legislative Council, *Debates* (1930), pp. 84–85. Lugard, *Dual Mandate*, p. 199.

[3] Lucy Mair, *Native Policies in Africa* (London, 1936), p. 12. This book contains a good discussion of indirect rule in general and of its application to the Gold Coast, pp. 12–18, 157–68, 264–9. It is written from the viewpoint of the anthropologist.

One of the leading English authorities in this field is Marjory Perham. See her 'A Re-statement of Indirect Rule', *Africa: Journal of the International Institute of African Languages and Cultures* (hereafter cited as *Africa*), vol. VII (1934), pp. 321–34; Hailey, *African Survey*, pp. 133–5, 527–45 *passim*.

Since a correct application of this theory requires a detailed knowledge of local institutions, much stimulus has been given to anthropological research in Africa. The Gold Coast government inaugurated a Department of Anthropology in 1921 under the direction of Captain R. S. Rattray. See *Report on the Department of Anthropology* (1921). This department remained in existence until the retirement of Rattray in 1930 when the government decided that it would be wiser to train selected political officers in this field rather than to confine the work to a special department. Legislative Council, *Debates* (1930), 'Governor's Address', p. 86.

The International Institute of African Languages and Cultures was founded in 1927 to encourage such studies. For a statement of its aims, see *Africa*, vol. VII (1934), pp. 1–27.

[4] Marjory Perham, in *Africa*, vol. X (1937), p. 397.

left itself open to the charge that it merely perpetuates the domination of an antiquated and oppressive authority. It must be remembered, however, that maintenance of tribal institutions was not its principal object, for its advocates expected them to undergo radical changes as they became subjected to the influence of modern social and economic conditions. It was their hope, furthermore, that this evolution would not be towards a slavish imitation of Western methods but rather towards a new development which would combine the best in both European and African cultures. As Miss Perham states, the aim of this theory was 'to hold the ring, to preserve a fair field within which Africans can strike their own balance between conservatism and adaptation'.[1]

Indirect rule has been criticized not only by certain students of colonial theory, but by some of the Africans as well.[2] In the Gold Coast, members of the educated class often held that it did not make sufficient provision for their talents and training in the administration of the colony, and that the government used it to keep illiterate, pro-British chiefs in office.

To understand this attitude on the part of the intelligentsia and to account for the difficulties which indirect rule in the Gold Coast encountered, it will be necessary to consider the provisions of the original Native Administration Ordinance, their unsatisfactory consequences, and the efforts of the government to better the situation by providing the Gold Coast in 1925 with a new constitution, and in 1927 with an improved legislation for native rule.

It will be remembered that throughout the early nineteenth century the British had interfered as little as possible with the rule of the local chiefs and had even considered, in accordance with the 1865 recommendation of parliament, eventual withdrawal from the Gold Coast. Merchants and missionaries, however, wished to retain their trade relations or religious establishments; and it was finally realized, after the Ashanti War of 1873-4, that if peace and order were to be secured the government must take more responsibility for its maintenance. The Colony was therefore annexed in 1874, while two years later a legislative council with appointed members was re-established, to be followed in 1878 by a native jurisdiction ordinance which provided for the recognition of the chiefs. This last measure was replaced in 1883 by a second law which remained the basis, until 1927, for all native administration.

---

[1] ibid., vol. VII (1934), p. 331.
[2] Legislative Council, *Debates* (1929), pp. 156, 170; (1935), pp. 121, 144; Padmore, *How Britain Rules Africa*, p. 383; P. D. Quartey, 'Indirect Rule from a Native's Point of View', *Negro Year-Book. An Annual Encyclopedia of the Negro, 1937-1938* (Tuskegee Institute, Alabama, 1937).

The ordinance of 1883 confirmed the authority of the paramount and divisional chiefs,[1] though it failed to recognize the right to be consulted which the native councils had formerly possessed by customary law. It gave the paramount chiefs the power to make by-laws covering a wide range of subjects, such as the administration of public lands and forests and the upkeep of roads. On the judicial side it recognized African tribunals, but only in minor civil and criminal cases; while at the same time their jurisdiction was merely concurrent with that of the British courts and they had no power to enforce decisions. The ordinance was silent on the subject of the election and destoolment of chiefs, thus indirectly recognizing that such matters were the affair, not of the British government, but of native law. No provision was made, furthermore, for direct taxation nor for the administration of those tribal revenues which custom allows the chiefs to collect from time to time for specified purposes.

The whole ordinance bore the mark of the *laissez-faire* spirit of the nineteenth century. The British government recognized the local institutions, but made no attempt, as did Lugard later in Nigeria, to adapt these old forms to modern conditions. In their desire to protect the position of the chief, the British gave him wide authority which he could use or misuse in his own way, but they took from him his former power over life and death and his position as the one source of justice. This was particularly unfortunate at the very time when the cessation of the Ashanti wars lessened the need for tribal cohesion and tempted dissatisfied elements to destool their rulers or to seek independence.[2] Another weakness lay in the fact that the government directly took over the bulk of administrative duties instead of sharing them with the chiefs, as should have been done according to the theory of indirect rule. To sum up, then, the British had left the chiefs their full powers in some fields but with no provision for official guidance or control; while in

---

[1] *British and Foreign State Papers, 1882–1883*, vol. LXXIV, p. 604.
The term 'paramount chief' includes those who are not subordinate to any other paramount. There is one at the head of each of the sixty-three native states. The term 'divisional chief' refers to those who are directly subordinate to a paramount. Beneath divisional chiefs are chiefs and headmen. See *Native Administration Ordinance, 1927*, for lists of paramount and divisional chiefs.
[2] 'Governor's Address', *Gold Coast Gazette* (25 April 1925), p. 632. Guggisberg gives the following tabulation of destoolments:

Period	Number of Destoolments
1904–08	7
1909–13	23
1914–18	38
1919–24	41

certain administrative matters they had unnecessarily deprived them of authority, thus preventing the development which comes of responsibility and the added prestige it would have given them in the eyes of their subjects.

Examples of this situation can be found, for instance, in the matter of the African tribunals where, official supervision being unprovided for, judicial practices were sometimes corrupt. Another case in point is that of the by-laws. Regulations for the establishment of forest reserves and for the destruction of diseased cocoa pods were passed—due to government insistence—by the local authorities, but the legislation was not satisfactorily enforced. The chiefs had neither sufficient experience to realize their necessity, nor adequate power to execute them.

The growing prosperity of the colony, with its resultant increase of education and wealth, tended to lessen respect for tribal authority; while the position of the chief, as it then stood, gave the Gold Coast the benefit of neither direct nor indirect rule. Such was the situation in 1919 when Guggisberg came into office. After several years as governor he was convinced that the only remedy lay in strengthening the position of the chiefs, rather than in developing a purely European type of government. He believed that if these traditional rulers could receive more educational advantages and improve their methods of local government, they would gradually be able to take a place of leadership and to win over the educated to work with them. This same opinion was shared by Nana Ofori Atta, one of the few educated chiefs at that time. In 1913 he had been elected paramount of an Eastern Province state and had been appointed to the legislative council three years later. He was to make this goal of raising the position of the chiefs and of encouraging them to mutual co-operation the principal achievement of his long political career, which did not end until his death in 1943.

It was for the purpose of improving the local administration that Guggisberg made a first, though unsuccessful, attempt in 1921 to introduce a new native jurisdiction ordinance to the legislative council. It provided merely for the consolidation of a number of existing laws, for the recognition of the authority of paramounts over chiefs in judicial matters, and for the reservation of all land cases to the courts of the provincial commissioners; but it met with so much opposition that the governor decided to delay it for further research. He then turned his attention to the preparation of a constitution which would give new form to the legislative council and, by providing for increased representation of chiefs, would help indirectly to rehabilitate their authority.

Once they had a stronger position in the council it would be easier to get support for a more efficient native administration ordinance.

In May 1925 the new constitution[1] was granted to the Gold Coast, giving for the first time the right of elected representation. It provided for fifteen official and fourteen unofficial members. Of the unofficial members five were Europeans—three appointed by the governor to represent the banking, shipping, and mercantile interests; one elected by the local chamber of commerce; and one chosen by the chamber of mines. Among the nine African members, three were elected to represent the towns of Accra, Cape Coast, and Sekondi, and the six others were paramount chiefs elected in each of the three provinces of the Colony by a provincial council of paramount chiefs. According to population, the provincial council of the Eastern Province elected three representatives, the Central Province two, and the Western Province one. At these councils each paramount was accompanied by eight of his subordinate chiefs whom he was obliged to consult before expressing his opinion. For purposes of election, the voting strength of each one was calculated in proportion to the number of his subjects. In the Eastern Province there were three divisions—the Akan, the Gã, and the Ewe —with a paramount representing each section.

It was the intention of the government that these provincial councils of chiefs should not only exercise an elective function, but should also help to strengthen African authority by providing an opportunity for discussion of matters of tribal interest and by advising the government on any proposed legislation affecting the people. Guggisberg believed they would be of great value and thus expressed himself:

It was at the preservation of native institutions that I aimed when devising what is the outstanding feature of the new Constitution: the Provincial Councils. These Provincial Councils are really the breakwaters, defending our native constitutions, institutions, and customs against the disintegrating waves of Western civilization. They are the chief means by which the nationality of the Africans of the Gold Coast will be built up out of many scattered tribes; for it must be remembered that, although each Council functions for its own Province, yet arrangements have been made by which these Councils can meet and discuss many questions. . . . As time goes on, the experience and knowledge gained . . . will help the Paramount Chiefs . . . to develop gradually into bodies carrying far greater responsibility than they do in the present day.[2]

[1] *Laws of the Gold Coast in Force, 1936*, vol. IV.
[2] *Events, 1920–1926*, p. 23.

Although the new constitution had finally granted the educated classes elective representation, they opposed it fiercely on the grounds that the chiefs had twice as many members in the council as had the municipalities. What many of them really wanted was a constitution which would give them a more predominate position in the council and which would replace African institutions as rapidly as possible by a parliamentary type of government. They feared, too, that the chiefs would be mere tools in the hands of British officials and use their increased power to hold up the political development of the Gold Coast. One African newspaper wrote of the new law:

The issue is one of life and death with us, for if you perpetuate the possibility of the return of dummies to the Legislature, our national independence is gone for ever. Probably that is what has been aimed at all the time, to so gag the people that while they have a machinery ostensibly of an advanced type, yet to be truly and really voiceless in the affairs of their own country.[1]

Deeply concerned by this bitterness which the new constitution was engendering between the chiefs and the intelligentsia, Dr. Aggrey wrote in the spring of 1926 to a friend in America:

The new Order in Council concerning the new Legislative Council has stirred up a hornets' nest. Part of the people of the Eastern Province, especially the educated, are against it. . . . The Paramount Chiefs of the Eastern Province . . . including Nana Ofori Atta[2] and Konor Mate Kole are heartily for it. . . . The political atmosphere is charged.[3]

As Dr. Aggrey had said, the atmosphere was indeed charged and the educated classes were determined to prevent the new constitution from going into effect. Members of the Aborigines' Rights Protection Society and of the British West African Congress agitated against the provincial councils in the Press, through members of the legislative council and, in the autumn of 1926, finally sent a delegation to London to petition for an amendment to the constitution.[4] When these measures failed, the

[1] Quoted by Buell, *The Native Problem in Africa*, vol. i, p. 839, from the *Gold Coast Leader* (22 May 1926). The Gold Coast newspapers were often extremely critical of both British policy and of the chiefs. This opinion, however, was probably representative of only a minority of the population.

[2] 'Nana' is an honorific title. 'Konor' is used to designate a chief of the Krobo tribe. In 1927 Nana Ofori Atta was knighted and was thereafter known as Nana Sir Orfori Atta or Sir Ofori Atta.

[3] Smith, *Aggrey of Africa*, pp. 259–60.

[4] Gold Coast Aborigines' Rights Protection Society, *Petition for the Amendment of the Gold Coast Colony (Legislative Council) Order in Council, 1925* (London, n.d.).

dissenters turned to the chiefs themselves and succeeded in persuading a number of them that provincial councils were contrary to customary law. The government answered by pointing out that in the past the chiefs had often met of their own accord to discuss matters of inter-tribal concern. In spite of the opposition, electoral arrangements were made and on 17 May 1926 the three provincial councils met for the first time. In the Eastern Province, which was largely in favour of the new law, eleven out of twelve chiefs assembled, but in the Central Province only half of the paramounts put in an appearance, while the Western Province, under the influence of the Aborigines' Rights Protection Society, flatly declined to elect its representative. The government therefore left the Western Province unrepresented, but provided for the sixth chief by appointing Nana Ofori Atta, even though he belonged to the Eastern Province.

Gradually the bitter opposition to the new constitution lessened, and by 1928 the Western Province had its own chief in the legislative council while twenty-five out of the twenty-eight states of the Central Province were represented at the provincial council.

To Guggisberg this legislation brought:

. . . the keenest personal satisfaction. . . . The new Constitution is far more solidly based on the institutions which the people of this country have found best suited to them, and far more likely to develop into something bigger and wider than any mushroom constitution based on the ballot-box and the eloquence of politicians over whom the people have no control except at election time.[1]

Once the new legislative council was functioning, Guggisberg determined to solve the problem of the inefficient native government by different tactics. He invited the six head chiefs on the council to make proposals for a more satisfactory native administration ordinance. After

---

[1] *Events, 1920–1926*, p. 23. Some writers did not fully approve of the new constitution. Professor Buell believed that the provincial councils should have been based on an ethnic rather than a geographic principle, since they are meant to be tribal institutions. He was also of the opinion that the true goal of the Gold Coast was not an African legislative council—which is a European device—but rather a united nation governed by institutions of local origin. Buell, *The Native Problem in Africa*, vol. I, pp. 842–3.

Professor MacMillan, on the other hand, expressed the belief that the economic and social development of the Gold Coast had already gone too far for indirect rule to be practical as it was in Nigeria, Tanganyika, and other less advanced colonies. He would prefer a strong central government rather than the preservation of native institutions. William MacMillan and others, *Europe and West Africa; Some Problems and Adjustments* (London, 1940), pp. 94, 106, and *passim*.

A fuller discussion of this matter will be found in a later chapter.

preliminary conferences, the councils of the Eastern and Central Provinces prepared in joint session, without any official assistance, the draft for a new Bill. When it had been revised by the attorney-general it was introduced—for the first time in the history of the Colony by an unofficial member, Nana Ofori Atta—to the legislative council and passed on 19 April 1927, just a few days before Guggisberg's extended term of office came to an end.

The purpose of the new ordinance was to arrest the decay that was threatening African institutions, to place the authority of the chiefs on a more stable basis, and to extend their powers in some fields. To implement this aim the authority of the *oman* or state council, with its traditional personnel of paramounts, lesser chiefs, and councillors, was recognized as the highest authority within each native state. It was made responsible, subject to appeal to the provincial council, for disputes over election and destoolment. The latter council was also given jurisdiction over the demands of subordinate chiefs for independence, but in all executive or constitutional matters the final decision rested with the governor, who was guided by the reports of the native councils and the practices of customary law. The ordinance further empowered the governor to refer any matter to the councils for hearing and determination, a provision which proved most valuable especially for inter-tribal disputes and cases which require a detailed knowledge of local conditions or native customs. The jurisdiction of the paramount chiefs' tribunal was extended in civil matters, and decisions were made enforceable by execution against property. Disputes between different provinces were to be referred to a joint session of the provincial councils of the provinces concerned.

Although these measures strengthened native authority and lessened certain defects, especially through the functions of the provincial councils,[1] fundamental weaknesses still remained. The government had given itself no power to vary the schedule of chiefs who could hold tribunals—of which there were too many—nor to make a chief's right of jurisdiction dependent on official recognition of his election. Since political officers, furthermore, were not empowered to supervise these tribunals the dispensation of justice often remained corrupt, and one of the most essential elements of successful indirect rule was thus neglected.

On the administrative side no increased powers were delegated to the chiefs, and it still remained necessary for the government to take official

[1] Legislative Council, *Debates* (1931-2), 'Governor's Address', p. 288; *G.C. An. Report, 1930*, p. 3.

action when the by-laws for such essentials as forest reserves and plant-disease control were not enforced. A certain amount of financial control is another essential of successful African rule, but this too was neglected, as no provision was made for required direct taxation nor for stool treasuries. As these weaknesses became increasingly evident during the following decade, the legislative council tried to remedy the defects by amendments, but it was not until the 1940's that a completely reorganized and more satisfactory type of native authority ordinance was finally adopted.

The same type of opposition which had been stirred up by the 1925 Constitution was also shown to the 1927 Native Administration Ordinance. Once the Africans realized, however, that increased authority was given, not to the paramount chief as an individual, but rather to the state council, criticism gradually ceased from all but the usual die-hards.[1]

---

[1] The municipal members of the legislative council tried to delay passage of the Bill. Minutes of the Legislative Council, *Gold Coast Gazette* (21 May 1927), p. 1055. Their criticism is to be found in Gold Coast Aborigines' Rights Protection Society, *Petition to the House of Commons* (London, 1935), Sections 51–56.

CHAPTER V

THE GOLD COAST COLONY, 1928–39

When in April 1927 Guggisberg's term of office ended, he left to his successor, Sir Ransford Slater, a Dependency which had made much recent progress and yet which had many difficulties still to solve. As has been seen in Chapter III, the preceding years had been ones of almost unbelievable material growth, and by 1927 external trade had reached a record peak. In the political field, however, the story was a different one. Chapter IV has given an account of the efforts of Guggisberg to strengthen the position of the chiefs and to increase African representation on the legislative council, both of which measures met with opposition from the educated class. The present chapter will be concerned with the story of this opposition and then with the gradual betterment of relations. The world-wide economic depression, with its attendant problems, various political developments, especially in the provincial councils' system, social developments, and an ever-increasing progress and maturity among the Africans of the Gold Coast, all combine to make the years 1928–39 very eventful ones.

It will be recalled that Dr. Aggrey had likened the quarrel between the chiefs and the intelligentsia over the 1925 constitution to the stirring up of a hornets' nest.[1] The municipalities were jealous because they had only three members on the legislative council, whereas the chiefs, representing the rural areas, had six. This was a fair division since the rural population of the Colony is far greater than that of the towns, but the urban leaders did not want to see the chiefs' powers increased. They complained that the tribal rulers were too ignorant to represent the country properly on the legislative council, and they criticized their methods of local administration as backward and often corrupt. Some of them held that the British policy of preserving traditional usages was unwise, and that it would be better if these customary practices were replaced by European governmental institutions. Underneath their objections, however, was the fear that the chiefs would become autocratic, or that the British would use them as tools in order to hold the

[1] See p. 49 above.

53

Colony back from a rapid transition to self-government. This was the key to the intelligentsia's opposition to improvements in the status of the chiefs. Fundamentally, however, there was never any real antagonism between the two groups, for they both belonged to the same upper class, and both were interested in winning from the British the right to eventual autonomy. Their disagreements concerned the means rather than the final goal, the provincial members preferring their traditional political system to the Western institutions favoured by the urban representatives. In the long run, the underlying division of forces in the Gold Coast was not between the chiefs and the intelligentsia, but between the Europeans and the Africans on the fundamental issue of constitutional development. Because of this basic unity, the disagreements between the rural and coastal groups lessened during the years following the quarrel over the 1925 constitution, and they gradually learned the value of political co-operation. Nevertheless, it must be pointed out that, in spite of this growing harmony, antagonisms appeared again from time to time, but they were usually the result of quarrels between individual chiefs and municipal leaders, or between certain extreme groups rather than between the rulers and the educated classes as such. Moreover, as the number of educated chiefs and the opportunities for political experiences increased during the thirties and forties, the former distinctions were further lessened and the unity of the two classes became more evident.

The first step towards this mutual understanding between the provincial and municipal members of the legislative council was largely the work of Casely-Hayford, one of the Gold Coast's outstanding statesmen. Since early in the century, Casely-Hayford, the originator of the British West African Congress, had been an influential leader of the educated classes. He was at first antagonistic to the 1925 constitution and to the provincial councils' system, but he later recognized their value and became, as Dr. Danquah, another African leader, has written of him:

... one of the few leaders of his time who had the imagination to see through the present constitutional guarantees of Provincial Councils and Tribunals of Chiefs to a future constitutional order in which all the Provincial Councils would cease to remain three separate interests in the Eastern, Western and Central Provinces of the Colony and come together in a national consultative assembly with a greater scope and a recognized constitution wider than what a 'protective society' could ever be.[1]

[1] Magnus Sampson, *Gold Coast Men of Affairs Past and Present*, p. 35. This statement occurs in the introduction which was written by Dr. Danquah.

Once Casely-Hayford saw that there was a greater future for the provincial councils than for the Aborigines' Rights Protection Society, he worked with Nana Sir Ofori Atta for their success. Thus these two great leaders of the educated classes and the chiefs were able to bring about a fusion of the hitherto divided interests. After this conciliation had taken place in the spring of 1929[1] the municipal and provincial members usually worked harmoniously together in the legislative council.

There was one small group of intelligentsia, the remnants of the Aborigines' Rights Protection Society at Cape Coast, however, which remained antagonistic to the provincial councils and on several occasions opposed their policy, most notably in the society's petitions to London against the 1925 constitution.[2] But even these Cape Coast extremists were probably in agreement with the majority group on the fundamental issues of Gold Coast development, even though they did not always see eye to eye on the methods to be used.

The most significant feature of the new constitution was the provincial council system. The new law established a council in each of the three administrative provinces of the colony 'which shall consist of the Head Chiefs whose headquarters are situated within the Province'.[3] Each paramount could be attended by as many as eight of his own council who, in turn, represented the various divisions of the state, and no decisions were to be taken without their consent. The paramounts then elected delegates to the national legislative council. Thus the democratic character of the native institutions was preserved, the more so in view of the fact that any chief could be destooled by his people if they found his leadership unsatisfactory.

Sir Gordon Guggisberg had planned that the provincial councils should not only perform an elective function but should also give the paramounts and their councillors an opportunity to consult on subjects of common welfare and to advise the government in any projected legislation affecting the people. He had also foreseen the value of inter-provincial meetings where the chiefs could discuss the interests of the colony as a whole and thus replace sectional views by a wider outlook. While there were several such inter-provincial conferences during the

[1] For a full account of this important reconciliation and for a detailed discussion of the relationship between the chiefs and the intelligentsia, see Wight, *Gold Coast Legislative Council*, Chapter V.
[2] Gold Coast Aborigines' Rights Protection Society, *Petition for Amendment of the Gold Coast Colony (Legislative Council) Order in Council, 1925; Petition to the House of Commons* (1935).
[3] *Gold Coast Colony (Legislative Council) Order in Council, 1925*, clause 16.

early 1930's, the joint provincial council system was not definitely established until 1932.

Besides the political problems of the early part of the 1930 decade there were economic and social ones as well. In 1928 the new port of Takoradi was opened. It was soon found, however, that further deepening of the harbour was necessary as well as the building of a berth for oil-tankers. A second loan of £1,170,000 at 4½ per cent was made in 1931 in addition to the earlier one of 1925. In view of the economic depression that was being felt in the Gold Coast as elsewhere by that time, it proved to be a heavy financial burden.

Results of the slump in world prosperity were evident as early as 1929, when the price of cocoa dropped suddenly from £50 to £41 a ton, and in 1930 to as low as £20.[1] By that year, too, the annual revenue of the Dependency was only about two and a half million pounds in contrast to over four million in 1927. This loss of revenue was due to three main causes. Because of lower cocoa prices less was collected from export taxes. Secondly, the import receipts on liquor fell some 50 per cent in 1930, due to ordinances which provided for gradual restriction of the importation of geneva and gin. In the third place, the accustomed revenues from the railways dropped sharply. These reductions led to large budget deficits for the first time since 1924.

The question now arose as to whether there was any reserve on which the Colony could draw in such an emergency, or would it be necessary to balance the budget by sharp curtailment of expenses? It will be remembered that Guggisberg had so reorganized the finances of the Gold Coast in 1923 that the Colony had gradually built up a general reserve fund which at this time amounted to £1,200,000. This sum, however, was not to be used except with permission of London and only in the wholly exceptional case of complete failure of trade. In addition to the reserve fund, the Gold Coast had an accumulated surplus of over £2,000,000. This last sum might ease the situation for a time, but with a depreciated revenue of some £1,500,000 a year and with no assurance as to how long the depression would last, the government was faced with the necessity of drastic reduction of expenses. It was in such a crisis that the danger of a one-crop economy became evident. Sir Ransford Slater therefore increased import taxes, curtailed development projects of every kind, lessened social services, and compulsorily retired over 200 European and African officials before the end of their term of

[1] G.C. An. Report, 1930.

office.[1] When even these reductions did not appear sufficient, in his budget address of 1931 he suggested that an income tax be levied throughout the Gold Coast Colony. Up to this time all revenues had resulted from indirect levies, the bulk coming from import and export duties. The Africans had always felt a strong resentment against any form of direct taxation and earlier attempts to introduce it had failed. The rate suggested by Slater—six shillings in the pound—aroused widespread criticism from both the African and European inhabitants. In the legislative council the provincial and municipal members gave evidence of their growing unanimity of purpose by a joint opposition to the Bill. They argued that it was unjust to introduce an income tax until every source of revenue had been tapped. They suggested that the salaries of the British staff be cut, since this was being done in England and in other countries faced with depression deficits. They saw no reason why the general reserve fund should not be used. The representative from Accra, Dr. Nanka-Bruce, who was Accra's leading physician, stressed the fact that the people in the cities were suffering from unemployment and that their health was beginning to show the strain of hard times. He believed that it was a most unpropitious time to introduce a measure which would only serve to increase suffering and unrest. The people, he held, would prefer to have all government services—even those for health—cut still further rather than pay an income tax.[2] He argued moreover that it was unjust to impose a levy without an increase in self-government:

In every country where direct taxation is imposed there must be equal representation. I will only put the proposition: Is the government prepared to give this country full representation and is the government prepared to give control of our finances to the people of this country? If not, it is better that we remain where we are and try to balance our budget in some other way.[3]

The colonial secretary answered these objections with the statement that he did not see why responsible government was any more necessary for direct taxation than it was for indirect; that the prejudice of the Gold Coast against taxation would have to be dropped in these bad times; that if salaries were cut, the Colony could no longer expect to get able

[1] Legislative Council, *Debates* (1930), p. 16 and (1931) p. 266.
[2] ibid. (1931), pp. 367–84. It is probable that the greater majority of the people, not understanding the true nature of an income tax, were influenced by the criticism of an interested minority. There has always been, however, a prejudice against any form of regular taxation.
[3] ibid. (1931), p. 385.

officials, and finally that the one great weakness of the Dependency was its lack of a sense of personal responsibility to contribute towards the expenses of the state.

The governor finally ended this prolonged budget session by telling the councillors that he had never intended to leave the unofficial members unrepresented on a commission of investigation. A finance committee was then formed which included Nana Sir Ofori Atta and Dr. Nanka-Bruce as well as both official and unofficial European members.

The Africans eventually won their point, for the next budget made no provision for an income tax, and in 1932 an ordinance was passed which required a 4–10 per cent levy on all official salaries.

The following year the Gold Coast still faced a budget deficit, due largely to the heavy charges of the loans made in the 1920's. Sir Shenton Thomas, who replaced Slater as governor in the autumn of 1932, now suggested a local or stool tax to be collected by the chiefs. This would enable each state to pay for its own needs and thus relieve the central government. In addition it would be of immense value in training the Africans to civic responsibility. He promised that the matter of the income tax would be dropped until the depression was over. The chiefs, however, did not approve of his suggestion for a local tax, and nothing more was done about it at the time.

By 1934 world trade had begun to improve and the danger of budget deficits was apparently over. In comparison to other colonies the Gold Coast had come through those trying years with relative ease and with its reserve fund untouched. During one of the legislative sessions of that year, the chiefs thanked the governor for the cut which had been made in official salaries, and voted that this reduction be discontinued.

Before leaving the discussion of the Gold Coast finances during these years, there is one more point it would be wise to consider. The government loan of £4,000,000 made in 1920 bore an interest rate of 6 per cent. Those made in 1925 and 1931 amounted to £5,750,000 at 4½ per cent. These debt charges proved a very heavy burden during the early 1930's, and both the African and unofficial European members of the council suggested conversions at a lower rate of interest. If this action had been taken the Colony would have saved at least £177,500 a year. When pressed to give reasons for his refusal to convert the loans, Thomas answered that the Gold Coast had greatly benefited by the increased transportation facilities which this money had made possible. It would be unfair to ask the shareholders to lower their income for improvements received by another country.[1] High interest rates were, of course, common during the 1920's; but the failure to convert these loans during the depression, and the earlier mistake of not having used equity capital, have been the subject of much criticism, not only by the Africans but by Englishmen interested in colonial welfare.[2]

The spring session of the 1934 legislative council opened auspiciously with Sir Shenton Thomas's congratulations on the improving financial condition of the Colony. But before the session was over, it had developed into one of the most difficult a Gold Coast governor ever had to face. The chief cause of the dissatisfaction was two new ordinances proposed by the government, one concerned with the water supply, and the other with the prosecution of seditious acts.

The purpose of the former, the waterworks ordinance, was to shift the cost of the pipe-borne water supply in Accra, Sekondi, and Cape Coast from the general revenue of the Colony to the cities' inhabitants. The attorney-general very justly pointed out that it was not fair to use money supplied by the Colony as a whole to provide for the improvements of individual cities, and that in all other parts of the world, municipalities expected to pay for such services. As was usual on questions of direct taxation, not only the municipal representatives but all the African councillors objected to the Bill. They argued that the citizens were too poor at this time to bear another levy in addition to the local house rates. Probably they feared the criticism of their own people on so delicate a point as further taxation, especially as so much unrest had been caused by the recent proposal for an income tax. More fundamental than either of these reasons was the fact that the Bill left the control of the water rate entirely in the hands of the governor and his executive council. In spite of the protests of the African councillors, the Bill was passed by the usual vote of 20 to 9—twenty ayes of the European official and unofficial members against the nine nays of the Africans.[3] The Africans, feeling themselves helpless before the official majority, wrote: 'the waterworks ordinance reeks with unfettered bureaucracy'.[4]

[1] Legislative Council, *Debates* (1933), p. 7.
[2] See, for example, Rita Hinden, *Plan for Africa*, pp. 149–55, 171; Lord Hailey, *African Survey*, p. 1324; M. Dowuona, 'Economic and Social Development of the Gold Coast', *Quo Vadimus or Gold Coast Future*, p. 13. In 1945 a part of the 6 per cent £4,000,000 loan was repaid from the Gold Coast sinking fund, while the remainder was converted to a 3 per cent basis. This conversion reduced the annual loan charges from £265,000 to £80,400.
[3] Legislative Council, *Debates* (1934), p. 114.
[4] Gold Coast Aborigines' Rights Protection Society, *Petition to the House of Commons*, Section 58.

If the Waterworks Bill aroused such dissatisfaction, the Sedition amendment was to cause far greater unrest and lead to very strained relations between the government and the Africans. Ordinance 21 of 1934 provided for various changes in the criminal code of the Colony, including Clauses 4 and 5 which extended the former definition of sedition and the manner in which it was to be punished. The reason for this new policy was not so much that literature of a radical nature had been imported into the Gold Coast, but rather the general political unrest which was evident during these years of economic crisis. The government believed that the extremist views taken by certain sections of the local Press at that time would only serve to intensify dissatisfaction and foster race prejudice.[1] During the debates over the ordinance, the attorney-general explained that writings which tended to incite one class or one race against another were particularly dangerous in a colony with so many illiterates.[2] The Africans answered that they understood the necessity of a law against sedition, which, in fact, the Colony had had since 1892. It was the manner in which it differed from the sedition law in England to which they objected. According to the Gold Coast version it was a criminal offence even to have seditious material in one's possession and the onus of proof was put on the defendant rather than on the prosecutor. Moreover, it was the governor rather than the courts who was to decide what material was of a seditious nature. In reply, the government pointed out that the African was protected since no prosecution would take place without the consent of the attorney-general, and in that case the defendant would go before the courts for trial. The Africans were not satisfied with these explanations and the ordinance passed the second reading with the usual division between African and European votes.[3]

Two laws, then, the Waterworks Bill and the Sedition code ordinance, had been passed within the same session over the united protests of the African members. Public opinion was aroused and some of the population felt the time had come to demand of the Colonial Office in London an investigation of the recent legislation. In spite of some recent disagreements between the intelligentsia and the chiefs over local administration, the two groups were firmly united in their opposition to the 1934 ordinances. They believed that it was opportune to oppose not only this particular legislation, but to broaden their attack to the

[1] Legislative Council, *Debates* (1934), vol. I, p. 155.
[2] ibid., p. 132
[3] ibid., p. 56.

whole constitutional field and demand increased political powers. It is in this combined effort that the fundamental unity of the two groups is particularly evident. Though conflicts appeared again in later years this ground of common purpose must not be forgotten. As a result of this co-operation a committee of Accra citizens, organized to arrange for a Gold Coast delegation to England, obtained the chiefs' full political and financial support. Nana Sir Ofori Atta, the provincial leader, and Dr. Frederick Nanka-Bruce and Mr. Korsah, municipal representatives of Accra and Cape Coast respectively, headed the delegation, which included five other outstanding men from both the Colony and Ashanti. The members decided not to confine their requests merely to a withdrawal of the unpopular Bills, but to ask for general constitutional reforms. The petition which they presented to the secretary of state for the colonies in July 1934 included, therefore, demands for the elimination of the official majority on the legislative council, for permanent African representation on the governor's executive council, and for the eligibility of non-chiefs as provincial members of the legislative council.[1] While the petition was refused at the time and the delegates returned home with practically nothing to repay them for the time and considerable expense involved, the decade of the 1940's was eventually to see their requests granted. The strong opposition put up by the African members of the legislative council against the Water and Sedition Bills indirectly had a beneficial result, however, for it made the general populace realize for the first time that the unofficial members were really interested in public opinion and not just in their own personal welfare.

During this same summer of 1934 the Aborigines' Rights Protection Society decided to send its own delegation to England. The members of the society represented the extremist group of the intelligentsia who were still dissatisfied with the 1925 constitution and who had not taken part in the conciliatory movement which was uniting the chiefs and many of the educated leaders for co-operative political action. Since it did not agree with the petition of this group, it prepared one of its own. When the society's delegates were refused a hearing by the King-in-Council, they turned in desperation to the House of Commons. On 29 May 1935 Sir Arnold Wilson presented the society's petition to the House.[2] This document asked, as did Ofori Atta's petition, for a withdrawal of the 1934 legislation, but herein the resemblance ended.

---

[1] ibid., pp. 225–7. *Papers relating to the Petition of the Delegation from the Gold Coast Colony and Ashanti*, Sessional Paper No. XI of 1934 (Accra, 1934).
[2] *Parliamentary Debates*, 5th ser., Commons, vol. CCCII, col. 1103; Aborigines' Rights Protection Society, *Petition to the House of Commons*.

Instead of accepting the 1925 constitution and going on from there to ask for further political rights, it returned to conditions as they existed in the nineteenth century and contrasted the 'liberal and considerate spirit' shown by the British in the 1844 treaty with present policy. The whole argument lacked a realistic outlook and showed that the Aborigines' Rights Protection Society was still fostering an antagonism against the provincial councils and against the position of the chiefs.

On 16 August 1935, over a year after their arrival in London, the representatives of the Aborigines' Rights Protection Society were finally received by the under-secretary of state for the colonies. Though the legal advisers of the two delegates were not allowed at the meeting, the Africans were able to state their case fully. Their demand for an inquiry into the affairs of the Gold Coast by the Colonial Office, however, was rejected.[1] They then determined to remain in London until they received satisfaction. Several Labour members of the House of Commons believed that the delegation had been unfairly treated, and they endeavoured to help the Africans. From time to time throughout 1935–6 they brought the case of the Gold Coast to the attention of the House.[2] Though the society's petition was never reconsidered, and the Africans eventually returned home, some good appears to have resulted from the efforts of the two delegations. The Water Bill was not enforced until 1938, when the population could better afford to pay the rates, and very few prosecutions took place as a result of the Sedition ordinance.

When a new governor, Sir Arnold Hodson, replaced Sir Shenton Thomas in the autumn of 1934, it was evident from the tone of the new governor's first address to the legislative council that he was determined to show more sympathy for the interests of the Africans than had been done in recent years. It is only fair to point out, however, that the governorships of Slater and Thomas had coincided with the difficult and trying years of the depression. Now that prosperity was returning, Hodson had the pleasant task of initiating developmental projects and of appointing Africans to at least some of the positions which these new activities made possible. Ofori Atta and others remarked in the council that since his coming the co-operation between the government and the people was 'very much closer and more cordial than it had been in the past'.[3]

[1] *Parliamentary Debates*, 5th ser., Commons, vol. CCCXII, cols. 374, 1024.
[2] ibid., vol. CCCIV, cols. 2065–6, 2126; vol. CCCXII, col. 1505; vol. CCCXIII, cols. 1013–14.
[3] Legislative Council, *Debates* (1936), p. 119; ibid. (1935), p. 127; for criticism of Hodson, however, see J. B. Danquah, *Liberty of the Subject* (Kibi, Gold Coast, n.d.), pp. 21–24.

Hodson came to the Gold Coast in the autumn of 1934, and in November gave his first address to the legislative council. At this time he confined his remarks to generalities, and carefully avoided any of the issues which had caused so much friction in the past. The promulgation of the Waterworks ordinance, as has been seen, was delayed until 1938, while little was done to enforce the new Sedition law, and the imposition of an income tax was never attempted during Hodson's term of office. Although these problems were avoided for the time being, it was growing increasingly evident that some changes must be made in the ordinance governing native administration. In the first place, the Bill had been poorly drafted. It was so intricate that the Africans easily misunderstood it, and the law courts found it hard to apply. On one occasion the attorney-general of the Gold Coast remarked that 'the architects of this measure left a somewhat unwelcome legacy to their successors who tore their hair in despair in endeavours to get it in shape'.[1]

In addition to its poor form the ordinance was faulty in that it made provision neither for stool treasuries nor for proper judicial supervision by British officials. Unless the government of the chiefs were efficiently carried on, they could never hope to merit the respect of the educated Africans or to obtain their co-operation in local affairs. Due to the *laissez-faire* policy of the period prior to 1920, the paramounts had not received the training and supervision which would have helped them to improve local government according to modern needs.

Though the intelligentsia had often co-operated with the chiefs in the legislative council, they still remained critical of their methods of government. They had much to criticize, of course, for rural administration was inefficient and sometimes corrupt. In spite of this attitude, however, the municipal members usually opposed native administration amendments intended to improve local government. They were suspicious of any measure which would give the British further power of supervision over rural institutions. They feared that if the chiefs had increased powers they might become, on the one hand, autocratic or, on the other, mere puppets of the government officials. The British in their turn urged the educated citizens of each state to take an interest in local government and become members of the various councils—village, divisional, or *oman*—so that the old complaint that there was no place for the intelligentsia in the civic life of the Gold Coast would no longer be true. Once on these councils, they could use their influence and training to raise the standard of native administration.

[1] Legislative Council, *Debates* (1936), p. 60.

During the 1930 decade the government made several attempts to introduce regular local taxation, sound treasury systems, and more efficient courts. Sometimes the chiefs themselves objected to these measures, but usually it was the municipal members who tried to prevent the passage of such legislation. On one occasion when an urban representative was blocking an amendment which would strengthen local government, Nana Sir Ofori Atta broke out in disgust:

> If I listen to these Barristers I often wonder what they really think of the Chiefs. One day they would say to the Chiefs 'You are our Almighty God' and the next day the Chiefs would not be worthy of the respect due to the scavenger.[1]

Similarly Nana Acquah III, the paramount of Winneba, added that if the municipal members were not curbed, the authority of the chiefs would soon be completely undermined.[2]

The lack of definite annual revenue and efficiently managed treasuries was perhaps the outstanding weakness of the native government. Most of the population objected to the establishment of stool treasuries because they feared it would lead to the imposition of regular local taxes. In 1931 an amendment (Ordinance 23) allowed the chiefs to inaugurate treasuries, but no use was made of the permission. The paramounts feared destoolment. In some of the native states, especially in the Western Province where the large gold-mines were located, substantial royalties were annually paid to various stools by European companies. This money was sometimes extravagantly spent by African officials rather than applied to those social and economic improvements which were pressingly needed and which would have benefited the entire population. In other states which had neither mines nor cocoa plantations as sources of wealth, a wisely controlled budget was even more necessary.

Prior to 1936 such states depended on court fees or occasional levies for their finances. No public accounting was made as to how the money was spent, and there was often much dissatisfaction on this score. Since the 1931 ordinance already permitted state treasuries, the present problem was to get the chiefs to avail themselves of this right. Two other ordinances were introduced in 1936 and 1939, making it legal for a chief

[1] Legislative Council, *Debates* (1936), p. 85. Several of the chiefs spoke very good English. Others had not a full command of the language, but they managed, nevertheless, to express themselves clearly and forcefully. There was a very marked improvement in the debates of the chiefs over the years 1926–46.

[2] ibid.

to impose regular taxation, provided his state council agreed and had the governor's permission. The British officials did all they could to get the various chiefs to apply the ordinances, as improvement in local government and the expansion of needed social services depended so largely on a sound financial structure. Response was slow at first, but gradually opposition weakened, especially after the governor promised a share of central government funds to those states which had satisfactory treasury systems.

Another amendment which made possible further improvements was Ordinance 18 of 1935 which allowed the district commissioners a right of supervision over the native tribunals, which were sometimes notoriously corrupt, and gave them a restricted authority to review judgements.

The native administration was also strengthened by an increasing use of the provincial councils. Sir Gordon Guggisberg had hoped that they would be of much value in uniting the sixty-three small states and in widening the outlook of the various chiefs. His hopes were not in vain, and once the first antagonism had broken down, these chiefs came to be regarded as the mouthpiece of the people. As early as 1929 occasional inter-council committees conferred on subjects of common interest. This movement led to the inauguration of joint provincial councils, which were meetings of the three councils as one, whenever united action was desirable. They also provided for a standing committee made up of four representatives from each province, with a chairman elected for a two-year term. Its purpose was to give advice or take action on matters referred to it by the councils, to consider the agenda for the annual sessions of the provincial councils, and to make recommendations for their adoption or rejection. Its successful development has been thus described:

The Standing Committee has within a very short time of its existence made its influence felt and is fast becoming an indispensable factor in the Provincial Council system. Guided, therefore, along right channels and with the State Councils and the State Treasury developed, the Provincial Councils may in the near future grow to be a strong bulwark of our heritage.[1]

This quotation, showing the high place the council had come to hold in the political life of the Gold Coast was probably representative of general public opinion. Appreciation of native government by the intelligentsia had at first, as we have seen, been characteristic of only a

[1] Magnus Sampson, 'A Starting Point in Native Institutions', Achimota Dicussion Group, *Pointers to Progress*, edited by C. T. Shaw (Achimota, 1942), p. 34.

few far-sighted leaders. Only very gradually did this prejudice begin to break down. It was possibly the united action of the paramounts in 1937 in putting over an economic boycott against European firms which won these chiefs the greatest respect of the professional classes.

This boycott, or 'cocoa hold-up' as it was popularly termed, was the direct result of an agreement on the part of European companies to control the cocoa market in both the Gold Coast and Nigeria.[1] As has been seen, the economic life of the country depends to a very large extent on cocoa because in some years as much as two-thirds of the entire revenue has come from the tax levied on its export. The world price fluctuated severely during the period 1918–38, going as high as £122 a ton in 1920 and dropping to £18 in 1930. This unfortunate dependence on a one-crop economy caused much distress and uncertainty in the Colony and led the peasant farmer, in his ignorance of the forces of world economics, to suspect that alien capitalists were to blame for the situation. In actual fact, the trouble was due in part to a faulty organization of the cocoa industry within the Colony itself, in part to the situation resulting from the intense competition among the cocoa-buying firms of West Africa, and to some extent also to the unsatisfactory state of the world market for primary produce.[2]

In the mid-thirties the price per ton averaged about £21, but in 1936 various local and foreign influences combined to send it up to £44. The following year the fourteen major firms dealing in Gold Coast and Nigerian cocoa made a secret buying agreement whose purpose was to control the price and prevent the ruinous intercompany rivalry. Several of these firms, especially the United Africa Company, also controlled the bulk of imports into the Gold Coast and had established merchandise stores throughout the Dependency. If the agreement had succeeded, the African would probably have found that both the buying of his products and the sale of European imports would have been in the hands of a single combine.

In the autumn of 1937 rumour of the pending agreement began to leak out among the Africans. Seven years earlier they had suffered in

---

[1] The text of the agreement is given in *Report of the Commission on the Marketing of West African Cocoa*, Cmd. 5845 (1938), Appendix J. (Hereafter cited as *Report on Cocoa*, Cmd. 5845 (1938).)
[2] A further discussion of the cocoa industry will be found in Chapter VIII. Several good accounts of this problem have been written. Besides the excellent parliamentary report of 1938, there is a thought-provoking discussion in MacMillan, *Europe and West Africa*, pp. 80–92. A survey of a typical cocoa village is given by W. R. Beckett, *Akokoaso: A Survey of a Gold Coast Village* (London, 1943). The *Gold Coast Annual Report* has good summaries on the cocoa industry.

a similar situation and the price of their cocoa had been greatly lowered. This time they decided to reject it. By October the farmers of the Gold Coast Colony, of Togoland, and of Ashanti had united under the guidance of their chiefs or of farmers' unions in a solid determination to resist to the bitter end. Not only did they refuse to sell any cocoa whatsoever, but they boycotted the retail stores of the firms connected with the pool. The hold-up lasted from October until the end of April and involved an almost complete stoppage of the economic life of the Dependency. The great personal suffering it entailed was borne bravely, in the hope that once and for all the threat of a monopoly might be removed.[1]

Sir Arnold Hodson believed that he should maintain a strictly neutral policy throughout the crisis. That he endeavoured to do so can perhaps be concluded from the fact that both the European firms and the Africans accused him of favouring the opposite side.[2]

In November representatives of the government, of the buyers' firms, and of the Africans met in Accra for conferences, in the hope of reaching a satisfactory settlement. As the European merchants refused to give up their agreement, Hodson suggested that, in view of the great harm the boycott was causing, the producers give the plan one season's trial, with the understanding that they could resubmit their case if they were dissatisfied. Because of the remarkable co-operation which the joint provincial council and the farmers' leaders were able to obtain from the entire population, Ofori Atta, the representative of the Africans, was in a position to refuse the governor's plan and to hold out for a complete abandonment of the agreement. Consequently the boycott continued, and in March a parliamentary committee, under the chairmanship of William Nowell, arrived in the Gold Coast to study the whole problem of the West African cocoa market. By the end of April it succeeded in negotiating a truce between the producers and the buyers, and within the next four months the whole of the accumulated stocks, amounting to some 476,000 tons, were sold.

The Nowell Commission afterwards published a very full report covering the cocoa problem in general, the history of the hold-up, and its recommendations for future policy. It strongly condemned not only the merchants' attempt to control the price, but also the inefficient and often dishonest methods of the African brokers and middlemen.

---

[1] J. B. Danquah, *Liberty of the Subject* (Kibi, Gold Coast, n.d.), pp. 9–24. This pamphlet gives an interesting account of the hold-up by an African writer.
[2] *Report on Cocoa*, Cmd. 5845 (1938), Sections 181, 219.

During the boycott, the European companies complained that the strike was not the wish of the farmers at all, but was fomented by radical agitators and encouraged by the chiefs for reasons of personal gain. They condemned the government for a weak policy in not forcibly breaking the hold-up. The Nowell Commission, however, reported that the Africans had been almost 100 per cent behind the movement and had supported the chiefs' actions. It approved of Hodson's efforts to remain neutral and stated that 'we consider that the local government acted throughout with tact and that credit is due to Sir Arnold Hodson and his officers for their handling of a very delicate situation'.[1] It recommended that for the future the government help the producers to combine into some sort of co-operative selling organization of their own, and in conclusion it forthrightly stated that *'in all the circumstances it is our opinion that the Agreements should be finally withdrawn'*.[2]

Hodson consequently appointed a Gold Coast committee to study the possibilities of a local organization. The outbreak of the war in 1939 delayed the adoption of such a plan and during the war years the British government itself marketed the cocoa.

One of the outstanding results of the cocoa hold-up was that the successful leadership of the chiefs in this affair strengthened the confidence and respect, both of the common people and the educated classes, for their authority. Thenceforth there appears to have been more co-operation between these two groups, though disagreements were sometimes to reappear. After the establishment of the joint provincial council, the chiefs took an ever more active part in the affairs of the Gold Coast as a whole, for these meetings opened their eyes to the general as well as to the purely local aspect of their problems. Among the topics discussed, the question of advanced government positions for Africans was one of those most frequently introduced. Sir Gordon Guggisberg had made definite plans for the gradual increase of Africans in positions usually held only by Europeans. According to this programme 'the number of Africans holding European appointments should steadily grow from 27 in 1925–6 to 151 in 1935–6'.[3] But the plan was not carried out, and in 1938 only 41 Africans were in such positions. This failure to carry out Guggisberg's plan was naturally most disappointing, both to the educational institutions which had trained the

[1] *Report on Cocoa*, Cmd. 5845 (1938), section 230.
[2] ibid., Section 489.
[3] *Events, 1920–1926*, para. 225; see also Chapter IV above.

youth of the Gold Coast and to the Africans themselves. The latter made many complaints,[1] and in 1938 the joint provincial council directed Ofori Atta to make another strong representation in the legislative council concerning the matter. The governor, in reply, promised to discuss the problem at the forthcoming conference of colonial governors,[2] and the next year, 1939, he announced a new policy of government appointments. Plans were being made to establish an intermediate grade of officer. If a man proved competent he would then be given a scholarship for further training in England as a direct preparation for advancement.[3]

The sympathy between the chiefs and the educated classes which was increasing during the late 1930's was evident in the establishment of the Gold Coast Youth Conference. This association was not a society, but merely a convention, a calling together, from time to time, of the various societies and clubs of the Gold Coast to discuss affairs of common interest to their members. Its aim was not meant to be political, but rather to awaken the young people to the economic and social needs of their country.[4] One of the interesting characteristics of this association was that, while it was organized by Dr. Danquah and other professional men, it also counted many of the most important chiefs among its patrons. In one of its earliest publications it spoke with pride of the excellent work done by the joint provincial council and recognized that this body was in a position to win the co-operation of the various sections of the country and to guide them to united action.

Another organization of a somewhat different type was begun in the winter of 1939, namely, the Achimota Discussion Group, at first made up only of members of the college staff, but later enlarged to include representatives of the missions, the government, the provincial councils, and private citizens.

Here was an opportunity for that meeting of minds between the two races which was so necessary if co-operative action were to go on. The members planned to meet unofficially from time to time in order to talk over the various problems of the Gold Coast and to suggest possible solutions. The results of these conferences were published and they gave an excellent picture, not only of a certain section of public opinion but also of the friendly spirit which characterized the meetings. The

[1] See, for example, Legislative Council, *Debates* (1929), pp. 153ff.; and (1937) p. 97.
[2] ibid. (1938), pp. 91, 100.
[3] ibid. (1939), vol. I, pp. 23, 196–7; see also chapter above.
[4] 'Gold Coast Youth Conference; Its Constitution and History', *First Steps towards a National Fund* (Accra, 1938), pp. 23–24.

idea of these study groups later spread to Ashanti, and a successful conference was held in Kumasi.[1]

The opinions expressed by both the Youth Conference and the Achimota Discussion Group pointed to the need for greater economic and social progress, but a progress based on research and scientific knowledge rather than on spasmodic and unco-ordinated development. Of these matters something will be said in a later chapter. They also stressed, though from somewhat different viewpoints, the necessity for political growth and increased self-government. Some of the younger and more radical of the Africans made use of every chance to demand immediate and complete autonomy.[2] But the older men, especially the chiefs, though they wanted an African majority on the legislative council and other reforms, appeared more willing to wait for a gradual evolution towards independence. Most of the Africans were loyal to the British connexion, wishing to remain within the Empire if they could achieve, in the not too distant future, the status of a dominion. As Casely Hayford once remarked,

... every son and daughter of the whole territory is well and rightly persuaded that our destiny is linked with Great Britain, and that under her tutelage, we shall succeed in achieving the best of every phase of life. Our quarrels and bickerings are domestic affairs ... on the larger issues we are agreed, and no one can shake the African's firm belief in the virtues that have made England the model state for the world.[3]

In reviewing the events of the 1919–39 period they seem to fall into two divisions. There was a time of rapid growth from 1919 to 1929 when

[1] Achimota and Kumasi Discussion Groups, *Towards National Development; Post-War Gold Coast* (Achimota, 1945).

An Anglo-American mission group, when making an educational survey in West Africa, noticed this same friendly spirit. 'In no other territory visited was co-operation between the government and missions so close, nor did we anywhere else meet Africans with a greater sense of public service or find such free and natural professional and social contacts between Africans and Europeans.' Jackson Davis, *Africa Advancing: A Study of Rural Education and Agriculture in West Africa and the Belgian Congo* (New York, 1945), p. 66.

The discussion group movement was particularly valuable since, at the time, there was no first-class Press. Some of the newspapers were immoderate in tone and the Africans themselves recognized the need for better journalism. Lugard considered that such publications were a serious danger to racial peace. Lugard, *Dual Mandate*, p. 80.

[2] For example, see N. Azikiwe, *Renascent Africa* (Lagos, 1937). Azikiwe was editor of the *African Morning Post*, a Gold Coast newspaper, during the mid-1930's. He was eventually fined and imprisoned for seditious writings. Later he was acquitted by the West African Court of Appeal and went to Nigeria, where he became a leader in the nationalist movement. His writings, which are a plea to the youth of Africa to assert itself and demand complete autonomy, are very popular among many of the younger generation. See also A. A. Nwafor Orizu, *Without Bitterness* (New York, 1944), p. 293.

[3] J. W. de Graft Johnson, *Towards Nationhood in West Africa* (London, 1928), p. 79.

trade and revenue increased by leaps and bounds and when an equally surprising expansion of communications, public utilities, and social services was therefore possible. At the same time, the government permitted additional African representation on the legislative council and endeavoured, by the 1927 Native Administration Ordinance, to strengthen the authority of the traditional chiefs.

The depression years followed this prosperous period when the drop in revenue, the resultant suffering, the administrative attempt to introduce an income tax and to curtail civil rights by a new sedition policy, all combined to cause unrest in the Gold Coast. With the governorship of Sir Arnold Hodson in 1935, the authorities appeared to take a more sympathetic attitude. The next four years saw some improvement in local government. Certain states inaugurated stool treasuries; the joint provincial council made unified political action possible; and the chiefs' leadership in the cocoa hold-up strengthened their position. By 1939 the Colony was ready to take advantage of the stimulation to general development which the exigencies of war were to bring to all of West Africa. Before the 1939–46 years are considered, however, it would be wise to give some attention to the other divisions of the Dependency and to the economic and social progress of the previous period. Only after this survey has been made can the reader appreciate the problems of the Dependency as a whole.

CHAPTER VI

ASHANTI

While the years 1919–39 saw great development in the Gold Coast Colony itself, the other sections of the Dependency, namely, Ashanti, the Northern Territories, and Togoland, were also making good progress. After the powerful Ashanti Confederacy was conquered in the late nineteenth century by the British, the federation was dissolved and its king was deported to the Seychelles. In 1901 the British annexed the territory and entrusted its control to the governor of the Gold Coast. The Order-in-Council which implemented this change[1] gave the governor authority to provide by ordinance for the administration of justice, the collection of revenue, and for all that was necessary to maintain peace and good government. He was to exercise his authority through a chief commissioner who in turn would be aided by district commissioners and other officers. There was, therefore, no need for either a legislative or an executive council in Ashanti.

In the days of the old confederacy, the various chiefs had owed allegiance to the paramount of the Kumasi, since it was his predecessor, Osei Tutu, who in the eighteenth century had first organized the Ashanti groups on a federal basis.[2] Since that time, this king had been recognized as head chief in his own state but as Asantehene with reference to the entire country. When in 1896 the British deported King Prempeh, the federal form of government was dissolved and the various units remained isolated, each under the rule of its own chief. But the state of Kumasi had lost its paramount, so that native administration was thrown out of line and much disorder ensued. As a result the British decided in 1905 to replace him by a state council. The eighteen divisional chiefs who would have held this right under the former dynasty and who resented their loss of power, were invited to form a Kumasi Council under the chairmanship of the chief

[1] *British and Foreign State Papers, 1903–1904*, vol. xcvii, p. 988. Ordinance for the Administration of Ashanti (1902), *Laws of the Gold Coast in Force, 1936*, Chapter 94 (hereafter cited as *Laws, 1936*).
[2] R. S. Rattray, *Ashanti Law and Constitution* (Oxford, 1929), p. 76.

commissioner.[1] Their authority, however, was limited to their own state in contrast to the federal powers they had held before 1896. Gradually the bitterness of the chiefs and people against the conquering power began to disappear, through the willingness of the various commissioners to adapt policy to local needs. Governor Sir Gordon Guggisberg attributed the progress of Ashanti to its economic prosperity, to the wisdom of its commissioners, and to the elasticity and common sense of British rule which seemed instinctively to adapt itself to the successive phases in the evolution of the race.[2]

The economic prosperity of which he spoke resulted in great part from the cocoa farms. Shortly after the annexation of Ashanti, this form of agriculture was introduced, especially into the western half where large areas were suitable for it. Rubber and kola also did well in these same districts. As soon as the *Pax Britannica* had assured steady commercial conditions, European and Hausa traders moved into Kumasi, which remained the capital of the colony. In 1903 the railway connecting it with Sekondi on the coast was completed. Eventually good roads were also built, and in 1923 a second railway was opened, running from Kumasi to Accra. Little by little the capital itself gradually changed from an entirely African town to a well-laid-out European city which in 1938 had a population of over 44,000.

Yet such development came gradually and, during the years 1901–20, progress must often have seemed slow to the British officials. There were not sufficient funds to provide for all the schools, roads, hospitals, and other social services necessary to transform the forest area into a modern colony. Although Kumasi improved, the rate of development was not evenly distributed throughout the territory, so that many sections still remained primitive. The inhabitants in Ashanti were not any more ready to accept direct taxation than those in the colony, and even the chiefs' levies were most irregular and only grudgingly accepted by the people. It was still the policy of the British Empire to expect each colony to pay for its own improvements, as the idea of a Colonial Development Fund was not to come for many a year. Ashanti, therefore, had to get along as best it could on local fees and on its share of the import and export taxes of the Dependency.

If there had been more revenue, much of it would probably have

[1] Sir Francis Fuller, *A Vanished Dynasty* (London, 1921), p. 216. Fuller was chief commissioner in Ashanti from 1902 to 1920 and did much by his sympathy and common sense to help its people adjust themselves to British rule. His book gives an excellent account of these early years. See also the Ashanti Annual Reports.

[2] *Events, 1920–1926*, p. 234.

been spent on education, for the Ashantis were anxious for an increased number of government schools. In 1925 there were five such institutions, besides twenty-eight assisted schools, and some one hundred and fifty-eight in the non-assisted class.[1] Non-government institutions were conducted either by missionaries or by Africans.

The first Christian church was built in Kumasi as early as 1841 by a Methodist missionary, but the numerous wars of the nineteenth century naturally prevented almost all missionary activity. Even in the twentieth century progress was slow. Many of the early converts gave up their allegiance to the chiefs and to native customs, which aroused such antagonism that the schools of the missionaries were not well supported. But the Ashantis were eager for education and for the advantages enjoyed by the inhabitants of the coastal areas, so they clamoured for government schools. Eventually the missionaries succeeded in getting converts to remain loyal to their tribes. Christianity then spread more rapidly, and by 1925 there were nearly thirty denominational schools. The Methodists opened a training college in 1923 at Kumasi, where they spent some £25,000 on its fireproof building and extensive grounds.

During the world war of 1914–18, though practically all troops were withdrawn from Ashanti for the Togoland campaigns, the Africans remained thoroughly loyal and contributed generously to Great Britain's war expenses. After the war Ashanti felt, in a limited way, the wave of restlessness and desire for increased freedom which swept over much of colonial Africa. It was particularly evident in a growing rift between the older and younger members of most of the tribes. The young men resented the authority of illiterate chiefs and the levies required to pay for the heavy debts which encumbered many of the Ashanti stools. It was clear that the very existence of African institutions was threatened unless a strong counter-balance could be introduced. As in the Gold Coast Colony, the British officials determined to improve the position of the chiefs by more efficient forms of local government. A new native jurisdiction ordinance would have to be prepared, but it would be necessary first to have a thorough knowledge of Ashanti law and customs if the best of the past was to be preserved.

In 1921 an anthropology department was inaugurated by the Gold Coast government under the direction of Captain Robert Rattray, an anthropologist and former commissioner, who had had much experience in Ashanti. It was part of a more general movement, as we have seen,

[1] *Ashanti Annual Report, 1925.* In 1925 only 7,209 children out of a total population of 486,000 were in school.

to implement the policy of indirect rule in British Africa. Rattray believed that the people of Ashanti had come to the parting of the ways where there was a choice either of giving up African institutions in favour of European ones or of trying to preserve what was best in their own culture that it might be adapted to modern conditions.[1] He preferred the latter course, and found that the greater majority of the inhabitants shared his views. During the years 1920–7 he spent much of his time travelling among the various Ashanti tribes, where he won the confidence of the old men and women who were still steeped in the ancient beliefs and practices of their people. He was thus able to make a complete study of their religion, constitution, law, and folk-lore.[2] Such material would be helpful to the British officials, to missionaries, and to the Africans themselves.

It was found that the old Ashanti Confederacy, though autocratic in appearance, was 'in correct practice democratic to a degree',[3] since the chief was dependent on his council, which in turn represented the various divisions of the state. The federation, moreover, had been of great value in that it welded the Ashantis into one nation, restricted the powers and ambitions of great chiefs, and satisfied the West African's love of a titular head.

Because of this early tradition of united action, it would probably be easier to make a success of indirect rule among the Ashantis than in the Colony. Besides being among the most gifted tribes of West Africa, they had not been misled, as was so often the case in the Colony, by the bad example of slave trading or unprincipled Europeans.

In 1921 an interesting event occurred which showed that most of the Ashantis were still very loyal to their traditions. It will be remembered that the golden stool was their symbol of nationhood; it contained the *sunsum* or soul of the people. Since the fatal British attempt to gain possession of this stool in 1901, the people had kept it carefully hidden. Twenty years later a group of African road-builders accidentally came across its hiding-place, whereupon several Ashantis, having robbed the stool of its ornaments, sold them for the gold they contained. News of the sacrilege soon crept out and. the whole nation was aroused. As a

---

[1] *Report on the Anthropological Department, 1926–1927*, p. 6. See Agnes Donohugh, 'Essentials of African Culture', *Africa*, vol. VIII (July 1935), pp. 329–38, for a good discussion of this problem.

[2] The results of Rattray's research can be found in the reports of the anthropological department, and in fuller form in his four books; *Ashanti* (Oxford, 1923); *Religion and Art in Ashanti* (Oxford, 1927); *Ashanti Law and Constitution* (Oxford, 1929); *Tribes of the Ashanti Hinterland* (Oxford, 1932).

[3] Rattray, *Ashanti Law and Constitution*, p. 82.

result of Captain Rattray's studies, the British officials understood the gravity of the situation and took a wise course of action. The culprits were arrested and the Kumasi Council of Chiefs allowed to try them in their own local fashion. So serious did they consider the crime that the death penalty was imposed. The British, fearing an internal revolt, later commuted the sentence to perpetual banishment. As for the stool itself, the chief commissioner explained to the Ashantis that the government held no claim to it and that it remained the property of the nation. This action helped to atone for the earlier attempt of a British governor to seize the stool, and it deepened the loyalty of the people.[1]

Shortly afterwards the Queen Mother of Mampong, one of the Ashanti states, sent a replica of her own silver stool to Princess Mary of England on the occasion of her wedding.

It may be that the King's child [Princess Mary] has heard of the Golden Stool of Ashanti. That is the Stool which contains the soul of the Ashanti nation. All we women of Ashanti thank the governor exceedingly because he has declared to us that the English will never again ask us to hand over that Stool. This stool we give gladly. It does not contain our soul, as our Golden Stool does, but it contains all the love of us Queen Mothers and of our women. The spirit of this love we have bound to the stool with silver fetters, just as we are accustomed to bind our own spirits to the base of our stools.[2]

If the relations between the government officials and the chiefs were improving, this was not the case with reference to the African rulers and the 'young men'.[3] The ever-increasing need for a law which would strengthen the position of the chiefs was finally met in 1924 by the Native Jurisdiction Ordinance of that year. This Bill set down definite regulations for the legal election and destoolment of chiefs, making them subject to the confirmation of the chief commissioner. It made more definite provision for local courts and included a schedule of a select number of chiefs and subchiefs to whom jurisdiction was granted. The ordinance appears to have been well received, and some of the rulers not included in the schedule began to demand this privilege. The report of the following year states that there was steady improvement in its application, but that it was difficult for the tribunals to function properly without trained registrars who were evidently very scarce in Ashanti. Of

[1] *Ashanti Annual Report, 1921*, pp. 21–29.
[2] *Report on the Anthropological Department, 1922*, p. 12.
[3] The term 'young men' was used by the chiefs to refer to the ordinary citizens as distinct from the chiefs and elders.

1,667 cases disposed of by native courts that year, only 75 were appealed to the district commissioners. Eventually the commissioners were able to train the African clerks in the intricacies of legal procedure, and affairs then went more smoothly, especially as no lawyers were allowed in the tribunals of Ashanti.[1]

Two years later Ordinance 10 of 1927 provided for native treasuries. These were not compulsory, but the commissioners encouraged them in districts which were the least unfavourable to sound finance. By 1929 only thirteen areas had taken advantage of the law. One report states that it was difficult for the Africans to see any connexion between revenue received and expenditure made. In the next decade, however, the Ashantis began to realize that the publication of stool accounts prevented much corruption. The chiefs were required to open bank accounts whenever possible, and no withdrawals of funds nor contraction of stool debts was allowed without the signature of the district commissioner.

Another step forward came in connexion with the city of Kumasi. Since it was the commercial as well as political centre of Ashanti, it had been growing rapidly since 1901. The entire area within the city limits was a Crown estate, where the land was rented to the inhabitants. Little was done in the early years to control municipal growth by carefully prepared plans. In 1924, however, a serious plague broke out in the Zongo area, which was the quarters of the Hausa traders. This disaster appears to have hastened the modernization of the city. The next year a public health board was inaugurated with both European and African members, appointed by the chief commissioner, or nominated by the chiefs and chamber of commerce. It was made responsible, under the control of the chief commissioner, for the sanitation and development of the city. Its main source of revenue was the land rents which the government turned over to it for some years, as a grant-in-aid. There were also various fees for licences and markets, and after 1928 the board levied house rates. An excellent town-planning scheme was prepared, and before the depression in 1930 almost £1,000,000 had been spent on the commercial section by the government public works department, the public health board, and by private owners.[2] In 1942 the British restored the Crown lands of Kumasi to the Asantehene, but in such a way as to preserve the rights already granted to other parties. During the

---

[1] Ordinances 1 and 2 of 1933 eventually allowed lawyers in native courts, but only for certain types of cases. For the criticism of the Gold Coast lawyers against this restriction, see Legislative Council, *Debates* (1933), p. 84.

[2] ibid. (1930), p. 90. Of this sum £320,604 was spent by people of Ashanti.

war period also, further plans were made for the modernization of
Kumasi, which developed into one of the most attractive cities in
West Africa.

Interest in better building spread to the villages, and what is known
as the Ashanti-type compound was advocated by the government
engineers. This is a concrete house built around a plot 60 by 80 feet
with a courtyard in the centre. Some chiefs co-operated with the
authorities by following layout agreements for the correct development
of their towns. While the depression held up much progress, the late
1930's saw a renewal of building activity. Many of the poorer areas still
remained, however, with inadequate water supplies and sanitation, and
with the most primitive wattle and daub huts. As in the Gold Coast
Colony, the advantages of social services were not evenly distributed.

Among the members of the first Kumasi public health board was the
former Asantehene, Prempeh I. He had been exiled in 1896, as we have
seen, and the confederacy had been broken up. He was but a youth at
the time and had lived ever since with members of his family in the
Seychelles Islands, where he had become a Christian and had received
some education. In the early 1920's he wrote some of his Ashanti relations that he would like to return, if not as king, at least as a private
citizen. The British authorities, impressed by the loyalty and self-control
which the Ashanti people had shown during the golden stool incident,
decided in 1924 to allow Prempeh to return to Kumasi.[1] The chiefs and
the government co-operated in supplying a maintenance fund. A suitable
home and 150-acre plantation were prepared for him, and he was given
a place in the municipal government. He remained a private citizen until
1926, when he was again installed as head chief of Kumasi but not as
Asantehene. This involved the abolition of the Kumasi Council of
Chiefs which had faithfully replaced him since 1905. Prempeh's former
subjects were deeply grateful for his return and came in great crowds
to welcome him back to Ashanti. When he died in 1932 he was succeeded
by his nephew under the title of Nana Osei Tutu Agyeman Prempeh II.
About this time investigations by the British authorities revealed that
the great majority of the people wanted the restoration of the old
confederacy. On 1 January 1935 the Ashanti kingdom was officially
recognized, with Prempeh II assuming the ancient title of Otumufuo
Asantehene.[2] The great durbar held at Kumasi in honour of the event
was a most colourful affair, revealing the beauty and dignity of the

[1] *Ashanti Annual Report, 1924*, p. 29; *Events, 1920–1926*, pp. 234ff.
[2] *G.C. An. Report, 1934–1935*, p. 76.

pageantry of the Ashanti people. The governor said later that the perfect order and discipline among the 50,000 African participants was 'a proof of national unity and concord'.[1]

The Asantehene was to be assisted in government by a confederacy council, made up of the paramounts from each division of the country and of the chiefs of the seven Kumasi clans.

In the same year two new ordinances, not directly connected with the restoration of the confederacy, came into effect. Ordinance 1, the Native Authority Ordinance, marked a further advance in introducing into Ashanti the type of indirect rule which had proved successful in both Nigeria and Tanganyika. It gave the governor power

. . . to declare there shall be a native authority for any specified area and to appoint as such native authority any chief, or other native or any native council or group of native councils. The Ordinance imposes on such native authorities the obligations generally of maintaining order and good government.[2]

It will be noticed that the governor could choose to appoint a group of native councils as the native authority in any area. This made it possible for him to combine the various chiefs of a number of small divisions into one unit of government and thus secure the economy and increased efficiency that comes of co-ordinated social services. If such a combination were made, however, the chiefs concerned did not thereby lose their individual authority in local matters.

The Ashanti Confederacy Council was named as the supreme native authority for the nation. A second Bill, the Native Courts Ordinance, set up four grades of tribunals. These courts differed in jurisdiction, according to the importance of the chief concerned. The district commissioners exercised supervision over them and could remove cases to their own courts.

The Asantehene presided over a tribunal of first instance for the Kumasi division, and over a court of appeal for the entire confederacy. This latter consisted of the head chiefs of the divisions and clans and had: (a) power to hear appeals in land cases from head chiefs' courts; (b) original jurisdiction in land cases between chiefs of different divisions. Appeals from head chiefs' courts, in other matters, went to the government magistrates' courts.

[1] Legislative Council, *Debates* (1935), p. 3.
[2] *G.C. An. Report, 1934–1935*, p. 76.

The new ordinances and the changes brought about by the restoration of the confederacy developed on the lines envisaged, with surprisingly little disturbance in the lives of the ordinary people. Under the guidance of the Asantehene, the policy of consolidation was carried forward so that Ashanti began once again to assume something of its old importance as a complete unit. This was particularly evident in 1937, during the cocoa hold-up, when the Ashanti people were as solidly united as those of the Gold Coast Colony.

While stool treasuries became more efficient under the new régime, material progress was delayed by the lack of regular taxation. It was not until 1942 that the Ashanti Confederacy adopted a small annual levy for the entire area. One-third of the sum collected went to the central confederacy and two-thirds to the divisional native authorities for development purposes. In 1944 total revenue was over £100,000 and the Ashanti institutions were rapidly adapting themselves to modern conditions.

Throughout this period the municipal members of the Gold Coast legislative council occasionally asked that Ashanti might be represented on that body.[1] The Colony African Press also suggested the union of the two sections. On the occasion of the restoration of King Prempeh one paper said:

The Ashanti and the people of the Gold Coast are cousins . . . they are destined in the order of Providence to become welded together in one national unity and entity.

It ought to be a proud thing for Great Britain to help to rear a nation in the Gold Coast and Ashanti which will form the nucleus of the yet greater nation to be, namely, that of British West Africa, with a Parliament of its own, in the way of self-government at some distant date leading up to the Dominion Status.[2]

Some of the ancient jealousy between the two divisions still remained, however, and political union did not come until the inauguration of the 1946 constitution.

Looking back over this period, many of the advances made by the Ashantis appear remarkable. They had shifted from the warfare or slave trading of the nineteenth century to the cocoa farming of the twentieth. Their confederacy was restored and the rule of their chiefs strengthened,

[1] Legislative Council, *Debates* (1929), pp. 156, 170; (1935), pp. 121, 142.
[2] *Gold Coast Leader* (27 November 1926), p. 6, quoted in Buell, *The Native Problem in Africa*, vol. 1, p. 843.

to some extent by the new native administration ordinances. As in the Gold Coast Colony very much remained to be done, especially in the field of a more even distribution of social services. While the older and younger members of the community often differed as to the speed at which new development[1] should take place, nevertheless there seems to have been a widespread respect for the culture of the past and for the tradition of Ashanti unity. These characteristics were to be markedly evident in later years when many of the Ashantis found themselves in disagreement with the Convention People's Party on the constitutional issues raised by the question of Gold Coast independence. A full discussion of this problem will be found in a later chapter.[2]

[1] Excellent discussions of these problems by both Gold Coast and Ashanti leaders can be found in the published record of the Discussion Conference held in May 1945 at Kumasi. Both the British Chief Commissioner and the Asantehene gave their unofficial support by attending the closing meeting. The editor remarks in the Foreword that while there were points of difference on controversial subjects, 'the general impression was that the people in the Colony and Ashanti are both thinking along the same lines as regards the main problems of National Development'. M. A. Ribeiro, ed., *Towards National Development: Post-War Gold Coast* (Achimota, 1945), p. vii.

[2] See Chapter 10.

CHAPTER VII

NORTHERN TERRITORIES AND TOGOLAND
THE PROTECTORATE OF THE NORTHERN
TERRITORIES AND NORTH TOGOLAND

The Gold Coast Dependency included the three great divisions of the coastal Colony, Ashanti, the Protectorate of the Northern Territories, and—for administrative purposes—a fourth area, the former mandate of British Togoland, which became a trusteeship in December 1946. Since the history of the Gold Coast Colony and of Ashanti has been considered, this chapter will be concerned with the last two divisions. Because the northern part of Togoland contained sections of tribes who also lived in the Protectorate, the League of Nations mandate in 1922 gave the Gold Coast government the right to administer them as a unit. This arrangement satisfied the inhabitants, who had been discontented since the Anglo-German Treaty of 1890 had broken up their tribal life. On account of these tribal connexions, it has seemed wise to deal with the history and development of the Northern Territories and of north Togoland as a unit.[1] The story of south Togoland will be considered in the second part of this chapter.

The savannah areas in the hinterland of the Gold Coast and of Togoland are occupied by Negroid peoples speaking, for the most part, languages of either the Gur or Gonja groups. In 1931 the population of the Northern Territories was 717,275 and of the mandate, 293,671. According to the 1948 census the population of the Northern Territories was 866,503 and that of Togoland 382,768. The inhabitants depend on agriculture or cattle raising for a living. Even in the 1950's they were in a primitive condition in comparison to the tribes of the Colony and of Ashanti.

During the last quarter of the nineteenth century much of the area between the Guinea Coast and the Sudan was being explored by French,

[1] The account given in this section has been taken largely from *Northern Territories Annual Report; Gold Coast Annual Report; Report of the British Mandated Sphere of Togoland;* A. W. Cardinall, *The Natives of the Northern Territories of the Gold Coast, their Customs, Religion and Folklore* (London, n.d.). The film, *A Mamprussi Village,* which was taken in the Northern Territories gives an excellent picture of the life of these very interesting tribes. British Information Services circulate this film.

British, and German nationals. International rivalry soon developed, and these agents endeavoured to secure territory by getting the various chiefs to sign treaties of protection. Into Togoland and into the hinterland of Ashanti during these years, the British government sent representatives to make maps and to secure treaties from the local rulers. Later, military expeditions went north to quell the disturbances which slave raiders from the surrounding areas were causing. In 1897 the British definitely occupied this section, and in 1901 they annexed it as the Protectorate of the Northern Territories.[1] Meanwhile, boundary treaties had been made on the east with the Germans, who had by this time annexed Togoland, and on the north and west with the French.

For a time the Protectorate was administered in a semi-military fashion by a chief commissioner and the officers of the second battalion of the Gold Coast regiment, who had both civil and military duties. This measure was necessary because of the unsettled condition of the country, but the disorder caused by foreign slave raiders and by several turbulent tribes of the north-western section gradually subsided, so that in 1907 it was possible to replace the troops by a constabulary and to put the administration on a purely civil basis.

It became evident, once the British had established order, that the majority of the inhabitants were peaceful, industrious, and law-abiding. They are still primarily an agricultural people, though in some areas cattle raising is possible. They live by family groups in large compounds, which consist of a series of round huts connected by a wall and surrounding a central courtyard where the cattle are kept. There are also shelters for sheep, goats, fowl, and the grain supply. The older children in the family have their own huts, and a wealthy man has one for each of his wives. These buildings are connected by passages as in a maze, but with low walls to separate them. Made of mud, they are waterproofed with a glaze prepared from a mixture of locust bean pods and cow dung, and often painted in bright colours and designs. The average compound houses ten to twenty persons, though before the *Pax Britannica* some were built for over a hundred occupants, who thus sought the protection of numbers. A single narrow entrance with a stout gate is another remnant of less peaceful times.

The compounds are not usually grouped in compact villages but are surrounded by the farm lands of the family. Such land is obtained from the *tendana*, priest of the earth, in return for an annual tithe, which is generally a basket of grain. These baskets are exchanged in turn for a

---

[1] *British and Foreign State Papers, 1905–1906*, vol. xcix, p. 495.

sheep which is sacrificed to the deity. The title to land is permanent and remains within the family, so that while it may be leased, it is never sold. Land tenure is, accordingly, so much more secure in the Northern Territories than in Ashanti and the Gold Coast that litigation is very rare. Since both the chief and the poor man originally got their land from the *tendana*, the ruler would never dare incur the earth god's anger by seizing the property of his subjects.

In the north and north-eastern sections of the Protectorate, the population is very dense, and farms average from only four and one-half to five and one-half acres for a compound, housing ten to fifteen people. Seventy-five per cent of the crop is millet and guinea corn. As the dry season lasts for almost half the year, there can be no cultivation at this time, and the farmers must live on stored grain. Thus land is precious and only small sections can be allowed to lie fallow each year.

Large areas of the Protectorate, especially the Gonja state, are infested with tsetse fly, so that danger of trypanosomiasis makes them unsuited for cattle. The soil, moreover, is usually poor and rainfall insufficient, with a resultant low population density. Much of Dagomba, Mamprussi, and Lawra-Tuma, on the other hand, are good cattle and agricultural areas. Scant rainfall is a serious drawback, but geological surveys have revealed large underground supplies of water. If the revenue were obtainable, wells and pipe lines could change the whole aspect of the Northern Territories.

When the British established the Protectorate, they soon realized that the only hope of economic development lay in the improvement of agriculture and cattle raising. The latter industry would be particularly valuable since the southern areas had to depend almost entirely upon imports for their meat supply. There was also the possibility of mining, if the mineral deposits were to prove sufficiently rich to warrant exploitation.

Agricultural experiment stations, which were soon set up, attempted to improve indigenous methods of farming and to test the possibilities of cotton culture. The extensive development of the latter product was finally given up, for though it grew fairly well in both the Protectorate and in Togoland, it could not be produced cheaply enough for export.

As for food crops, the government believed that the Northern Territories could eventually supply the southern colonies, where interest in cocoa led the farmers to neglect subsistence agriculture. Besides groundnuts, cassava, legumes, and yams, this area could also produce the shea nut which is rich in a fat known as shea butter, or commercially as 'karite'. Proper care of these trees would ensure an increased supply of nuts which always found a ready market in the south. The essential foundation for trade, however, was a sufficient transport system.[1] In 1901 the territory had practically nothing but bush trails. Road-building, therefore, became one of the earliest activities of the British administration. By 1920 motor vehicles began to run between Kumasi and Tamale, the capital of the Protectorate, and eventually throughout the entire area. For a time there was a question of continuing the Kumasi railway farther north, but it was finally decided that motor transport was less expensive and more practical.

When the British first took over the Northern Territories, they found that what trade did exist was almost entirely in the hands of the foreign Hausa. The native was primarily a farmer and not interested in commerce. Cattle, from near-by French territory and from the Protectorate itself, were driven south and sold in the markets of Kumasi and the Gold Coast. On the return trip the traders brought kola nuts from the Ashanti forests to be sold in the Muslim areas to the north, or manufactured articles which, little by little, began to attract the primitive peoples of the Protectorate. Desire for European goods, however, grew very slowly among these simple agriculturalists who had little contact with the white man, and who clung more tenaciously than the inhabitants in the south to their ancient customs and superstitions. For the same reason they were not easily persuaded to migrate as seasonal labourers to the mines and cocoa plantations in the Colony and Ashanti. Each year an ever-increasing number of unskilled workers came from the surrounding French possessions, and passed through the Protectorate on their way south. As a result, the entire group was sometimes classified as Northern Territories labourers, but of the total only a fairly small percentage actually used to come from that area. It was only in the 1930's that almost as many British as French subjects began to take advantage of the higher wage rates of the south.

The contrast between the people of the north and those of Ashanti is quite marked. The highly organized tribal government of the latter group, combined with their intellectual capacity, put them in a position to profit by the commercial advantages which came with British rule. The northerners, on the contrary, lived in small, unco-ordinated groups; and their country was poor. As a result they took no interest in commercial possibilities, left all trade to the foreign Hausa, and preferred to

---

[1] In 1901 it cost £2½ a 60-pound load to transport goods from the Gold Coast to the Northern Territories.

maintain their primitive habits. Those who actually did try a season or two in the south often refused to return because they felt little need for money. They disliked the unaccustomed food and underground mine work. They were sometimes unfairly treated and, when they got home, there was always the danger that their farms, women, and cattle would be gone. The tribal elders and missionaries, moreover, disapproved of the ways of life with which the young men came in contact during their stay in the 'more civilized' south.

Before the motor roads were built, the Hausa traders followed the old slave-trading caravan trails which united the Gold Coast with the vast Sudanese plains to the north. Along them each year passed thousands of cattle, sheep, and donkeys, or African porters with their head loads of yams and shea nuts for the coast, or with salt and kola for the north. In the early days caravan tolls supplied the Protectorate's only source of revenue, so that it had to depend in large part on government grants. In 1907 even these were dropped, through fear that such taxation would force the trade into the neighbouring French or German colonies. Thereafter revenue was scanty, but the government believed that eventually economic development would come. The labour supply, too, once the young men began to go south in considerable numbers, was to be an indispensable factor in the growth of the mining and cocoa industries of Ashanti and the Colony.

Before studying further the material growth of the Protectorate, it would perhaps be wise to consider the manner of local government, because with a primitive agricultural people these two phases of daily life are very closely linked. It was, moreover, only because the British were eventually able to introduce a satisfactory form of indirect rule in the Northern Territories that, in later years, there was real co-operation between rulers and people in economic matters. The story of the gradual development of this indirect rule is probably one of the most interesting phases in the history of the Dependency.

In 1897 the government found that tribal organization had been all but destroyed by the slave raiding which had been so common in this area. Then, too, the coming of the white man had not helped matters. Eventually, however, the British worked out, in an even more successful manner than in Ashanti, a complete reinstatement of native authority. To understand the problems involved and the methods used, it will be necessary to consider something of the historical background of the Northern Territories.

The story of these peoples was only vaguely known until 1927, when an anthropological investigation was made of this area.[1] Before this study, it was generally believed that the Protectorate and the surrounding territory had been invaded some four or five centuries earlier by a mass migration from the north-east. The new-comers set up the Mamprussi, Dagomba, and Gonja kingdoms in localities which still bear these names, and forced their language and customs on the original inhabitants. Inquiries among the population led to the conclusion that this account was only partially true. It appeared that instead of whole tribes descending upon the Northern Territories, merely small bands of warriors had come. Because they were better armed than the original inhabitants and possessed a more developed idea of chieftainship, they were able to obtain political power. They were apparently clever enough to realize, however, that their only chance for permanent control lay in identifying themselves as much as possible with the existing customs of the land, which they did. Though the resident peoples were divided into three great language groups, they 'possessed a practically uniform religion, a uniform tribal and totemic organization, and an identical political constitution or system of tribal government'.[2] The outstanding feature of the last was a *tendana* or priest-king.

This *tendana* would undoubtedly have evolved into the type of native ruler with whom we are familiar among the Akan; that is, a ruler who was not only high priest and custodian of the land of his tribe and of the ancestral spirits, but one who was also a chief or king on a territorial basis and whose sanctions were secular and physical rather than spiritual; in other words, what the average European implies when he uses the word 'king' or 'chief'. Here in the north, this natural evolution from the priest-king to the territorial ruler was interrupted by external influences which produced a really remarkable state of affairs.

These external influences were, of course, the coming of strangers from the north-east. The invaders had already developed the idea of a political and secular rule which they took over for themselves, leaving the *tendana* the spiritual leadership and his trusteeship of the land. They married into the tribes among whom they settled, adopted many of their manners and customs, and their descendants came to speak the language

---

[1] Captain Robert Rattray of the Gold Coast anthropological department, who had already made a study of the people of Ashanti, spent several years in the Northern Territories. He traced the early history, language, constitutions, and customs of the inhabitants. The results of his findings were published in 1932. See R. S. Rattray, *Tribes of the Ashanti Hinterland* (Oxford, 1932), 2 vols.

[2] ibid., p. xi.

of the country. One important change they did make was the shift from a matrilineal to a patrilineal line of succession, so that they could keep the kingship in their own families. In contrast to Ashanti and the Gold Coast these foreign rulers usually appointed their successors, and the elders elected them only when there were several candidates in the princely families who had the right to rule.

As a result of the retention of the *tendana*, there appears, therefore, to have grown up a kind of dual mandate. There was the secular ruler, descended from the leader of the warrior bands, recognized by everyone as a titular head, but rarely interfering with the private life of the masses. All religious concerns continued to be managed and conducted by the former priestly rulers, who now, however, functioned nominally under the territorial chief. The new foreign ruler and the old native *tendana* thus came to work hand in hand, 'The people belong to me, the land belongs to the *tendana*,' was a statement which such chiefs often made.[1]

The sphere of influence which these soldiers of fortune came to control did not, however, embrace all the Northern Territories, but only the north-east, west, south-east, and south-west. Down the centre and radiating from it was a large section where their power was felt so little that the *tendana* kept his original authority. When the white man came in, demanding to see 'the king' and expecting to be supplied with water, firewood, and carriers, these old priestly rulers, aristocrats in their way, would remain aloof and thrust forward some unimportant person, often a slave or the descendant of a slave, as the supposed chief. For a while he would act as an intermediary between the *tendana* and the white man, despised by his fellows for being willing to play a false part. Then, backed as they were by the unknowing Europeans, in the course of time many of them began to dig themselves in, confident of a permanent chieftainship. The real ruler, often before he realized just what was happening, gradually found himself becoming of less importance in the eyes of his own people. There were many such petty, unconstitutional, European-made chiefs in the Northern Territories. They were usually efficient rulers, very willing to carry out the suggestions of the district commissioners because they realized their position depended entirely on European support.

It will be apparent from the foregoing discussion that the chiefs of the Northern Territories fell into three groups: (1) a few rare cases where the traditional ruler, the priest-king, still functioned, but in the dual

[1] R. S. Rattray, *Tribes of the Ashanti Hinterland*, p. xv.

rôle of secular and spiritual leader, that is, as a chief in the modern sense; (2) those chiefs, originally aliens, whose title to that office dated from long before the advent of the European in these parts; such rulers were, for example, those of Mamprussi, Dagomba, and Gonja; (3) chiefs whose title dated only from the time of European intervention, and was created by it. These were often persons without a vestige of the traditional qualifications necessary to hold such office.[1]

As a result of this investigation, it was suggested that for the reorganization of native administration which the government was contemplating in 1929–32, the chiefs of the *tendana* class should certainly be retained since they were the true rulers. As for the second category, they too could be kept, as they had succeeded before the advent of the Europeans, in working out quite an equitable system of government. There had been a tendency for them in recent times, however, to ignore the advice of the council of elders and become autocratic, a condition which is entirely opposed to the fundamentally democratic spirit which underlies the true African constitution of this area. The third category, of European-made rulers, should be required to acknowledge the rightful *tendana* and his hereditary elders as his councillors. When any one of these chiefs died, every effort should be made to reinstate the rightful ruler in his place.

Finally, as a general conclusion of these years of research, it was decided that the Northern Territories could be regarded as 'a more or less homogeneous cultural and—to a lesser extent—linguistic area rather than as a mosaic comprising a welter of tongues and divergent customs'.[2] If this were true, it should not be hard to reunite some of the old states and to introduce the idea of native authorities with increased judicial power, stool treasuries, and the right to guide and improve the economic life of their peoples.

Some very definite ordinance would have to be drawn up, however, for the success of such a plan, since during the years 1901–29 no reorganization of native government had been attempted. When the British first took over the territory, they had merely allowed the chiefs to continue exercising the jurisdiction which they had formerly held. No effort was made to define more exactly its extent, or to recognize native tribunals. As a result of so vague a policy, a process of disintegration began to set in, and even chiefs with a long tradition of rule found it hard to hold their authority. Matters were not helped by the separation of tribes caused by the Anglo-German boundary of 1890, or by the

[1] ibid., p. xviii.   [2] ibid., p. 2.

sometimes arbitrary formation of administrative districts within the Protectorate itself.

Mamprussi and Dagomba in the east, and Wa and the Gonjas in the west and south-west, were among the principal areas that had formerly been organized into strong native states by descendants of the early invaders. Even these states, once so firmly knit, were now weakening. At the end of the nineteenth century, when the Germans annexed Togoland, the Nas (paramount chiefs or kings) of Mamprussi and Dagomba had lost considerable portions of their kingdoms. Ever on the look-out for an opportunity to regain these lands, during the world war of 1914–18 they eagerly supported the Anglo-French invasion of that colony.

As soon as the war broke out in the summer of 1914, British forces from the Gold Coast Dependency and French forces from Dahomey co-operated in an immediate attack upon Togoland. The efficiency of their invasion and the limited strength of the resident German contingent combined to make possible its speedy reduction. By 7 August 1914 the town of Lome was in the hands of the British, and by 26 August, after several engagements and the destruction of the great German wireless station at Kamina, the acting governor unconditionally surrendered the entire colony to the invading forces.[1]

The British and French then divided Togoland on provisional lines, and remained in occupation until the victorious Allied powers could make a decision as to its future status. Before the German annexation of this territory in 1886, some of the tribes had acknowledged the protection of Great Britain. The British reports to the Permanent Mandates Commission stated that the inhabitants appeared more satisfied to return to their rule than to remain under German administration. One story is told, for example, of a Togo chief whose grandfather had buried his Union Jack rather than surrender it when the Germans annexed his land. Upon the return of the English, the old flag was dug up and proudly displayed.[2]

In the northern part of Togoland there were several native states that

[1] Report of the British Mandated Sphere of Togoland for 1920–21, p. 4; Sir Charles Lucas, The Gold Coast and the War (London, 1920), contains a full account of the occupation of Togoland.

[2] British Togo Mandate Report, 1923, p. 38. See also Correspondence relating to the wishes of the Natives of the German Colonies as to their Future Government, Cd. 9210 (1918). It is difficult to know if this report of the satisfaction of the natives at a return to British rule were true of all the inhabitants of Togoland. Mary Townsend in her The Rise and Fall of Germany's Colonial Empire (New York, 1930) came to the conclusion that German colonial administration was no better and no worse than that of any other power similarly circumstanced.

were split by the Anglo-German boundary. Among these the Dagomba kingdom was the largest. Its head chief or 'Na' had his capital at Yendi, in German territory. After the British invasion, he signed a treaty acknowledging their sovereignty, and asking that his former state be reunited.[1] Mamprussi and a small part of Gonja had likewise been separated by the former frontier.

With this situation in view, it was decided at the Paris Peace Conference that Togoland should be divided in such a way as to reunite these tribes.[2] The Supreme Council, therefore, mandated an area of some 13,000 square miles in the western portion to Great Britain, while the French received the larger and more important eastern section containing 19,960 square miles, having access to the coast at the port of Lome, and containing the railway which the Germans had built.[3]

The cause of this uneven division was the desire to reunite certain separated tribes in the northern section of Togoland and, for the same reason, the British were allowed, by Section 9 of the mandate, to administer the area as an integral part of the Gold Coast Dependency.[4] If the new boundary joined tribes in the north once again, however, it had the opposite effect in the south where the Anglo-French frontier now split the Ewe-speaking tribes into separate groups. Though there was some agitation among the Africans, and though they sent a petition to the British government protesting against the partition of Eweland, the territory was divided as had already been determined by the Paris Peace Conference.

In the first report on Togoland to the League of Nations, the British pointed out that the acceptance of the mandate would involve additional expense for the Gold Coast. Since the new boundary reunited the northern tribes, however, the government was reconciled to the prospect of a temporary financial liability.[5] It hoped that the mandate would

[1] *Correspondence relating to the Military Operations in Togoland*, Cd. 7872 (1915), pp. 31–34.
[2] G. L. Beer, *African Questions at the Paris Peace Conference* (New York, 1923), p. 433.
[3] The boundary between French and British Togoland was settled by the Milner-Simon Agreement of July 1919. See *Official Journal of the League of Nations* (August 1922), p. 883. Though the British administered the western portion as a mandate from 1919 on, and sent a 1920–1 report on Togoland to the League of Nations, the actual document of mandate was not confirmed until July 1922. This postponement appears to have been due to difficulties over the boundary and to a delay in getting the consent of the United States. Buell, *The Native Problem in Africa*, vol. II, p. 278. For the text of the mandate, see *Official Journal of the League of Nations* (August 1922), p. 874.
[4] Permanent Mandates Commission, *Minutes*, Fifth Session, p. 42.
[5] *British Togo Mandate Report, 1920–1921*, covering dispatch by Governor Sir Gordon Guggisberg.

eventually become independent of government grants. Throughout the following years, however, the deficit between revenue and expenditure continued to exist, amounting in 1938, for example, to some £67,000.

Since the mandate was to be administered as a part of the Gold Coast Dependency, the northern section was placed under the chief commissioners of the Northern Territories, while south Togoland was made a district of the Eastern Province of the Colony. The advantages of a union between so small an area as British Togoland and the well-established government of the Gold Coast were obvious, but the Permanent Mandates Commission had no intention of letting the mandatory power think that the territory thus administered was eventually to drift into annexation. An examination of the minutes of the commission reveals its attitude on this point.[1] It was because of tribal relationships that some two-thirds of the mandate was united with the Northern Territories, while only a small part was left for south Togoland. Until 1932 this northern portion included the following districts:[2]

District	Area in Sq. Miles	Population
Kete-Krachi . .	3,911	25,244
Eastern Dagomba .	4,609	58,929
Eastern Mamprussi .	1,528	4,518
Kusasi . . .	385	12,093

As can be seen on the map, Kete-Krachi was the most southerly of these four divisions. It was occupied by several different tribes among whom no previous link had apparently ever existed. The next section, Eastern Dagomba, was only one portion of a large native state which had about half its territory in the Protectorate itself. The capital, Yendi, seat of government for its paramount—the Ya Na—lay in the mandated sphere, which accounted for the paramount's desire that the British occupy Togoland. Cattle raising and agriculture, as in most of this area, were the principal occupations of its people along with some simple crafts such as weaving, rope, leather, and pottery making. North of Dagomba was the Mamprussi district, divided also between Togoland and the Protectorate, although in this case the capital and the bulk of the land lay on the Northern Territories' side of the boundary. In the far north-east corner of the mandate was the Kusasi district which,

[1] See, for example, Permanent Mandates Commission, *Minutes*, Fifth Session pp. 17–18, 31, 190.
[2] *British Togo Mandate Report, 1927*, p. 51. During the years 1920–32, several shifts were made in the arrangement of these districts. The various reports give an account of these changes.

though small in area, had a population of 12,000 with a density of 137 to the square mile. The tribes of both Eastern Mamprussi and Kusasi had formerly owed allegiance to the Na of the old Mamprussi state, but with the disintegration of native authority during the period 1890–1930, this bond was greatly loosened.

It will be remembered that such weakening of native constitutions had been noticeable, not only in the mandate, but throughout the entire Northern Territories. It was with a view to re-establishing the former unity by a system of indirect rule that Captain Rattray's study of these tribes had been undertaken. His research enabled the government to ascertain, in most cases, to what paramounts the numerous small divisions had previously owed allegiance. Long experience in the Gold Coast Colony had taught the British the necessity of gaining the full consent of the Africans before any changes were made. With this fact in mind, in 1930–1 they invited the chiefs, the elders, and their followers to preliminary conferences.[1] At these meetings the Africans and the commissioners talked over disputed points of customary law and endeavoured to restore, as far as possible, the original native constitution. The principal aim of the conferences, however, was to persuade the subchiefs once again to acknowledge the authority of the state paramount, from whose jurisdiction they had been free for some thirty years. Force was not applied, but the advantages of union were demonstrated so effectively that, in almost every case, the subchiefs willingly and often enthusiastically joined the reconstituted state. This action, like that of the restored Ashanti Confederacy, was a striking example of the respect which the West African peoples have for their traditional organizations.

As a result of these conferences, the numerous small divisions of the Northern Territories and north Togoland were reunited into several large states. Thus the tribes of the former districts of Kusasi, and East and West Mamprussi, became the single state of Mamprussi under the paramountcy of the Na of Nalerigu. The Ya Na of Yendi restored the hereditary kingdom of his ancestors when he amalgamated all but one of the tribes of eastern and western Dagomba into a unified Dagomba state. The one group which did not accept his headship was that of the Nanumbas. These people, however, had never been dependent on the Ya Na and were therefore justified in remaining a separate state.

As for the Kete-Krachi district, it was found that two small tribes on its western boundary had formerly belonged to the great Gonja state of

[1] *G.C. An. Report, 1930*, p. 3. *British Togo Mandate Report, 1930*, pp. 6–10.

the Protectorate, so they were allowed to reaffirm their allegiance to the head chief of that area. Some of the other tribes of this district had no former connexion with the Krachi paramount, so remained independent, but by 1935 a large enough population acknowledged his overlordship to justify his appointment as a native authority. To the reconstituted states of Mamprussi, Dagomba, Gonja, and of a section of Krachi can also be added those of Wa and Lawra-Tumu in the far north-west. In the Northern Territories and the north section of Togoland it was hoped that the process of tribal disintegration had thus been halted.

Once these small divisions were reunited into several strong states, there was no reason to delay the establishment of native administrations based on an adequate representation of the aboriginal population. To this end, during the year 1933, three new ordinances were promulgated providing for executive, judicial, and financial reorganization.

The Native Authority Ordinance[1] was very like the one which the government was to provide for Ashanti in 1935 and with which we have gained some acquaintance in a previous chapter. It gave the chief commissioner, with the approval of the governor, the right to appoint any chief or group of chiefs as the native authorities, and placed in their hands the duty and power to provide for good government. In contrast to Ashanti and the Gold Coast, there was to be more stress on the executive than on the judicial. It will be remembered that on the coast especially, the chiefs had great difficulty in carrying out such measures as the establishment of forest reserves, the destruction of diseased cocoa trees, and, above all, the collection of taxes. Their subjects, sometimes under the leadership of educated Africans, often refused obedience. Here in the north the inhabitants were still in a primitive state, and though before the reorganization of 1932 the dependence of subchiefs on paramount chiefs had been insufficient, the common people still had much respect for authority. The chiefs were therefore able to use the powers given them by the new law to carry out widespread economic and social reforms, especially in the matter of agriculture and cattle raising. A further consideration of this matter will be taken up shortly.

The judicial power of the chiefs was established by the Native Tribunals Ordinance.[2] Prior to this time African courts in the north were most inadequate, with a vague jurisdiction and no provision for enforcing decisions except through the district commissioners. The tribal elders settled most cases merely by arbitration. The new law permitted the chief commissioners to establish a tribunal for any native

[1] Ordinance 2 of 1932.   [2] Ordinance 1 of 1932.

authority area and to define the extent of its civil and criminal jurisdiction. This measure was in marked contrast to the judicial ordinances
of Ashanti and the Colony where the amount of jurisdiction was
definitely stated. It was probably the intention of the government to
leave the commissioner free to go rather slowly in the matter of courts,
which had been the cause of much abuse in the south. He would thus
be able to watch the development of each state and assign it as much
jurisdiction as he thought it was capable of handling. At any rate, three
years later a second judicial ordinance was promulgated which provided
for three grades of courts with the extent of jurisdiction definitely
stated. Grade A courts, for the higher chiefs, had civil and criminal
jurisdiction up to £50 or six months' imprisonment, while Grade C
courts were limited to £10 in civil affairs and to £5 or one month's
imprisonment in criminal affairs.[1]

The third aspect of the 1932 Native Authority reorganization was
financial. Up to this time all revenue had come from indirect taxes such
as ferry tolls, market and licence fees, and import duties, on the small
amount of European goods which reached the north. Prior to 1914 the
Germans had collected a direct tax in Togoland, but the British dropped
it in favour of indirect taxation. As for the chiefs, they had depended on
occasional levies and small court fees for revenue, as well as on the
forced labour of their people for the upkeep of roads and other public
property. The British believed that in the Northern Territories there
could be no true development of local government without regular
taxation, any more than there could be in Ashanti or in the Colony.
Fortunately there did not exist in the Protectorate the prejudice against
it that hampered progress in the south. The government therefore
passed in 1932 a Native Treasuries Ordinance[2] which gave the chief
commissioner the right not only to establish treasuries in all native
authority areas but also to define the sources of revenue, to provide for
specified forms and amounts of taxation, and to regulate the preparation
of annual estimates. Here was the first law to introduce direct taxation
in any section of the Gold Coast Dependency. The authorities, however,
did not immediately apply all its clauses. Treasuries were introduced in
the reorganized states and subdivisions, and the people were gradually
prepared to acknowledge the need for regular assessments. In 1936,
when the effects of the depression had all but disappeared, the new tax
was collected for the first time. To the pleasant surprise of the British,
who had not forgotten the recent commotion in the Gold Coast over a

[1] Ordinance 31 of 1935.   [2] Ordinance 10 of 1932.

like measure, the tax was not only peacefully collected but the actual returns exceeded the estimates. The account in the *Gold Coast Annual Report* of the new legislation is written in a most laudatory manner, and with the evident intention of impressing the southern sections with the benefits which had come to the Protectorate from such docile acceptance of government advice.

The Northern Territories have seen the greatest advance in native administration so far recorded in the history of the Gold Coast. Chiefs and councillors have been granted limited powers in the government of their divisions, tribunals have been set up, each under the direct supervision of the District Commissioner and direct taxation has been introduced, the assessment and collection of which is carried out almost entirely by the native authorities, the administrative officers acting in a purely advisory capacity. The introduction and successful operation of this tax is an event of unique historical significance, for not since the later years of the nineteenth century has any form of direct taxation been paid by any section of the people of the Gold Coast. Moreover, the keenness displayed by the Protectorate chiefs and their sense of responsibility have been such that the estimated revenue from the tax was exceeded in every division and there were no instances of abuse, embezzlement or evasion. This result reflects the greatest credit on the native authorities and gives cause for considerable confidence in the future development of the territory.

The revenue, which is administered through properly constituted native treasuries, has been applied to the general welfare of the people in a manner which should act as a great incentive and example to the States in other parts of the Gold Coast. Roads, wells, cattle kraals, dispensaries and sanitary conveniences have been provided in every division, while the chiefs and tribunal members, together with the staff necessary for the various services, have for the first time been paid regular salaries. As a result, the reliability and efficiency of these services have increased to a degree unthought of a few years ago.[1]

As can be seen from this quotation, the assurance of definite revenue now made possible a real progress in local government. The payment of regular salaries to the chiefs and their officials seems to have had some indirect results of great value, for it both enhanced these officials' position in the eyes of their people and taught them the reality of their powers and responsibilities.

The entire proceeds of this tax were paid directly into the local

---

[1] *G.C. An. Report, 1936*, p. 8. The film, *A Mamprussi Village*, gives interesting scenes of the collection of this tax and of the budget session which the district commissioner held with the various chiefs. See p. 82 above, note 1.

treasuries; for it was meant not to be something new but merely the commutation to a regular levy of the former customary tribute in labour and in kind. The district commissioners helped the African officials to make out the rolls of taxpayers and to decide what was the average annual income of each area. A flat rate was assessed on each adult male according to the economic condition of his section. The maximum rate was 7 shillings (later scaled down to 5 shillings) and the minimum 1 shilling, except in a few divisions where it was found wiser to apportion a lump sum to each family group and let the elders determine what individuals could pay.[1]

As a result, both of the tax and of a more systematic collection of market fees, &c., the revenue of the native administrations increased from £860 in 1933 to £98,000 in 1946.[2] The district commissioners supervised the drawing up of the annual estimates which were regularly published in the Gold Coast Gazette. These statements were given in great detail and a study of them reveals, perhaps better than anything else, the gradual progress which the native administrations made. Expenditures for such items as market buildings, sanitary structures, model farms, and dispensaries began to appear. This is all the more surprising when one considers that in 1934 there were only seven or eight primary schools in the entire area and that, except in the towns, the inhabitants were still living under the most primitive conditions.

A question naturally occurs to the reader of these reports, however, as to how the Africans of so poor a section were able to pay any tax at all. The answer can be found in the fact that the economic growth of this area was steadily going on, due largely to government efforts to improve both the agricultural and cattle-raising industries.

In 1922 the veterinarian department at Tamale, administrative centre of the Northern Territories, began work on breeding livestock and poultry with a view to improving the poor native strains. At the same time a strict quarantine was imposed on imported cattle, and attempts made to stamp out the rinderpest epidemics which had annually been destroying some 20 per cent of the cattle herds. The department soon realized that the only hope for eradicating the plague was the immunization of all the stock of the Protectorate. Though it seemed an almost impossible task, in view of the ignorance of the African owners, an up-to-date laboratory with piped water and electricity—the first to be used in the Northern Territories—was opened in 1932 at Pong Tamale by means of a grant from the British Colonial Development Fund. Here

[1] Hailey, *African Survey*, p. 586.   [2] *G.C. An. Report, 1946*, p. 127.

anti-rinderpest serum was prepared and young Africans were taught to administer it. Within two years the entire stock of the area was immunized and the illiterate inhabitants were won over to appreciate its necessity.[1]

With the danger of rinderpest out of the way, the laboratory turned its attention to a study of the tsetse fly and trypanosomiasis problem. This proved a far more difficult task, because about half of the area of the Protectorate was fly-infested. Five years of experimentation at Pong Tamale showed that the complete clearance of a district required far more than the conventional removal of the primary breeding foci. An anti-tsetse campaign, concerned with both human and animal trypanosomiasis, was begun in 1935, but it was to be a long and expensive process,[2] especially as the recession of the forest in the southern cocoa areas was leaving ever-increasing bush regions open to infection.

Once the cattle were freed from rinderpest, the animal husbandry department was able to turn its attention to better breeding. The same government grant which built the Pong Tamale laboratory also financed experimental farms where trials were made until satisfactory types of cows, pigs, and poultry had been obtained. In 1926 a tariff was levied on all cattle imported from French territory, and the funds thus obtained paid the running expenses of the department. One of its aims was to provide a model farm where young Africans could be trained in modern husbandry and where the various chiefs and elders of the Protectorate could see the actual result of combined scientific agriculture and livestock raising. It was hoped that eventually each chief would have his own model farm with a communal breeding bull which would thus form the nucleus of an area of improved husbandry. The whole economic future of the Protectorate depended, to a large extent, on the success of this plan. Great efforts to carry it out were made at the beginning of the 1930's, and the annual reports thereafter contained the encouraging story of its implementation.

Because the political reorganization of 1932 had enlarged and strengthened the various units of local government, and because the new tax had given them a regular source of revenue, the head chiefs were able to set up model farms as suggested by the government. By

[1] *G.C. An. Report, 1930*, pp. 28 ff.
[2] Legislative Council, *Debates* (1936), p. 13; *G.C. An. Report, 1934*, p. 14. In 1944 a 'Tsetse Fly and Trypanosomiasis Committee' was set up by the secretary of state for the colonies in order to co-ordinate the work of the entire Empire. Bush clearance in the Gold Coast continued during the war and some hundreds of square miles have been freed for human habitation and cattle breeding. British Information Services, *Weekly War Notes* (21 December 1944), p. 33. See also *G.C. An .Report, 1949*, p. 56.

the end of the thirties, twenty such centres were completed with substantial stone buildings and stocked with the improved types of cattle which the Pong Tamale station had developed. The central government gave two-thirds and the native authority one-third of the funds necessary for their support. The farms were managed by tribal elders aided by young men who had been educated at the Pong Tamale centre or on the model farms connected with each of the Northern Territories' primary schools. Each head chief planned gradually to increase the development of his area by encouraging the subchiefs to open up smaller centres in their own divisions.

As cattle raising is impossible in the forested areas of Ashanti and the Gold Coast, the Dependency had to rely almost entirely on the Protectorate or on foreign import for its meat supply. There is a small area east of Accra which is also a cattle centre, but it cannot begin to fulfil the needs of the peoples on the coast. If the tsetse-fly regions can be cleared and sufficient water supplies developed, the day may come when the present large import of French cattle and canned meats will be lessened in favour of domestic production.

Along with the economic progress of the 1930 decade, some social development was also taking place. This can be seen in the steady though slow increase of interest in education, health, and Christianity.

The first school in the Northern Territories was a primary one opened in 1909 by the government at Tamale. In 1925 Sir Gordon Guggisberg published a memorandum on education for the Protectorate.[1] He advocated that the government keep a strict control so that no inferior schools be opened, as had happened in the south. He wanted all teachers trained at Achimota and supervision exercised from that institution. Very little, however, was done to carry out this policy. Probably the depression interfered with development, but in 1930 there were only five government primary schools and two technical schools in the area.

After the establishment of stronger local rule in 1932, the government turned all its educational institutions over to the native authority, except for the agricultural centre and a middle school (Standards IV–VII) which it later established at Tamale. By 1946 there were seventeen native authority primary schools, entirely financed by local funds except for the teachers' salaries which were assumed by the government. The majority of these institutions were for boarders only, where the boys were housed by groups in African-type compounds. The discipline was

---

[1] *British Togo Mandate Report, 1926*, Appendix E.

usually organized on civic lines with chiefs, subchiefs, and elders chosen from the student body to share responsibility and thus obtain valuable experience for the future. Much stress was laid on crafts and each institution had a well-run farm for the purpose of demonstration and practice as well as for food production.

Aside from these few schools, the Protectorate and the northern section of Togoland had no others except for five institutions conducted by Catholic missionaries. The White Fathers, a society founded for the evangelization of Muslims and Negroes in Africa, had entered this area in 1906 and had established themselves in the far northern section with a centre at Navrongo. Gradually they spread towards the north-western corner, founding missions, schools, and dispensaries. When Principal Fraser of Achimota toured the Protectorate as government educational inspector, he found the White Fathers' institutions the best in the area, because of the strong link they had established between school and village life.[1] This was particularly necessary in the Northern Territories, where education must be closely bound up with native life if the danger of an educated class, wholly out of sympathy with the agricultural community, was to be avoided.

The only other missionary effort made in this area was that of the Methodists who settled in 1913 at Tamale, the capital of the Protectorate. They withdrew, however, in 1920 and did not return. In the mandated sphere there were several other missions, but they will be considered in connexion with the southern section of Togoland. The Africans of the Northern Territories were deeply attached to their animistic faith, and Christianity made very slow progress. In later years, however, there was something of a mass movement towards conversion among the Dagatis, one of the more industrious and intelligent tribes of the Lawra-Tumu area.[2]

As for health and sanitation, the Northern Territories, like Ashanti and the Gold Coast, did not receive an evenly shared development and very much remained to be done. There were several small hospitals, leper and sleeping-sickness camps, and some sixteen dispensaries, most of which were supported by native authority funds. Yaws, guinea worm, and other diseases were very widespread in the entire area, but until sufficient water supplies could be obtained so that better sanitation and a larger food supply could be introduced, this condition was bound to remain. The chiefs were beginning to realize the need for improvement

[1] Legislative Council, *Debates* (1929), 'Governor's Address', p. 51.
[2] Donald Attwater, *The White Fathers in Africa* (London, 1937), p. 59.

and to set aside fair sums for this purpose in their annual estimates.[1] It was really too big a task for them, however, and needed the help of the central government or the Colonial Welfare Fund on a large enough scale to clear up all the tsetse-fly areas, to build sufficient health centres, and to develop an adequate water supply.

Before leaving the subject of the Protectorate, it is encouraging to review the consequences which followed from the 1932 reorganization of native institutions on the lines of indirect rule. These northern chiefs seemed to possess a keen civic sense, and the increased responsibility given them by the native authority ordinances brought out the best that is in them. The peasant population, too, benefited by the change. They felt a sense of pride and ownership in experimental farms, schools, and dispensaries which were managed by their own rulers rather than by alien officials. Throughout the reports the statement is often repeated that the revival of rule through indigenous institutions caused a return of mental activity and an interest in the work of government which did not exist previously. When Nana Sir Ofori Atta and other Gold Coast chiefs visited the Northern Territories in 1937, they were astonished at the social progress which this section, so much poorer in natural resources than the coastal colony, had made.

The following year all the chiefs and most of the subchiefs of the Protectorate and north Togoland met at the capital for a conference on the general needs of their people. It was the first meeting of its kind ever to be held, but it was most successful in helping each ruler to shift his viewpoint from the confines of his own division to the larger problems of the entire area. In 1946 a Northern Territories council, representative of all the chiefs, was established. The 1951 constitution gave the Northern Territories a share in the central government of the Dependency by enabling it to send nineteen representatives to the legislative assembly.

SOUTH TOGOLAND

In turning from the Northern Territories of the Dependency to south Togoland, one comes to a section which in many ways was not unlike the Gold Coast Colony itself. About one-fifth of the mandate —later a trusteeship—with an area of 2,607 square miles was known as

[1] In the Mamprussi State Estimates for 1938–9, for example, over £4,000 were set aside for medical, sanitary, and water supply development out of a total expenditure of £17,915. See *British Togo Mandate Report, 1938*, Appendix III.

the Southern Section or Ho District, and was connected for administrative purposes with the Eastern Province of the Colony. Even though so small, this portion contained nearly one-half of British Togoland's population—about 170,000 in 1948—and was richer in natural resources than the larger northern part.

Generally speaking, Togoland is hilly and picturesque. A mountain range, commencing near Accra, runs in a north-easterly direction, cuts across south Togoland, and continues along the Anglo-French boundary into the Krachi district. A second and smaller range parallels the Volta River in the western part of south Togoland. Forested areas, suitable for cocoa growing, are found in these two mountainous regions and provide the inhabitants with their greatest single source of wealth. The rest of this Ho District is covered with scrub or park lands which gradually give place to savannah types of vegetation as the Northern Territories are approached.

The Volta River runs along the western boundary of Togoland for some distance, but eventually flows into purely Gold Coast territory until it reaches its outlet in the Gulf of Guinea. The southern boundary of British Togoland stopped abruptly some thirty miles inland from the coast, while the far eastern corner of the Gold Coast Colony jutted over into this area, forming what was known as the Volta triangle and cut off the British mandated sphere from any access to the sea. For this reason it was necessary to connect Togoland by a road system with the ports of Accra and Ada on the west, and with the French port of Lome on the east.

The climate in the southern section, like that of the Colony, is so tropical and humid as to make it an undesirable area for European settlers. The river valleys and forest areas are quite fertile, but for the rest the soil is poor and rainfall uncertain, so that some sections are entirely uninhabited. Besides cocoa, cotton, and tobacco some fruits and vegetables can be grown. The district is therefore a predominantly agricultural area, as cattle raising is impossible and the iron, gold, chromite, bauxite, and limestone deposits are not well situated for transportation facilities. A few of the inhabitants engage in handicrafts, but such production is entirely for local use. As a result of an intensive campaign for road-building during the 1920's, trade has been much stimulated. Meat, flour, textiles, an occasional motor-car or truck, and some building materials are imported through the Gold Coast, while an annually increasing amount of cocoa and other foodstuffs leaves the country by British ports on the west and the French one on the east.

The inhabitants of southern Togoland form, in the main, one linguistic group—the Ewe—which is made up of a number of petty tribes with more or less similar customs, but at different stages of development. These peoples are believed to have come originally from Yorubaland in south-western Nigeria.[1] They migrated in waves westward, probably in the fifteenth or sixteenth centuries, and built up settlements at Tado near the River Mono and at Notsie, now in French Togoland. As the settlement at Notsie grew, groups of Ewes travelled farther west, fanning out to south, west, and north-west—that is, to the coastal lagoons, to the Volta River area, and to the uplands of the north. Other peoples from different areas also made their permanent homes among the Ewes.

Broadly speaking, therefore, the land of the Ewe people lies between the Mono River on the east and the Volta on the west, extending northward from the Gulf of Guinea as far as the uplands of Central Togoland. In this area of nearly ten thousand square miles there are close to a million inhabitants. In the period under discussion Ewe-speaking people were found in British and French Togoland and in the south-east section of the Gold Coast Colony.

The early Ewe settlements were few and far between, but in the course of time the original villages and their offshoots increased in population and ultimately various politically independent local states came into being. These divisions vary from 50 to 300 square miles and from 500 to 50,000 inhabitants. Poor communications and the stretches of unexplored lands between the states account for the small size of these units. In the eighteenth and nineteenth centuries, moreover, there was considerable disorganization in the country resulting from quarrels over fishing and trading rights, slave raids, the Ashanti invasion of northern Eweland, and the various expeditions undertaken by the Europeans to pacify the country. Such disorders left their mark on the inhabitants so that when the Germans came they did not find such large or well-organized political units as, for example, existed among the Ashantis. In 1884 the Germans annexed Togoland as a protectorate, and in the following years concluded boundary agreements with their French and British neighbours. During their thirty years of occupation they made thorough and careful preparation to develop the economic resources of the colony in conjunction with the needs of the homeland. Roads were built and plantations and forest reserves begun. The Germans apparently hoped to develop the cotton-growing industry

[1] *The Ewe News-Letter,* No. 1 (May 1945).

sufficiently to make themselves independent of imports from America. Most of the good cotton land was in French Togoland, however, and production has not been particularly successful in the British area.

The Germans appear to have governed Togo largely by direct rule, and no effort was made to amalgamate the tribal divisions. About 1908, however, the colonial office in Berlin initiated a policy of preserving and utilizing native institutions. Though self-government, to the extent that it was developed by British indirect rule, was probably never intended, the chiefs were given a very limited jurisdiction and some responsibility for maintaining law and order.[1] Direct taxation in the form of a head tax (6 marks annually) was imposed, so that for some years Togoland was the only self-supported German colony.

After the British took possession of the western part of the country in 1914, they dropped this head tax in favour of indirect taxation which was more to the satisfaction of the population. But they retained most of the German laws during the war period and in some cases for several years thereafter.

In 1923 a royal order-in-council finally made definite provision for the government of the mandate.[2] It divided the area into northern and southern sections, placing it under the authority of the governor of the Gold Coast in accordance with Section 9 of the mandate treaty which stated:

This area shall be administered in accordance with the laws of the Mandatory as an integral part of his territory . . .

The Mandatory shall therefore be at liberty to apply his laws to the territory subject to the mandate with such modifications as may be required by local conditions.[3]

Thereafter the ordinances of the Gold Coast Colony were applied to southern Togoland, while those for the Northern Territories were promulgated in northern Togoland, unless unsuitable or contrary to the conditions of the mandate.

In 1924 an administration ordinance[4] provided for some simple forms of local government. Because of the numerous tribal divisions and the

[1] Mary Townsend, *The Rise and Fall of Germany's Colonial Empire, 1884–1914,* p. 278. In contrast to Townsend's account of the German policy, the British reports state that they made mere figureheads of the chiefs. *British Togo Mandate Report, 1920,* p. 9.
[2] *British Togo Mandate Report, 1923,* Appendix J.
[3] *Official Journal of the League of Nations* (August 1922), p. 880.
[4] Ordinance 1 of 1924.

backwardness of the people in civic matters, the British decided that it was too soon to attempt advanced forms of indirect rule. The ordinance therefore retained most of the earlier German arrangements. The native courts had only civil jurisdiction, while the chiefs were limited to fines of £5 and the subchiefs to £2½. They had no authority to enforce decisions, which power was left to the district commissioner.

Since this same ordinance provided that southern Togoland be united with the eastern province of the Gold Coast, there was no need for chief commissioners. The five districts of the mandate—Ho in the south and four others in the north—were managed by district commissioners responsible to their respective superiors in the Dependency itself. The commissioner of the Ho area had his own court with jurisdiction up to £100 for both civil and criminal cases, but any matter beyond this had to go to Gold Coast courts.

This method of administration remained in force in south Togoland until the early 1930's. About that time, the government was endeavouring, as we have seen, to strengthen the African institutions in the various sections of the Dependency by an amalgamation of small tribal groups and by an introduction, wherever possible, of fuller indirect rule. In the mandated sphere the same type of policy was carried out. But in the southern section, unfortunately, there were no remains of large native states as in Ashanti and the Northern Territories on which to build. A common language and customs were the only bonds which united the sixty-eight independent divisions which existed before 1932. The British therefore encouraged the various rulers to form larger states by acknowledging the headship of some acceptable chief within their own area. If unification took place efficient treasuries and native courts could be set up and the chiefs could pool their slender resources for the establishment of schools, dispensaries, agricultural experiment stations, and other much-needed benefits for their people.

Following this plan of the British officials, by 1939 all but 15 of the 68 divisions had amalgamated into four larger states. Though the Ewes recognized the value of such unification, some of them believed that these independent units should have formed confederacies rather than becoming merely subdivisions of enlarged native states. While this difference of opinion caused some political unrest, the new states did, nevertheless, make real progress during the following years.[1]

Once the amalgamation had begun to take place, it was possible to

[1] There is a full discussion of this political problem in *The Ewe News-Letter*, No. 13 (May 1946).

introduce some of the advantages of indirect rule, and accordingly an administrative ordinance[1] was promulgated in 1932 which provided for the strengthening of local institutions. On general lines it was not unlike those which have already been studied in connexion with the Dependency. It gave the governor the usual right to declare chiefs, councils, or natives as the local authority in any given area with the power and duty to provide for order and good government. Both divisional and state councils were recognized and allowed to investigate political and constitutional disputes within their own areas. An individual might appeal from the divisional to the state council in such affairs and then to the governor, whose decision was final. The state council, since it was made up of the chiefs of the various divisions under the presidency of the paramount, could make by-laws on matters pertaining to the general good of the area, such as establishing state treasuries, for example.[2] The head chief, as an individual, however, had no executive authority over the entire state as had those in the Gold Coast. Such power remained in the hands of the divisional chiefs since they were to remain independent in local matters. Their only obligation was to accept his presidency of the state council and, when registering their election as chiefs, to submit their names through him for the necessary government confirmation.

These clauses cover the administrative sections of the ordinance. Part IV had to do with judicial matters and gave the governor power to establish tribunals in any native authority area under the supervision of the district officers. This general provision was implemented the following year by a governor's order[3] which set up courts in each division of the four new states and on certain defined matters up to £25 gave them both civil and criminal jurisdiction. Appeals lay from the chief's to the paramount's tribunal and hence through the Gold Coast courts all the way up to the Privy Council in London, if necessary. The order also provided for a president, other than the paramount, in cases in which the head chief's interests were concerned.[4] It is to be noted that these courts were only established in divisions which belonged to the new states and not in the independent areas. The government hoped to

---

[1] Ordinance 1 of 1932. This ordinance combines the administrative and judicial clauses which are usually treated in separate ordinances in the Dependency.

[2] It is interesting to note that in the Northern Territories there are no by-laws, for the chief commissioner issues the orders of this type.

[3] Governor's Order No. 2 of 1933. See *British Togo Mandate Report, 1933*, Appendix III.

[4] Land cases, as in the Gold Coast, went—not to the head chief's court—but to the state council which was considered a fairer tribunal for such matters.

encourage further amalgamation with this bait of increased jurisdiction. Divisions in which the new ordinance did not apply had to be content with the very limited powers granted by the old German law and with dependence on the district commissioner for enforcing all judgements.

The 1932 ordinance made no provision for local revenue beyond granting the divisions the general right to set up stool treasuries and collect taxes. The government hoped that each state would establish a central treasury and levy a regular tax as was done in the Northern Territories, but in south Togoland great difficulties stood in the way. In the first place, the states were artificial creations and the individual divisions felt they would derive little benefit from pooling their funds. Secondly, the Africans were willing to accept occasional levies, but they saw no need for regular taxes. Because in past years the central government had financed a water supply and markets in the capital city of Ho, they now expected the same thing to be done in other areas. Finally, the Gold Coast Colony had no direct taxation at that time and seemed to have developed very well without it.[1] In the face of such prejudice regular revenue could not easily be obtained and, indeed, in several instances the people threatened chiefs with destoolment if they insisted on forcing the issue. By 1939, then, only two state treasuries had been set up and no attempts made to collect taxes.

Besides the political changes of these years, there was some parallel growth on social and economic lines. In the mandated sphere there were no government schools, and in the southern section education was entirely in the hands of missionaries, who were assisted by government funds whenever their institutions reached the required standards. During the German occupancy, Lutheran and Catholic mission societies had established some excellent primary and technical schools. The former group had also succeeded in translating the Bible into the Ewe language and had done a fine piece of work. When the British entered the territory, all German missionaries were deported. From 1916 to 1923 the government conducted the Bremen Society (Lutheran) schools. Scottish Presbyterians then took over these institutions and were later aided by some of the former German missionaries who were allowed to return. Eventually an Ewe Presbyterian Church, made up largely of African clergymen and almost entirely supported by local funds, developed from the efforts of the early missionaries.

A Catholic institution working in the Gold Coast—the Society for

[1] *British Togo Mandate Report, 1937*, pp. 6 ff.; Hailey, *African Survey*, p. 479.

African Missions—took over the German Catholic schools, and later two orders of religious women began to teach and to do medical work among the inhabitants of the mandate.

The Gold Coast Education Ordinance of 1927 was also applied in south Togoland, requiring a reorganization of all assisted schools on a more efficient basis. Both Catholic and Presbyterian schools made great efforts to raise their standards, so that in 1938 there were eighty-three assisted and thirty-seven non-assisted schools. The assisted schools received a government grant of £11,336, together with some funds from the native authorities. Out of a population of 128,377, nearly 6,000 boys and 1,500 girls were attending school. Red Cross and Boy Scout associations were established in some centres, and Ewe boys and girls occasionally went to Achimota or missionary colleges for higher education.[1]

Medical work was carried on by both the government and the missions. This was a field in which there was much room for improvement, and the Permanent Mandates Commission, on several occasions, expressed the opinion that more medical officers were needed. The British representative answered that one doctor for every 60,000 natives was a better proportion than was to be found in the Gold Coast, and no increase in the medical staff was made.[2] Leprosy and hookworm as well as the other usual tropical diseases were widespread. As in the Dependency the infant mortality rate was always over 100 deaths to every 1,000 births.[3] The only answer to the problem seemed to be a larger revenue, or further grants from the British or Gold Coast governments.

There was some economic development during the years 1920–39, resulting especially from an increased production of cocoa which rose from 3,542 tons in 1923 to 12,316 in 1938. Coffee held second place on the export list with a value of £4,722, but as trade was largely local, there were no other important items. Revenue in 1938 only amounted to £28,375 (largely from import and export duties), whereas expenditure was £95,904. This meant a government grant of £67,529 was necessary

[1] *British Togo Mandate Report, 1938*, pp. 47–49.

[2] Permanent Mandates Commission, *Minutes*, 5th Session, p. 40; 28th Session, pp. 73, 91; 31st Session, p. 107.

[3] *British Togo Mandate Report, 1928*, p. 42, states that the infant mortality rate was probably as high as 400 and the 1927 report, p. 47, declares that perhaps 70 per cent died before reaching the age of five in the far northern Kusasi area.

See Robert Kuczynski, *The Cameroons and Togoland: A Demographic Study* (London, 1939), under the auspices of the Royal Institute of International Affairs, pp. 525–45. This demographer has made a scientific study of population in four West African mandates. He found that though several tropical diseases, especially sleeping sickness and leprosy, were on the increase in British Togoland, the government had not taken sufficient steps to combat them. Expenditure for medical care was only about 6d. per head in Togo as compared with 2s. in the Gold Coast.

to balance the budget. Such grants were paid annually from Gold Coast funds, since the mandate was first assumed.[1] But even with this aid, the mandate was not spending sufficient money, according to modern standards, on necessary social services. In 1938, for example, the amounts budgeted were as follows:[2] education, £12,147; agriculture, £6,718; public health, £13,997; public works, £9,658.

It is evident from the fact that the mandated sphere was not self-supporting during the 1919–39 period that it had not made as much economic progress as had the Gold Coast itself. Because of the differences in area, natural resources, population, tribal organization, and political background, it is almost impossible to compare justly the two areas. There are some factors, however, which may help to explain the slower rate of development.

In the first place, British Togoland had neither the rich mineral resources nor as large a cocoa-growing area as had the Gold Coast. While some exporting was done, it was less profitable than it should have been, since the mandate was separated by artificial frontiers from access to the coast. The railway, built by the Germans to serve the entire Togoland area, was in the French section. In the western part of the mandate transportation was also an expensive item since the nearest ports were in the Colony proper. In addition, the division of the Togoland tribes into so many small groups made economic and social development difficult—unless, of course, British policy had been one of direct and paternalistic rule. Even though some amalgamation took place during this twenty-year period, lack of a unified or national outlook—due in large part to widespread illiteracy—still hampered all forms of progress.

A further and perhaps more fundamental reason for the slower development was the fact that Togoland was a mandate rather than a British colony. It is natural that both governments and private individuals should prefer to spend their money in territories which belong to the metropolitan power, and whose future is therefore more secure than that of an area under international control. In the 1930's there was a section of public opinion in England which advocated a surrender of the mandates because they did not pay. A Member of Parliament, for example, voiced the opinion in the House of Commons that 'so long as you have large areas of territory which have no certain future, you cannot

[1] *British Togo Mandate Report, 1938*, Appendix XIII. However, it should be pointed out that Togo expenses always include a share in the general administrative costs of the Gold Coast central government. This share is decided on the basis of population and is therefore not very great.   [2] ibid.

attract capital and you cannot have any development plan'.[1] Looking at the progress of British Togoland during the 1919–39 period, then, it appears clear that the mandate, just because it was under international supervision, did not fare any better than the Colony. On the contrary, it seems to have come out less well in some instances, principally as a result of the British hesitancy to invest in a territory whose future status was uncertain.

While the 1939–46 period has not yet been considered in connexion with the Dependency as a whole, it will be helpful, perhaps, to go somewhat ahead of the main narrative in order to complete the account of the Togoland mandate and of its transfer, after the Second World War, to the status of a trust territory.

During the war years Togoland shared to a limited extent in the economic acceleration which was common to all of West Africa. If the war brought a certain amount of economic development, however, it was also the occasion of new difficulties for the country. These difficulties arose from the fact that, after the fall of France in 1940, the Vichy government closed the frontier between French and British Togoland. The attendant hardships for those families and tribal groups with interests in both areas sharpened their natural resentment at the division of their native land under two administrations. As a result, a movement for unification began to take shape. Among certain members of the various Ewe tribes located in both zones of Togoland as well as in the south-eastern corner of the Gold Coast Colony the movement eventually assumed the character of a campaign—not merely for the amalgamation of the two zones, but for a fusion of all Ewe peoples in a united Eweland.

In May 1945 Daniel Ahmling Chapman, an Ewe from the British sphere who had had the advantage of an Oxford education and who was on the Achimota College staff, began to publish a monthly newsletter designed to acquaint his fellow tribesmen with the plan for unification and to prepare them 'to play a more effective part in the affairs of our country and in shaping its future'.[2] The movement thus started aimed at increasing co-operation between the various states and at a more progressive system of native administration as well as at the eventual unification of the separated tribes.

At the same time that the All-Ewe movement was beginning, preparations were being made in San Francisco for the United Nations

---

[1] *Parliamentary Debates*, 5th ser., Commons, vol. CDII, col. 434.
[2] *The Ewe News-Letter*, No. 1 (May 1945).

Organization. Since British and French Togoland had been League of Nations Mandates, the question of their transfer to the new authority would eventually arise.

In June 1945 the United Nations Charter, as drafted at the San Francisco Conference, was finally signed. Chapters 12 and 13 of this document made provision for the establishment of an international trusteeship system. This system could be applied by means of trustee-ship agreements to mandated areas, as well as to other categories of territories. It did not differ greatly from the former mandate system since individual states would continue to administer the trust territories under the general supervision of the Trusteeship Council. This council had more power, however, than the Permanent Mandates Commission in that it could visit the respective trust territories at the times agreed upon by the administering authority, and could receive petitions directly from these territories. One notable feature was the inclusion of a general declaration of principles for the administration of all dependencies, mentioning among others the following aim:

To promote the political, economic, social and educational advancement of the inhabitants of the Trust Territories, and their progressive development towards self-government or independence as may be appropriate to the particular circumstances of each territory and its peoples and the freely expressed wishes of the people concerned, and as may be provided by the terms of each trusteeship agreement. . . .[1]

During the first session of the General Assembly of the United Nations in January 1946, Great Britain took the initiative in putting the new provisions into practical execution by placing her mandated territories of Tanganyika, the Cameroons, and Togoland under the trusteeship system. The following October the British government filed a draft of the terms of trusteeship with the Secretary-General of the United Nations for presentation during the ensuing session of the General Assembly.[2] At the same time, the French government also presented a trusteeship agreement for the former mandate of French

[1] *Charter of the United Nations*, Chapter XII, 'International Trusteeship System', Article 76.

[2] The original draft for the British Togoland trust can be found in *Togoland and the Cameroons under United Kingdom Mandate* (July 1946), Cmd. 6863. The second draft is given in *Territories in Africa under United Kingdom Mandate* (revised texts, October 1946), Cmd. 6935. The final text is in United Nations Trusteeship Document T/8 (25 March 1947). *Trusteeship Agreements; Texts of the Eight Trusteeship Agreements approved by the General Assembly at the Sixty-second Meeting of its First Session, 13 December 1946.*

Togoland. In spite of the Ewes' desire for the unification of the territory, the new agreements thus provided for a continuation of the old divisions. Both drafts were accepted by the General Assembly in December 1946. The first meeting of the Trusteeship Council did not take place until March 1947.

During the 1946 trusteeship discussions in the United Nations, the Ewes, through their organization, the All-Ewe Conference, continued to work for unification, and petitions were sent to the Secretary-General[1] and later to the Trusteeship Council.[2] In December 1947 the council, meeting in New York, heard an oral statement from Sylvanus E. Olympio, the Ewe representative, again asking for unification. His petition was not granted, but the British and French administering authorities agreed to set up an Anglo-French Standing Consultative Commission,[3] on which both the administration and population of the two sections would be represented, and which would endeavour to mitigate the difficulties caused by the frontier. The commission met several times during 1948 and 1949 and was able to remove many of the problems caused by the frontier, but not to solve the problem of unification.

The question was complicated by the fact that all the African groups concerned did not agree on the same solution. Considered at almost every session of the Trusteeship Council and the General Assembly during the 1947–56 period, the issue built up a massive documentation and became one of the most persistent problems to face the United Nations. Conflicting viewpoints have been presented by many Togolanders to United Nations visiting missions, through written requests and even by representatives who made the trip to New York for oral petitions to the United Nations. Among these various groups the All-Ewe Conference (AEC), mentioned above, with its counterpart in French Togoland—the *Comité de l'unité Togolaise* (CUT)—continued to demand a united Eweland for the Ewes of both Togolands as well as for those who lived in the south-east corner of the Gold Coast. But others, fearful lest the Gold Coast Ewes exercise a predominating influence, preferred to confine unification to the two Togolands proper as a step towards a separate independent state. Their party was known as the Togoland Congress Party (TC). Still a fourth group in French

---

[1] U.N. Doc. T/5.
[2] U.N. Doc. T/Pet. 6/1.
[3] *Report by His Majesty's Government in the United Kingdom of Great Britain and Northern Ireland to the General Assembly of the U.N. on the Administration of Togoland under U.K. Trusteeship for the year 1948* (London, 1949).

Togo, the *Parti Togolaise du Progrès* (PTP), favoured a bond with the French Union to the exclusion of any other association. They were a very small minority, however. To add to the complication the tribes in the northern section of British Togoland wanted a closer union with the Northern Territories, rather than with an independent Togoland, in order to preserve the very close cultural and historical unity which binds their tribes. It was not surprising that the United Nations Trusteeship Council Mission which visited Togoland in December 1949 was unable to provide a formula for unification. Its report pointed out that

any appraisal of the political development of Togoland under British administration must depend to considerable degree on the solution of the problems raised by the demands for unification of the two Togolands. The Territory under British adminstration is small in size and population . . . and it is difficult to contemplate its future political and economic development except in association either with Togoland under French administration or with the neighbouring Gold Coast Colony and protectorate or possibly both.[1]

In 1948, as indicated above, the British and French had set up a common Togoland council known as the Consultative Commission to deal with frontier grievances and to facilitate exchange of persons and goods between the two areas. In 1949 and again in 1951 the United Nations authorities recommended the enlargement of this organ so that it would be more fully representative of the population. Though the administering authorities somewhat expanded its rôle—it then became known as the Joint Council—they were not disposed to give it either executive or legislative powers. But when the council actually tried to function it was boycotted by the very groups which had been suggesting unification, because they were dissatisfied with its limited powers and with the type of indirect electoral system set up by the British and French. It would have been impossible, in any case, given the great divergence of opinion among the population, to have made a success of joint institutions. As a result, after a first brief meeting in August 1952, the Joint Council never met again. Moreover, after 1951, the dramatic constitutional changes taking place in the Gold Coast began to affect conditions in Togoland. The continuation of this phase of Togoland history therefore belongs to a later chapter.[2]

[1] U.N. Trusteeship Council, *Report of the First Visiting Mission to the Trust Territory of Togoland under British Administration*, U.N. Doc. T/465 (February 1950), p. 19.
[2] An excellent treatment of Togoland as a trust area is given in James Coleman, 'Togoland', *International Conciliation*, No. 509 (September 1956).

CHAPTER VIII

ECONOMIC AND SOCIAL PROGRESS, 1919–39

The history and political development of the four divisions of the Gold Coast Dependency from 1919 to 1939 have now been considered. It is evident that even in the latter year marked differences in the manner and rate of progress still existed. There were the Northern Territories with a subsistence economy, with insufficient communications to the south, and with social and political circumstances not much beyond those of the more primitive sections of Africa, although reunited native states and an apparently successful form of indirect rule promised much for the future. Then there was Ashanti with its long tradition of war and of federal action which gave this section a homogeneous character and led to a happy restoration of the former confederacy and to a surprisingly rapid adaptation to Western civilization. In contrast to both the Northern Territories and to Ashanti, in 1939 the coastal area remained divided into numerous petty states with at least three big linguistic groups. Due to the rapid development of the cocoa industry it had reached a more advanced economic status than the rest of the Dependency, with the resultant growth of a moneyed middle class interested in commerce, and with an educated professional group often politically minded and determined to obtain a speedy increase in self-government. The bulk of the population, however, remained living in rural areas under the traditional rule of their chiefs. Certain differences in viewpoint and interests consequently grew up between the rural and urban areas. The government, recognizing the mistakes of its early *laissez-faire* policy, attempted to draw together the rulers of the various divisions through the joint provincial council and to co-ordinate and harmonize the aims of conservative and progressive groups.

A fourth section of the Dependency—the mandated sphere of British Togoland—was itself divided in two parts, that of the north sharing the characteristics of the Protectorate, while the south had the same type of problems, though in a less acute form, as the Gold Coast Colony itself.

With this picture of the various departments of the Dependency in mind, it will be possible to consider the development which took place from 1919 to 1939 in economic and social matters. Since an inter-relation of the four divisions often exists in these fields, they will be treated, as far as possible, from the standpoint of the whole, rather than as separate units.

ECONOMIC DEVELOPMENT

The economic history[1] of the Gold Coast, since its first contacts with Europeans, can be divided into three main periods, though the characteristics of each occasionally overlap one another. During the first period (sixteenth–eighteenth centuries) various European nations carried on the lucrative business of slave trading until the British outlawed it in 1807, and English companies, encouraged by humanitarian groups, tried to replace it with a 'legitimate commerce' of such native products as palm-oil, gold-dust, and timber. In return for these exports the Gold Coast received fire-arms, rum, tobacco, beads, and cotton textiles. This 'trader's era' lasted until the mid-nineteenth century when parliament finally decided to take control of the coastal settlements, and thus inaugurated the third or Crown colony period, during which the Gold Coast was considered to be of economic value, since: (1) it could produce tropical commodities in demand in the English market; (2) it possessed considerable mineral deposits of gold and—as was later discovered—diamonds, manganese, and bauxite; (3) it could provide an expanding market for British manufactured goods, especially cotton textiles.

The administration, during this last period, had the aim of en-couraging exports and imports, and to this end the *Pax Britannica* was imposed on the entire Dependency, adequate government systems set up, and means of transportation developed. The system was not a difficult one to inaugurate, for the Gold Coast possessed great natural wealth; crops, especially cacao, which was introduced in the 1890's, were easily grown, and world markets were constantly expanding. The years between the opening of the century and the great depression were marked by what has been aptly called 'a leap to prosperity'. The export and import duties, especially those on cocoa, provided sufficient revenue to finance the administration and, for the time being at least, direct

[1] There is no economic history of the Gold Coast, although certain phases of its development have been treated in empire surveys or in separate monographs. See, for example, W. K. Hancock, *Survey of British Commonwealth Affairs*, vol. II; *Problems of Economic Policy, 1918–1939*, Part 2 (London, 1942); Hailey, *African Survey*; Hinden, *Plan for Africa*. See also the publications of the Achimota Discussion Groups for the best expression of native opinion on economic as well as political and social affairs. The annual reports and the legislative council debates also give details concerning economic and social development.

taxation seemed unnecessary. As has been seen, Governor Sir Gordon Guggisberg used this increased revenue, as well as government loans, to finance his Ten Year Plan which brought to the Gold Coast an enlarged transportation system and new educational, medical, and other public services. With the coming of the slump in world trade in the 1930's, however, the danger of an economy based on export goods was brought home to all; especially since the country was depending for its purchase of imported goods almost entirely on the proceeds of one main agricultural crop, which was extremely subject to world price fluctuations. By 1931 revenue dropped from the high 1927 level of over £4,000,000 to about half that amount. Fortunately for the Colony, the world premium on gold stimulated the mining industry, and the resultant increase of revenue from the gold export tax helped the administration, along with its policy of stringent economy, to weather the trade slump. As a result of this experience, the government made some attempts to foster more varied types of agriculture, but with only moderate success. The cattle and timber industries were also stimulated, but though far-seeing African leaders asked for the introduction of local industries, the administration did not, at that time, adopt a policy of official encouragement of manufacturing. It was to take the changed conditions and the challenge to Britain's colonial policy of the 1939–45 war years finally to procure strong governmental support of a more balanced economy.

Not only the Gold Coast administration but that of the entire colonial empire has been criticized for concentrating during the pre-war epoch on political development to the neglect of economic and social progress. As one author put it, this achievement in popular government and indirect rule had been very great:

But it will be jeopardized unless the Native Administrations and the European officials who give them guidance show themselves capable of solving the more pressing economic problems and thereby delivering those tangible goods which the people increasingly demand—better education, improved health, and the prospect of liberation from the ancient curse of abject poverty. Until quite recently, officials and writers have not paid sufficient attention to these matters. Anthropology has been the fashionable study, and it has been encouraged by intelligent administrators because of the help it can give them in improving the mechanism of indirect rule. This is all to the good. The partnership between anthropologists and administrators is a happy one. But it is a pity that the economists have not also been called in.[1]

[1] Hancock, *Problems of Economic Policy, 1918–1930*, p. 265.

But there were some signs during the latter part of the 1930's that both the Colonial Office in London and the administration in the Gold Coast were taking an increased interest in the economic life of the Dependency. In 1929 the first Colonial Development Fund was established, and about the same time a special section was organized by the secretary of state for the colonies to study and advise him on the economic problems of the empire. Though this policy did not come to full flowering until after 1939, a new attitude was just beginning to appear, during the pre-war years, towards social and economic matters in the various departments of the Gold Coast administration.

In turning from this over-all picture of the economic situation in the Dependency to the separate elements which made it up, the most basic one of agriculture will be considered first. During the nineteenth century it presents the story of a varied production for export purposes which gradually gave way to an unhealthy concentration on the single, easily grown, and highly popular cacao crop, until the 1930 drop in prices brought both the government and the Africans to the realization of their dangerous position and of the necessity for a more balanced development.

With the transfer in 1807 from slave trading to legitimate commerce, the Gold Coast began to export palm-oil and kernels, a little wild rubber, timber, and gold-dust, while there was also a considerable trade in kola nuts with the Muslim interior. In the nineteenth century the amount of these exports gradually increased, especially as there was a growing demand in Europe for all types of vegetable oils. It was found that the scrublands along the coast were suitable to coco-nuts, and a trade in copra, the dried meat of the kernels, was also developed.

Such was the situation in 1879 when an African labourer from the plantations of Fernando Po, an island off the coast of West Africa, returned to the Gold Coast bringing cocoa pods. The story has already been told how from this beginning the Gold Coast developed an industry which was contributing, by 1925, nearly 44 per cent of the total world cocoa exports. Probably the most interesting fact of all is that this amazing achievement was accomplished entirely by African farmers, with little help from the government beyond the provision of the necessary transportation system.

Throughout the colonial empire the British faced, during these years, the choice of allowing European capital to develop the plantation system or of protecting the native cultivator. In West Africa, the decision was almost always in favour of indigenous owners, even though Lord Leverhulme of the Unilever Company and other British financiers

prophesied that scientific large-scale producers would eventually monopolize the market and drive out the local agriculturalists. The cocoa
industry, though it was certainly not as efficiently run as it could be, was
nevertheless an example of African ability and of the possibility of
developing large-scale export crops from small native farms. There were
estimated to be some 300,000 such farms in the country (though no
exact survey was made), usually four to five acres in size and averaging
about one-ton output per farm.

The industry grew rapidly, as the establishment of a farm requires
little more than the clearing of the forest and the planting of trees. But
in contrast to the growers of South America and the West Indies the
African farmers neglected drainage, forking, pruning, disease control,
and the provision of sufficient shade trees. In the early years of the
industry's growth the government made little effort to guide it or to
introduce better methods of husbandry.

With a rapidly expanding market in Europe and America during the
first quarter of the twentieth century, success came easily to the Gold
Coast farmers. The following figures[1] give a picture of these forward
leaps:

Period						Five Year Average by Tons
1891–1895	.	.	.	.	.	5
1896–1900	.	.	.	.	.	230
1901–1905	.	.	.	.	.	3,172
1906–1910	.	.	.	.	.	14,784
1911–1915	.	.	.	.	.	51,819
1916–1920	.	.	.	.	.	106,072
1921–1925	.	.	.	.	.	186,329
1926–1930	.	.	.	.	.	218,895
1931–1934	.	.	.	.	.	236,088

In spite of the rapid development, however, the situation of the cocoa
farmer was not as favourable as at first appears. The finances of the
industry were poorly organized, or rather not organized at all, with
the result that the majority of the cocoa growers were deeply in debt
to money-lenders with little hope of ever being able to clear their
accounts. These money-lenders were mainly brokers for the European
firms. They were given money by the firms to advance to the farmers
as a guarantee that the forthcoming season's crop would be supplied to
the particular firm in question. The farmer got into debt if, owing to
bad weather, disease, or price fluctuations, he was unable to make good

[1] *Gold Coast Handbook, 1937*, p. 38.

the advance received. In some cases, of course, individuals got into debt through extravagant funeral observances, litigation expenses, or other causes.[1]

One cause of this financial difficulty was the changing character of land tenure which the cocoa industry itself brought about. West African practice has always been one of tribal ownership of land under the protection of the chief. In the beginning each farmer was a peasant cultivator who worked a few acres of soil with the aid of his family, and, if he wished to expand his cocoa holdings, no objections were raised as there was plenty of land for all. With the expansion of industry, however, hired labour from the Northern Territories or the neighbouring French colonies was also employed, which led to non-working absentee owners, who left the farms to managers relying entirely on paid labour. At the same time the land was increasing in value. Such a set of circumstances put the chiefs in a position to enrich themselves by selling their tribal lands, a practice hitherto unknown and contrary to customary native law. Accordingly, in the cocoa areas individual ownership began to replace the former communal right of occupancy. As unscrupulous local authorities often sold and resold the same acreage to different buyers, and as lack of surveys made definite boundaries impossible, endless disputes and costly litigation over land titles soon resulted. A further outcome was that land was no longer there for the taking, and an impoverished farmer could not help himself by expanded production.

With these new conditions, the need for cash increased. The farmer had to buy land, pay wages to his hired labourers, and support his family, for in many cases the older practice of growing local subsistence crops was so neglected that partial reliance on canned goods from England became increasingly common. If a farmer fell in debt he would usually turn to the African money-lender and borrow on his coming crop or, if necessary, mortgage his farm on the basis of a long-term loan. Due to lack of clear titles to land, the banks would not lend with the farm as security, nor was any government credit agency set up, so the money-lenders and cocoa brokers had their way and charged interest rates which were seldom less than 50 per cent. The whole system of uncertain land title, of obtaining advances on crops, of ever-increasing debts with no way of repaying them, not only threw the cocoa industry into a state of confusion and disrupted the land system of the Colony

---

[1] One of the agricultural officers of the Gold Coast made a survey of a typical cocoa village. See W. R. Beckett, *Akokoaso: A Survey of a Gold Coast Village* (London 1943).

but also had grave consequences of both political and social import. The sale of tribal lands, their rental to non-tribal strangers, or their unjust control by influential families of the district, often deprived the common folk of their share. As far as native authority was concerned, the new system also created difficulty. Non-tribal Africans who bought or rented land sometimes refused to give allegiance to the local chief or to pay their share in taxes. The migratory labourers from the north, moreover, had no chief to protect them in matters of just wages and were sometimes discriminated against in the local tribunals.

In addition to the unstable financial foundation of the cocoa industry and its resultant evils, there were many technical problems. Due to ignorance of scientific agriculture or to discouragement over low prices, the farmers often used negligent methods in both caring for the trees and preparing the cocoa for market. Proper care of the soil, pruning, drainage, manuring, pest control, and shade trees were neglected. Once the pods were ripe they were often so carelessly fermented and dried that diseased and mouldy beans resulted. In the end, Gold Coast cocoa, being rated on the world market as of inferior quality, consequently brought lower prices. In order to protect the quality of the Colony's exports,[1] in 1927 the government introduced a system of voluntary inspection, and seven years later made it compulsory. This legislation, along with the 1937 scheme for government grading, somewhat improved matters.

Added to these difficulties of finance, organization, and technique, a further one was to be found in the marketing of the product. As has been pointed out in an earlier chapter, almost the entire crop was purchased by thirteen European firms. From time to time the Africans united in hold-ups against the price agreements of these companies, some of which control also the bulk of imports and the retailing stores of West Africa. After the most serious and prolonged boycott—that of 1937–8—a parliamentary committee investigated the entire cocoa situation, and not only reported against the buyers' pool, but also recommended that marketing should be completely reorganized and, under government supervision, entrusted to a co-operative association of African farmers.[2] Though the governor appointed a committee to prepare for such an organization, the war prevented its formation and the administration controlled all marketing of cocoa.

---

[1] In one year the United States Department of Agriculture rejected 26,274 bags of cocoa out of a probable 400,000,000. Legislative Council, *Debates* (1930), p. 21.
[2] *Report on Cocoa*, Cmd. 5845 (1938), Sections 511–45; see Chapter V above.

The most serious threat to the cocoa industry, however, began to show itself in the 1930's with a rapid increase in the diseases affecting the cocoa trees themselves, particularly the 'swollen shoot' disease. The agricultural department made some attempts to get the Africans to apply methods of plant sanitation and pest control, but results were insufficient. Moreover, the basic causes of the diseases had not been discovered. Visiting agriculturists warned the government of the grave danger to the entire industry and in 1936 a colonial office expert finally spoke sharply. 'The Gold Coast,' he reported, 'with the largest cocoa industry in the world, is still contented with the present and is taking no steps to safeguard the future.'[1] Two years later, at long last, a research station was set up at New Tafo. During the war this centre did intensive work on the cocoa diseases, but the further account will be considered in a later chapter.

Looking back over the early story of the cocoa development, one cannot but regret that it was not properly organized from its very beginning. Here was a peasant industry which might have led to a fairly even distribution of wealth among the lower classes. In West Africa the British wisely held to the policy of safeguarding the land for the African rather than allowing European-controlled plantations, but such a method could not succeed unless the Africans were taught scientific techniques and were aided by the government to organize the marketing of the crop on the most modern lines. For the educated Africans of the coastal areas, this could best be done by agricultural co-operatives, while for the more primitive peoples of the interior, demonstration farms under the control of the native authorities would have been the wiser method. Unfortunately, until the 1930's no such policy was inaugurated. At that time the task of developing co-operatives was given into the hands of the Department of Agriculture. Its officers put much energy and enthusiasm into aiding the Africans to establish such associations, not only for cocoa farmers but for other producers as well.[2] In 1931 an ordinance[3] legalized them, and by 1938 the following types[4] had been organized:

[1] F. A. Stockdale, *Report . . . on His Visit to Nigeria, Gold Coast and Sierra Leone,* Oct. *1935–Feb. 1936*, p. 6, quoted by Hancock, *Economic Policy*, p. 250.

[2] Legislative Council, *Debates* (1937), pp. 23, 60; (1938), p. 107. See also Claude Strickland, *Co-operation for Africa* (Oxford, 1933); Hancock, op. cit., pp. 266 ff.; Jackson Davis, *Africa Advancing*, pp. 122–8. For an expression of favourable African opinion on co-operatives, see K. Sunkersette Obu, 'Economic Planning for National Development', Achimota and Kumasi Discussion Groups, *Towards National Development* (Achimota, 1945), pp. 48–49.

[3] No. 4 of 1931.

[4] *G.C. An. Report, 1938*, p. 28.

Types	Numbers	Members	Paid up Share Capital
Cocoa producers . . .	371	9,399	£28,298
Copra producers . . .	11	541	632
Fruit (banana) producers .	20	348	1,022
Citrus producers . . .	4	464	765
Coffee producers . . .	1	72	110
Total	407	10,824	£30,827

The 371 cocoa co-operatives, however, sold but 9,405 tons of cocoa in 1938, and though all lots were of high purity they commanded only the small price premium of some 6d. per load. This reward was scarcely worth the extra effort which co-operative action requires of the un-trained African. For this reason the Nowell Commission of 1937 recommended a Cocoa Farmers' Association to represent all the producers, and to sell on their behalf the entire crop of the Gold Coast.[1]

Another view advanced was that the whole cocoa problem was too complicated to be left in the hands of the native authorities who, owing to the *laissez-faire* attitude of the government in the nineteenth and early twentieth centuries, had not received sufficient training in administration to cope with the situation.[2]

On the fundamental question of native business morality, some observers pointed out that the Gold Coast African first learned commercial methods from hardened European slave traders. Some of the Africans were not professing Christians, and a few appeared to have no very high standard of business practice, being wholly material in outlook and interested only in financial gain.[3] The Africans themselves began to recognize this weakness. One of the Gold Coast intelligentsia speaking to the Achimota Discussion Group, for example, pointed out that 'Africans have often been known to be ruthless in dealing with other Africans' and that the future 'need will be greater business integrity and high moral purpose without which neither Europeans nor Africans, whose privilege it will be to re-make Africa, can succeed'.[4] Another African, a member of the legislative council, with a frankness not usually found in such addresses, warned the Gold Coast Youth Conference: 'Dishonesty keeps the country back from uniting together to carry on

[1] *Report on Cocoa*, Cmd. 5845, Sections 511–45.
[2] MacMillan, *Europe and West Africa*, pp. 80 ff.
[3] ibid., p. 84.
[4] M. Duwuona, 'Towards a New Social Economy', *Pointers to Progress: the Gold Coast in the Next Five Years*, ed. by C. Shaw (Achimota, 1942), pp. 61–62.

any trade, business, or anything that will place the people of this country on a good financial standing.'[1] Though unfair business practices were by no means universal, the problem was a serious one and left much for the Press, schools, and missions of the Dependency to accomplish.

Before leaving this discussion of agricultural development and its related problems, something should be said of the attempts which the government made to introduce a more balanced production. As has been seen, in the first quarter of this century palm-oil and local food crops were increasingly neglected for the easier and more profitable business of cocoa growing. With the depression, however, the low price for cocoa and the general financial condition led the farmers to cultivate subsistence crops both for themselves and the local market. At the same time, especially on derelict cocoa farms, the Department of Agriculture encouraged an increased and more efficient production of palm-oil products. The former wild-rubber industry, which since 1919 had been steadily decreasing, was also revived; while experiments were made in bringing new tropical products to the Gold Coast. In 1934 the production of bananas for export was begun, and three years later 59,000 bunches were exported.[2] The industry was a demanding one, however, and the farmers preferred the easier cocoa culture. Citrus fruits were somewhat more satisfactory. In 1934, likewise, grape-fruit orchards were begun, and the government set up a trial cannery, while in 1938 a European firm established a lime-juice plant, and £26,959 worth of lime products were exported. Since the coco-nut is the only crop which does well on the sandy beaches, the peasants of these districts often combine the production of copra with their ordinary fishing trade. By 1938 some 2,000 tons a year were produced, and the industry continued to expand.

Small quantities of rice and tobacco were also grown for local consumption, while kola did well in the forest areas and found a good market in the Muslim Sudan. The farmers of the Northern Territories and parts of Togoland produced maize, millet, yams, and peanuts, not only for their own use but for the markets of Ashanti and the Colony. The North had, moreover, quantities of unexploited shea-nut trees, whose fruit contains a solid fat suitable for food. The Department of Agriculture maintained a shea reserve near Yendi, where trials with the

[1] Kojo Thompson, 'Whither are we Drifting in Society?' Gold Coast Youth Conference, *Are We to Sit Down?* (Accra, 1942), p. 3.
[2] *G.C. An. Report, 1937*, p. 29; E. Worthington, *Science in Africa; A Review of Scientific Research relating to Tropical and Southern Africa* (Oxford, 1938), p. 367.

effects of cultivation on wild trees resulted in a marked increase of yield after 1932.

These efforts of the administration to broaden the base of Gold Coast agriculture bettered the situation, but they were not sufficient. The African leaders were not unconscious of the problem, and one section of the 1934 petition to the Colonial Office referred to this point:

> In regard to banana, the cotton plant, limes, etc., the Government has indeed made certain instalments towards improving or popularizing their culture, but the moneys voted for these have been niggardly, or otherwise they are expended in the wrong direction by employing local European officers in the Agricultural Department with no special business experience in these markets other than the academic training for their culture. We ask that a special commissioner with business experience be sent out to the coast to find a way of adding to the wealth of the country in addition to the cocoa they now cultivate.[1]

Of course the fault was not wholly that of the government, as this criticism might lead one to suppose. The Department of Agriculture made repeated attempts, as has been seen, to encourage other crops, but there was little hope of improvement until the illiterate farmer had been properly trained in more scientific methods. Governors and other public officials pointed out the danger, not only of a one-crop economy, but also of the malnutrition which was so widespread in the country.[2] From the early 1930's onwards the League of Nations, the International Labour Office, the British Colonial Office, and other organizations showed much interest in the nutrition of dependent peoples. Food surveys were made and malnutrition was found to be the predisposing cause of most of the African diseases, as well as of the low disease resistance so common among the inhabitants. In 1939 the Committee on Nutrition for the Colonial Empire published the results of its survey. The section on the Gold Coast reported:

> Broadly speaking, the diet is deficient in those animal and vegetable food-stuffs which provide fat, good protein, vitamins and mineral matter. It is believed, but not proved, that the calcium content of the diet is poor. The protein content is generally very low. This is especially noticeable in the miner's diet. There is also a definite deficiency of vitamin C in the diet of the poorer classes. . . .

[1] Sessional Papers No. 11 of 1934, *Papers relating to the Petition of the Delegation from the Gold Coast Colony and Ashanti* (Accra, 1934), p. 49.
[2] See, for example, Legislative Council, *Debates* (1930), 'Governor's Address', p. 39.

Food deficiency is a predisposing factor in many local disease conditions. Tuberculosis, the pneumonias and bronchitis are very prevalent and together account for 30 per cent of all registered male deaths. Over 70 per cent of persons in the coast town of Saltpond gave evidence of tubercle infection. . . . There seems to be a close relationship between undernutrition and the incidence of leprosy in certain areas.[1]

It is evident from this report that the people of the Gold Coast had need of a more balanced diet. The earlier discussion of the cattle industry in the Northern Territories showed its possibilities of further development, but much reorganization of the marketing technique was necessary if the cattle were not to be lost in transit and if a lower price and wider distribution were to bring meat supplies within the orbit of the lower classes.

In like manner, if health standards were to be raised, a more varied diet of fresh fruits and vegetables was obligatory. Practically every type of vegetable and many tropical fruits could be grown in the country. In past years between £1,000,000 and £2,000,000 had been spent, out of total import trade of only some £8,000,000, on all manner of foodstuffs from abroad, including canned fish and meat, flour, dried milk, and vegetable oils. If only the food economy of the country were properly organized, the inhabitants could save much money for more necessary imports; they could build up local trade and, above all, they could better their health by proper diet.[2]

Closely connected with the agricultural problems of the Gold Coast were those concerning land tenure and forest reserves. As for the land question and the litigation that grew up around it, one colonial official called it 'the curse of the country', and rightly so, for probably no single issue caused more trouble for the government, Europeans, and Africans, than this 'exasperating uncertainty' as to who holds title to the land.[3]

In the early days of British occupation, the government made no attempt to prevent alienation of tribal land to foreigners until, in the 1890's, European mining prospectors began a veritable rush for concessions. In ignorance, chiefs were easily persuaded to alienate their

---

[1] *Nutrition in the Colonial Empire,* Part 2, Cmd. 6051 (1939), pp. 35–36. *West Africa* (25 May 1946), p. 463, states that a nutrition survey conducted by the Gold Coast government itself, during the late 1930's, has been suppressed by the Colonial Office in London.

[2] The Africans of the Gold Coast realized the need for a more balanced diet. The Achimota Discussion Group often touched on this point. See, for example, C. Shaw (editor), *Pointers to Progress*, pp. 50–54, 64–72.

[3] Hailey, op. cit., Chapter XI, Part 2.

people's lands, even though it was not allowed by tribal law. In order to protect the heritage of the Africans, in 1894 the government attempted to vest all waste and forest lands in the Crown to be administered for the common good. When this Bill aroused much opposition, in 1897 a second ordinance was planned which would recognize the rights of the occupants as against the chiefs. The African leaders again offered such strong resistance that the matter was dropped, and in 1900 the government merely passed an ordinance which required that all concessions be validated by the Supreme Court of the Gold Coast. The Bill, however, was inadequate to protect the people's communal rights from the disregard of the chiefs, and by 1939 over 11,000 square miles of tribal lands had been alienated either to Africans or to Europeans.[1]

The gradual shift from communal to individual ownership further complicated the land situation. As insufficient surveys had been made, it was impossible to grant titles. In addition, the practice of individual ownership was recognized in only certain parts of the country. The Africans, furthermore, kept up continued litigation over cocoa farms, so that controversies supposedly settled were being constantly reopened. All these factors combined to make the issue one of great confusion.

Probably, as Lord Hailey suggested, the immediate aim should have been registration of documents, and the final goal not freehold but occupancy title, which would thus create a just balance between the rights of the individual and the oversight which the community should exercise over the land.[2]

The same factors which complicated the land situation also made it difficult for the government to set aside sufficient forest reserves. The early history of this problem has already been discussed, so that it will be sufficient to indicate only the later developments.[3] By 1938 some 5,659 out of the 30,012 square miles of forest zone had been either constituted or approved as reserves. The Forestry Department declared that 6,500 square miles were the minimum essential to protect cocoa

---

[1] Alienation to Europeans is almost entirely for mining purposes. Such alienation does not give the concession holder any land ownership but merely the right to develop mines. A few attempts were made in the past at European agricultural plantations, but they were not sufficiently successful to warrant continuance.

[2] Hailey, op. cit. In 1944 the government appointed the Havers Commission to study the land-litigation problem. Its report recommended the establishment of a boundary commission, land registration, short-term loans to indebted farmers, and simpler court procedure for land cases. A second commission was appointed in 1946 to prepare plans for implementing the recommendations made concerning debts. *Report of the Commission of Enquiry in the Litigation in the Gold Coast and Indebtedness Caused Thereby* (Gold Coast, 1945).

[3] See p. 32 above. *G.C. An. Report, 1938*, p. 26; Hancock, *Economic Policy*, pp. 251-3.

areas and water supplies; but this was far from the ideal, and large gaps in the forest zone where the dry *harmattan* can blow through had been so heavily farmed that even this recommended minimum was impossible. If water, soil, and forest conservation were to be properly handled and the very promising timber industry fully developed, there was a need for more African co-operation and an increased forestry personnel.

Besides agricultural and forest products, the third great natural resource of the country lies in its mineral wealth. European traders exported gold from the very earliest days of their occupation, and in later years the survey department discovered large quantities of bauxite, manganese, and diamonds, as well as lesser deposits of lime, granite, coal, and even oil. In the late nineteenth century, European capital began developing mines, and by the end of the thirties some very remarkable progress had been made, as the following export figures for 1937 will reveal:[1]

Mineral			Quantity	Value
Gold	.	.	557,764 fine ounces	£3,910,757
Diamonds	.	.	1,577,661 carats	648,057
Manganese	.	.	527,036 tons	1,025,091
Total	.	. . . .	.	£5,583,905

The Gold Coast in 1937 ranked as the third largest producer in the world for diamonds and for manganese. Its bauxite deposits, estimated at some 229,000,000 tons, are among the largest known to exist, though the lack of hydro-electric power has not yet allowed for much exploitation.[2] The gold-mine of the Ashanti Goldfields Corporation at Obuasi is one of the richest in the world. It is not surprising, then, that the Africans often represented to the government that some of the profits of these rich mines should be kept in the country. As was seen in the discussion of the land problem, in 1894 the British administration failed in its effort to gain control of mining concessions. As a result, ignorant chiefs often granted rights to European companies for very low annual rents, and with no provision for royalties. In more recent years the chiefs began to realize their mistake, and asked that the Concessions Ordinance be changed so as to ensure a percentage of profits to the landowners.

[1] *G.C. An. Report, 1937*, p. 50. The bauxite deposits were not mined until the 1940's.
[2] A. William Postel, *Mineral Resources of Africa*, p. 35.

This the government refused to do, on the grounds that such a measure would jeopardize further development. When the Africans in the legislative council asked for compulsory royalties, Governor Hodson stated:

. . . I feel sure it would be a short-sighted and extremely harmful policy for the Government to interfere in a matter of this sort, because capital is very sensitive and it might have the effect of driving it away to other parts of the world. . . .[1]

In spite of exports amounting to as high as £5,583,905 in a single year, the mines remained until 1944 with no levy on their exports other than insignificant rents to the chiefs and a slight tax to the government. All income tax was paid within England itself. Since the wages which the mining companies paid to African labour only amounted during these years to an annual sum of between £900,000 and £1,000,000, and since the highest yearly limit of taxation was £400,000, it is evident that the bulk of mining profits went to Europe rather than remaining within the Gold Coast.[2] The following excerpt gives an example of African opinion on this subject:

It should be the duty of a trustee government to see that the exploitation of minerals, while giving reasonable profits to shareholders, must contribute substantially to the increase of the revenue of the country in which the minerals are exploited. The large dividends paid by mining companies in recent years, show that they could shoulder more taxation without normal enterprise being discouraged, particularly when it is remembered that conditions of taxation and mining prospects in rival countries like South Africa and Australia are not as favourable as those in the Gold Coast.[3]

The Africans were dissatisfied, not only with the amount of mining profits kept within the Gold Coast, but also with the whole economic set-up as well. The loss of revenue which had accompanied the depression trade slump made them realize the insecurity of dependence on an export economy. In the petition which in 1934 Nana Sir Ofori Atta and

[1] Legislative Council, *Debates* (1939), Issue No. 1, p. 74.
[2] The Gold Coast government charged mining companies a 5 per cent royalty on profits. In addition, since 1934 there was an export tax on gold of 15 per cent of the gold premium; and a 6¼ per cent *ad valorem* tax on diamonds. See *Gold Coast Handbook, 1937*, p. 343.
[3] M. Dowuona, 'Economic and Social Development of the Gold Coast', Achimota Discussion Group, *Quo Vadimus or Gold Coast Future*, p. 26.

other Gold Coast leaders presented to the Colonial Office, their criticism of economic as well as political matters was expressed. During the legislative debates of these years, too, they often came back on the necessity of a more balanced system based on local manufacturers and a wider domestic commerce.[1] They believed no successful plan of direct taxation could be introduced until the Dependency's wealth remained within the country itself, and was more evenly divided among the bulk of the population to be taxed. To this end they suggested both an increased dependence on domestic foods and the gradual development of secondary industries, for it was estimated that a million pounds' worth of goods imported every year, such as soap, edible oils, and certain building materials, could be produced locally. The Youth Conference in 1938, for example, passed the following resolution:

Be it resolved . . . by the Youth Conference assembled at Cape Coast that the system of trade and commerce obtaining in the country by which its natural wealth is exploited mostly for the benefit of the foreigner at the expense of the native is dangerous to the economic stability and permanence of the people of this country and this Conference recommends that the matter be brought to the notice and attention of the Natural Rulers with a view to their taking suitable action to equate the said unbalanced conditions by means of a national fund and other means appropriate for the purpose.[2]

The remarks of the members of the legislative council came more bluntly to the point, and they openly expressed the opinion that it was the fear of harming British industry that deterred the government from allowing manufacturing to develop.

Now, Your Excellency, as industries are the mainstay of any country, I desire to emphasize the necessity of fostering native industries such as soap, salt, tobacco, sugar, rice, pottery, cloth-weaving, fishing, and palm-oil with a view to establishing good internal trade in this country. Why should crafts that have held the people from time immemorial be made to give way for a foreign cargo? Home weaving with all its beauty, for example, make way for Manchester and Japanese goods? Now the Department of Agriculture has often been severely criticized because of the failure of that Department to help the country in creating new industries . . . are we to understand, Sir, that our Agricultural Department is incapable of helping us to produce locally the articles mentioned in the notice? Surely they are capable, unless, in order to

[1] Legislative Council, *Debates* (1935), p. 135; (1936), p. 115.
[2] Gold Coast Youth Conference, *First Steps towards a National Fund* (Accra, 1938), p. 10.

protect the European trade, it is not intended to help us to develop economic-ally. It may be contested that this is a misconception, but I say, Sir, that this is what really exists in the minds of the people of this country. . . .[1]

In spite of this agitation, nothing was done during the period under consideration, and it was not until the war years that the administration made any attempts to encourage local manufacture.

Looking back at the economic development of the Gold Coast during the period 1919–39, it is clear that the first part up to 1929 was marked by great prosperity and rapid expansion with the increased revenue from customs duties. Guggisberg began and almost completed his Ten Year Plan for new railways, for a harbour at Takoradi, and for additional schools and hospitals. His successors in the governorship had the less pleasant task of pulling the Dependency through the second half of the period, 1929–39, when revenue dropped sharply and all development had to be curtailed. During these years both the administration and the Africans had to face the fact that a one-crop export economy was unwise, and they endeavoured to develop the cattle industry in the Northern Territories and to introduce new food crops for both domestic and export use. The Africans believed, too, that local manufacturing and commerce were also necessary, but, in spite of their increasing demands, the government took no definite steps towards such a policy except in so far as the encouragement of co-operatives, wider education, and more diverse agriculture can be considered as a preparation for a broader economic system.

Though the administration can perhaps be justly criticized during this period for not having made sufficient efforts to develop the economic life of the Gold Coast, it is only fair to point out that there is another side to the question. British policy in West Africa usually held that native ownership of the land is to be preferred to the European planta-tion system. While the latter method may ensure a faster production, a system of peasant agriculture is assuredly better because it preserves home life, leads to the social development of the people in a natural environment, and favours an eventual prosperity which has a more solid foundation than one built on the artificial and often harmful plantation system. In the Gold Coast the African still owned his land and, though he had much to learn of more efficient farming and marketing methods, his economic future was far more secure than it would have been if rapid development had been bought at the price of widespread European

---

[1] Legislative Council, *Debates* (1939), p. 155.

exploitation. Of course, in the long run his prosperity depended on the world market and for this reason he had to keep up with scientific methods if he was to compete successfully with modern production. British policy held that the native could be so guided that new techniques would demand, not the destruction of community life, but merely its adaptation to changed needs. During this period the Gold Coast government began to help the Africans towards such an adaptation and, if it was needlessly slow, it at least had the merit of having preserved the fundamental right of native ownership of the land.

SOCIAL DEVELOPMENT

As the missionaries were responsible, not only for the religious activity but also for much of the educational and welfare work in the Gold Coast, it is perhaps wise to begin an account of social development with a brief survey of their history.

The earliest missionaries to the Gold Coast were Franciscan friars who came in the fifteenth century along with the Portuguese traders. Little of their work remained, however, after Portugal withdrew from the territory. During the following centuries, except for a few Anglicans in the 1700's, almost no missionaries made attempts to introduce Christianity on this slave-trading coast. It was not until the nineteenth century that permanent missions were finally established. In 1827 Swiss missionaries of the Basel Society came to the Gold Coast, to be followed in 1835 by the Wesleyans, who established a strong centre at Cape Coast. Eventually other groups followed, all paying a heavy price in the loss of lives or of health: in 1847 the German Bremen Society to the Trans-Volta area; in 1881 the Catholics to Elmina; in 1898 an American Negro group—the African Methodist-Episcopalian Zion Mission; in 1906 the Anglicans; and during World War I Presbyterians from Scotland to replace the deported German missionaries.[1] Gradually each of these groups spread out from its original centre and worked to Christianize and build up an African clergy in the Gold Coast. Most of them founded schools as well as churches, and until 1882 education was entirely in their hands. Some of these mission schools have become deservedly famous and have had a marked influence on the life of the Gold Coast. Mfantsipim, the oldest secondary school in the Dependency, as well as the girls' high schools at Cape Coast and Aburi are

[1] *Gold Coast Handbook, 1937*, pp. 25-26.

among this number. At this period there were comparatively few government schools, and most of the work was done by religious institutions, aided by grants from public funds if they reached the required standard. Some idea of their position in 1937 can be gained from the following statistics:[1]

Denomination	Estimated Number of Followers	Number of Churches or Chapels
English Church Mission . . .	24,000	270
Methodist Mission Society . . .	125,225	767
Presbyterian Church of the Gold Coast .	58,454	286
Baptist Church Mission . . .	6,000	54
Roman Catholics:		
Colony-Ashanti	106,453	696
Lower Volta	36,383	191
Northern Territories . . .	24,200	24
Ewe Presbyterian Church . . .	27,000	137
Salvation Army	6,386	160
African Methodist-Episcopalian Zion Church	7,064	87

The missionaries' work in the Gold Coast was not easy. In the beginning, the climate and disease which had caused the country to be

---

[1] *Gold Coast Handbook, 1937*, p. 28. The Methodist Church was strongly established at this time in the Central and Western Provinces and in Ashanti. In 1931 it had forty-four African ministers and 427 catechists. It operated a good training college at Kumasi, a secondary school at Cape Coast, and many primary institutions. See J. Cooksey and A. McLeish, *Religion and Civilization in West Africa* (London, 1931), pp. 138-9, and 'Gold Coast Methodism; The First Hundred Years, 1835-1935', *Africa*, vol. VIII (1935), pp. 239-40.

The Basel Mission was confined to the Eastern Province, where it early developed strong vocational training and provided the country with some of its best craftsmen. The Bremen Mission worked in the colony and in south Togoland. During the 1914-18 war, and again in 1939, the Scottish Presbyterians took over the work of these German missionaries. A native Ewe Presbyterian Church later developed. It had ninety-two schools in Togoland. In the colony proper and in Ashanti there were many excellent Scottish Presbyterian schools. *British Togo Mandate Report, 1938*, p. 47; *Gold Coast Handbook, 1937*, p. 112.

The Catholic Missions of the Central and Western Provinces, Ashanti, and Togoland were directed by the Society of African Missions with the help of two Orders of nuns who did both educational and child welfare work. The Accra Vicariate was established in the Eastern Province in 1939 by the American branch of the Society of the Divine Word. The White Fathers came to the Northern Territories in 1906. In 1939 there were 117 priests, 57 sisters, and 182 schools and 12 dispensaries for the entire Dependency. *Report of the Vicariates of the Gold Coast* (1939).

The Anglican Society for the Propagation of the Gospel first sent missionaries to the Gold Coast in 1752, but their work had eventually to be given up. The Anglicans returned in 1906 and opened secondary and primary schools in various parts of the Colony and Ashanti. The Bishop resided at Accra. Cooksey and McLeish, *Religion and Civilization in West Africa*, p. 143.

called the 'white man's grave' led to early deaths among these mission-aries, sometimes within a few months of their arrival. Then many of the chiefs and elders opposed the spread of Christianity on the grounds that it weakened their subjects' allegiance to native custom and authority. Perhaps the most difficult problem of all, however, was the absorption of so many Africans in material affairs. The rapid increase of wealth during the early part of the century accentuated this tendency. The reports of the various missionaries refer to the ease with which converts slipped back into pagan ways, and to the lack of 'carry-over' of Christian principles from the church to the home, to social life, and to the business world.[1] In spite of these great difficulties missions did much for the Gold Coast, not only in purely religious matters but in their general civilizing influence as well. Many of these groups were self-supporting. Some missions had only made a start at an African clergy; while others, especially the Methodist and Ewe Presbyterian, already had a majority of African ministers. This training in responsibility had its effect on political life, for many Gold Coast leaders received their first experience in leadership in the councils of the missions. The Methodists can well be proud of Dr. James Kwegyir Aggrey, the man who did so much for the establishment of Achimota and who, perhaps more than any other man in the Gold Coast, furthered inter-racial understanding and co-operation.

Other results of missionary activity were the rooting out of repulsive pagan customs, the encouragement of vernacular languages, and the establishment of friendly contacts with other countries through the parent churches, which helped to broaden the African's outlook and to ennoble relationships between the white man and the black. In more recent years, too, the missions increasingly understood the neces-sity of basing education as far as possible on African culture, and of integrating the life of school, mission, and community. As a result the best missions achieved a position of marked influence among the Africans.

While the mission schools alone bore the burden of educational work during the greater part of the nineteenth century, the government began to take some responsibility in the matter, when in 1882 an ordinance was passed which provided for a board of education, official inspection, and grants-in-aid for satisfactory institutions. In the following years the administration established a few schools, and in 1909 it opened a

[1] ibid., pp. 135–7; Horn, 'The Achievements of the Missions', Achimota Discussion Group, *Quo Vadimus or Gold Coast Future*, p. 40.

technical institute and a normal training college at Accra. When Sir Gordon Guggisberg took over the governorship of the Gold Coast in 1919, there were nineteen government schools, 194 assisted mission schools, and some 400 unassisted ones, often of inferior quality. The budget of that year set aside £54,442 for educational purposes.[1] Guggisberg, who was keenly interested in education, did not consider this enough; he believed it to be the 'keystone of progress', and as such he gave it the first place in his plans for the development of the Gold Coast. The set of sixteen principles which he worked out as the basis for a higher educational standard included, among other things, provision for more fully qualified teachers, agricultural and technical as well as literary subjects in the curriculum, organized games, equal opportunities for girls as well as boys, and, above all, religious and character training as the foundation of the whole system. With these aims in view, the government passed an ordinance in 1925 requiring higher qualifications of non-assisted schools and their staffs if they wished to remain in existence; while at the same time it announced its intention of establishing a new secondary and normal school which would provide the best that both African and European culture had to offer. This latter plan eventually developed, under Guggisberg's enthusiastic guidance, into the world-famous Prince of Wales College at Achimota.

The new education ordinance went into effect in 1927, with the result that some 150 'bush schools' were closed during the following years. This action led to much criticism on the part of some missionary bodies as well as the Africans, who could not understand why institutions should be closed when, in spite of the increasing demand for education, only one child in ten could be accommodated.[2] By 1930 it was evident that the 1925 plan had probably been too drastic. Because the existing normal institutions of the Dependency could not satisfy the demand for teachers, it was impossible to open more schools of the approved standard. The government therefore decided to allow a two-year as well as a four-year course for rural teachers, and to encourage the establishment of more training centres by grants-in-aid. Consequently the missions were able to expand so that by 1938 the Gold Coast had seven normal institutions.

As for Achimota College, Guggisberg originally planned to have it

[1] *Report on the Department of Education, 1919*, Appendix D. The Gold Coast annual reports as well as the reports on the Department of Education are the best references on this subject. See also *Gold Coast Education Committee Report, 1937–1941* (Accra, 1941).
[2] Legislative Council, *Debates* (1929), pp. 168, 172, 218.

include only secondary and college departments, but the Reverend Alexander Fraser, the Anglican minister who was its first principal, insisted on both kindergarten and primary departments so that pupils could be trained from their earliest years to the high standard he wished to develop in the school.

The aim and first beginnings of Achimota were charmingly explained to an English radio audience in the autumn of 1925 by Dr. Kwegyir Aggrey, the first assistant vice-principal of the college, who was more responsible than anyone else for interpreting the new institution to his fellow Africans and for obtaining their support.

The greatest recent step forward in the co-operation between white and black, for the good of Africa, has come through the vision of Sir Gordon Guggisberg, Governor of the Gold Coast. He rightly believed that the great need of the movement was an educational institution which could meet the highest and broadest needs of Africans, and one where the leaders of the race would receive not only the best 'head' education, but an education of the 'heart' and 'hand' also.

The Gold Coast Government has therefore devoted half a million pounds to the foundation of the Prince of Wales College, Achimota, which, I believe, is the most significant thing in the whole of Africa today. . . .

With some fifty teachers selected from the five Continents of Europe, Asia, Africa, America, and Australia and with accommodation for about eight hundred students, it will be the aim of Achimota to correct the mistakes which have been made in the educational system of Africa. It will take the African boy and girl at the age of six, and carry them through the kindergarten to the University courses. It will give to the African, not only professional training, but also technical courses that will teach both boys and girls the dignity of labour. . . .

With the coming of Western civilization . . . African boys and girls tended to cut loose from tribal ties. In many instances the educated became neither Western nor African, losing the best in both and often imbibing the worst of both. . . .

The importance of the Gold Coast Government's experiment at Achimota is that it will retain and improve the best things in Africa and couple them with the best things Western. The pupils in this Government College will be trained to be Christian citizens, each one a part of the body politic to whom much has been given, and from whom much will be expected. . . . 'Christianity' will not be taught but a truly Christian spirit will be fostered, and the necessity of co-operation between white and black instilled. In the harmony of the world, as in the harmony of an organ or a piano, the black and the white keys are both essential. . . .

Achimota is destined to influence not only the Gold Coast, but directly and indirectly the entire African continent. And Africa is grateful for this daring and far-reaching experiment towards the true emancipation of her manhood and womanhood.[1]

The new building was dedicated by the Prince of Wales in 1925 and a few classes were begun the next year, but the school was only completed in 1931 at the cost of £617,000. The institution was situated near the small town of Achimota, some seven miles inland from Accra. Its extensive campus was attractively laid out with a large administration block, numerous residential units, a hospital, museum, printing press, swimming-pool, demonstration farm, and model native village for employees. Neither trouble nor expense seem to have been spared in obtaining an up-to-date plant and modern equipment.

The staff usually included about forty Europeans and sixty Africans, though some of the latter were for clerical rather than teaching purposes. Achimota had a faculty ranking with the finest to be found in any comparable institution in England or America. Most of its masters had Cambridge or Oxford degrees and were chosen because of their interest in this type of work.

In 1930 the college ceased to be a government institution by the creation of the Achimota Council,[2] a body made up of European and African members who had entire control of the institution. It continued, however, to receive an annual government grant[3] of £48,000, and the staff pensions were also a charge on Dependency funds. The administration believed that the college would be less open to political attack and would more easily gain the full confidence of the Africans if it became, as far as possible, a private institution. The interests of the government were safeguarded by a quinquennial inspection and by the appointment of official members to the council.

The curriculum included, until changes were made in the 1940's, the usual primary and secondary subjects, a commercial course, a one-year agricultural course, four years of teacher training, and a college department in which the students took intermediate courses to prepare for the external examination of the University of London in arts, science, economics, and engineering, and for the first medical examination.

---

[1] M. Sampson, 'James Emman Kwegyir Aggrey', *Gold Coast Men of Affairs*, pp. 64–66. See also *Report on Achimota College, 1926–1927*, and Smith, *Aggrey of Africa*, pp. 225–45 and *passim*, for Aggrey's own account of the joys and trials connected with the beginnings of Achimota.

[2] Ordinance 10 of 1930; Legislative Council, *Debates* (1929–30), p. 49.

[3] The grant was increased during the war to £54,000 and in 1946 to £64,000.

(These intermediate courses were somewhat like those of the American junior college.) The only college degree given was the B.Sc. in the fields of civil and mechanical engineering.

Classes were taught in the more important vernaculars as well as in English. Every attempt was made to give the students a well-balanced training with courses in handicrafts, farmwork, and domestic science, as well as in the literary subjects. The native history and customs of the Gold Coast were held in high honour, and the students were expected to take part in practice-teaching classes, first aid, sanitation, and agricultural demonstrations in near-by villages. Within the institution itself, discipline was largely on the lines of the English public schools, and the administration encouraged the pupils to develop habits of self-reliance and co-operation. There were both Catholic and Protestant resident chaplains, and the principal was always a Protestant minister. A Christian atmosphere was said to pervade the school.[1]

The government made one of its official inspections in 1938, and reported that the aims of Achimota 'are being in a great measure fulfilled', adding: 'The educational scheme presents itself, on a general view, as an ordered sequence from the lowest almost to the highest levels, conducted with notable ability and devotion on the part of the tutors, and with a high degree of industry in the pupils.'[2]

In spite of much successful work, however, Achimota was not without its critics. In the beginning many Africans disapproved of the expense involved and of its co-educational policy. Later, especially during the depression years, there were not always enough suitable positions for the Achimota graduates, and in 1935 the Africans therefore asked that more stress be put on agricultural training. Some of the missionary groups, too, doubted the wisdom of primary and secondary departments. They believed that Achimota would be more closely integrated with the educational life of the Colony if its students had received their early education in the regular schools of the Dependency,

---

[1] In 1938 there were 679 pupils enrolled at Achimota, 232 of whom were girls. They were divided into the following departments.

Kindergarten	.	.	.	60	Training college { boys	.	86
Lower primary	.	.	.	90	Training college { girls	.	66'
Upper primary	.	.	.	143	University .	.	.	.	32
Secondary	.	.	.	180	Special courses	.	.	22

G.C. An. Report, 1938, p. 81. During the Second World War the kindergarten and lower primary divisions were dissolved, leaving but three separate units, the School, the College, and the Training College. Further changes will be noted in a later chapter.

The film *Achimota*, distributed by the British Information Services, gives an interesting picture of this institution.

[2] *G.C. An. Report, 1938*, p. 81.

only going to the college for higher studies. Many felt that Achimota was too isolated from the educational life of the Gold Coast, and that if some of the large sums spent there had been used to raise the general level of all secondary institutions it would have resulted in benefits to a wider group of students.[1]

In later years local opinion grew more favourable to Achimota, and its increasing popularity was proved by the hundreds of students who applied for the few vacancies annually available. A splendid opportunity lay before this great institution—one of the finest in all Africa—for it was on its graduates that the future of the Gold Coast in large part depended. As Governor Slater once remarked of Sir Gordon Guggisberg: 'My predecessor's decision to create Achimota was an act of magnificent faith in the ultimate capacity of the African to govern himself.'[2]

In turning from Achimota to the educational situation in general, we find that during the years following Guggisberg's governorship, development was slowed up by lack of revenue resulting from the economic crisis. In 1938 there were only 24 government schools, 424 assisted, and about 457 unassisted institutions in the Gold Coast—some 905 in all. Of these the primary schools were providing education for 90,000 children. Though this was a good record for African colonies in general, it represented only about 15 per cent of the school population of the Dependency. At the rate of progress then prevailing, universal primary education would not be possible until the end of the century.[3] The money set aside for all educational purposes, including Achimota, in the 1938 budget was £270,000, which was 9·34 per cent of the total expenditure and about £3 to £4 for each child.[4] This is the highest expenditure of any African colony except Zanzibar, but it is unfortunate that these benefits were unevenly distributed. In some of the more prosperous areas of the Gold Coast nearly 30 per cent of the children were receiving an education, while in the Northern Territories, for example, only 1,000 attended school out of an estimated child population of nearly 200,000.[5]

In order to provide for a more rapid development of educational facilities, the government gave encouragement to schools supported by

---

[1] K. Horn, 'The Future of Education in the Gold Coast', Achimota Discussion Group, *Quo Vadimus or Gold Coast Future*, p. 44; Cooksey and McLeish, *Religion and Civilization in West Africa*, p. 130.
[2] Legislative Council, *Debates* (1929), 'Governor's Address', p. 51.
[3] *G.C. An. Report, 1938*, pp. 72 ff.
[4] *Report on the Finances and Accounts of the Gold Coast for the Year 1938–1939*, p. 11.
[5] Hinden, *Plan for Africa*, p. 184.

the local administrations. This appeared to be a wise policy, for if indirect rule were really to work and if schools were to give an education which would fit the child for a future in his own community, they must be as closely integrated with tribal life as possible.[1] Almost all the problems which then faced the Gold Coast, whether of a political, economic, or social nature, could be solved, in large part at least, by a wise system of education which would combine what is most suitable in Christian civilization with the best of the rich heritage of African life and culture. Such was the policy of the British administration and of the mission schools, which held that if growth has gone on more slowly than would be desirable, it at least had the tremendous advantage of being based on a solid and enduring foundation.

Turning from educational problems to those of health and sanitation, we find a much less hopeful situation. As vital statistics are only kept in the larger towns and even these are not always reliable, it is impossible to obtain any entirely accurate picture of the physical conditions of the population. The reports of the 1931 census, however, and of the medical department, do give some light on the situation. The infant mortality rate in 1931 was estimated to be 170 per thousand for the entire Dependency.[2] Although it was usually lower in the towns, it had been reported to go as high as 400 per thousand in the Kusasi area of north Togoland. The 1931 census also estimated that 40 per cent of the children of the Dependency died before reaching puberty. These figures, along with reports of almost universal malaria, widespread social disease, increasing incidence of tuberculosis and leprosy, as well as very serious malnutrition and poor housing conditions, combine to give evidence of a population rather generally handicapped by undernourishment and disease.[3] Such conditions were, of course, characteristic of many African colonies, but nevertheless in some areas, especially the Belgian Congo, great improvements were being made on these lines.[4]

The Gold Coast Medical Department, with its medical, public health, laboratory, and sleeping-sickness sections, was putting up a good fight, but it was handicapped by the usual barriers of insufficient staff and revenue, and also by the ignorance and superstition of the population. Most of the diseases which it had to combat were the result of bad

[1] For an excellent discussion of this problem, see E. Hussey, 'The Role of Education in Assisting the People of Africa to adjust themselves to the Changing Conditions due to European Contacts', *Europe and West Africa*, pp. 119 ff.
[2] Cardinall, *The Gold Coast, 1931,* p. 219.
[3] Summaries of the health situation are given in the annual reports, in Hailey, *African Survey*, and in *Nutrition in the Colonial Empire*, Cmd. 6051 (1939), pp. 35–38.
[4] Hailey, *African Survey*, pp. 1178–80.

sanitation and impure water, along with the weakened condition of the people resulting from malnutrition. The parliamentary report of the survey of nutrition made in 1938 in the entire colonial empire stated that 'food deficiency is a predisposing factor'[1] of much disease in the Gold Coast. Health education was therefore of prime necessity, and increased efforts were being made by the government and the Red Cross through the schools and radio.

For actual medical care, the Gold Coast in 1939 had thirty-eight African hospitals, including Korle Bu in Accra which was built at the cost of £254,000, and which was then the best in West Africa. The Basel Mission conducted a well-equipped hospital in Ashanti, and the Roman Catholic missions had a number of medical and infant welfare stations. There were also village dispensaries in the charge of African nurses trained and employed by the government. Some of the native authorities had established their own dispensaries, as a result of the growing appreciation for proper medical care.

Labour conditions presented another area in which further improvements could be made. A labour department was established in 1938 under the guidance of a trained expert from England, and it began by making an intensive study of the problems involved. By 1939 a labour exchange had been opened, and it was preparing legislation in such matters as juvenile employment, trade unionism, workmen's compensations, conciliation methods, and collective bargaining.[2]

Looking back over the Dependency's economic and social development it is evident that the Gold Coast made great progress during the period just considered. The establishment of the *Pax Britannica* and of a settled administration made a full development of natural resources possible, and brought with it an increase of revenue and trade which was ten times greater than it had been in 1900. At the same time, this survey has also revealed that expansion did not take place in the same ratio throughout the territory, and if the larger towns and coastal areas greatly benefited, the less prosperous sections did not receive their just share of the improvements. Development, moreover, was not always guided in the wisest channels as the chaotic conditions in the cocoa industry and the unbalanced character of the general economic situation

---

[1] *Nutrition in the Colonial Empire*, p. 36.
[2] *G.C. An. Report. 1938–1939*, p. 66. See also the excellent summary of labour conditions in the Gold Coast given by Major G. St. J. Orde Browne, *Labour Conditions in West Africa*, Cmd. 6277 (1941), pp. 87–113. There is also a very good survey of labour and other social problems for colonies in general in International Labour Office, *Social Policy in Dependent Territories* (Montreal, 1944).

clearly show. Besides the economic needs there were grave problems in the fields of education, public health, and social services yet to be solved. But in spite of these defects, the positive contribution of the British administration was great, as a comparison of the Gold Coast with such independent but less advanced states as Liberia and Ethiopia makes evident.[1] A strong colonial power could protect the economic interests of a comparatively backward area, in the complicated and highly competitive situation which characterized world trade in this period; it could provide capital for public utilities, and could give stability and continuity to clearly defined plans for a well-ordered development. This the British administration did and, although the support sometimes was insufficient or unwisely directed, the result of the whole appears heavily balanced in the favour of the Africans of the Gold Coast.

[1] The following are comparative statistics for the Gold Coast and Liberia in 1936 ($£ = 4.00):

	Gold Coast	Liberia
Population	3,618,376	c. 1–1,500,000
Area (sq. m.)	91,000	43,000
Revenue	$15,098,984	$770,414
Expenditure	$15,667,968	$708,443
Schools	c. 905	161
Pupil attendance	90,000	10,000

Statistics for the Gold Coast were taken from the annual reports and for Liberia from the *Statesman's Year Book, 1940*.

CHAPTER IX

THE GOLD COAST IN
THE SECOND WORLD WAR

When the Second World War broke out in the autumn of 1939, West Africa did not appear to be vitally affected. Until Dunkirk, the four British colonies were largely spectators, but from then on they were drawn ever more fully into the arena of battle. Britain had begun the war counting on the control of the Mediterranean. When Italy joined the Nazi camp, this life-line to the Far East was blocked and the ports and airfields of West Africa suddenly became of vital strategic importance. Then the fall of France not only prevented the use of North African air bases but also flanked the four British colonies with potential enemy territory. Finally, the Japanese seizure of the great Asiatic supply sources forced Britain and the United States to set a new value on the mineral and agricultural wealth of West Africa.

Almost overnight this great western bulge of the African continent was recognized as of strategic and economic importance to the Allies. As a result of the stimulus which was thus given to the whole life of the area, the war became for West Africa one of the most outstanding instruments of material progress which it had yet known. Under its impact, harbours and internal communications were developed, dozens of first-class airfields were built, a greater West African Frontier Force was recruited and trained for foreign service, and vital raw materials for export were increasingly produced, while at the same time local self-sufficiency was advanced to a degree which gave great hope for the economic future of the area. In all this West African activity, the Gold Coast was to play a major part and to share fully in the development thus achieved.

The outbreak of the war did not find the Gold Coast totally unprepared. Already in 1936 the uncertainty of international affairs had led Governor Hodson to create a volunteer naval force to assist in the defence of home waters, and early in 1939 to reorganize the Gold Coast Regiment and to provide for a motor corps unit. He had also developed a radio broadcasting system which was to prove invaluable as a means of spreading information and of gaining the Africans' fullest co-operation in the years of struggle which lay ahead.

With the declaration of war, the Africans immediately came forward with avowals of loyalty and promises of support so that, in his Christmas message of 1939, the governor could congratulate them on their cheerful and willing collaboration in the sacrifices which had been asked of them.[1] While this attachment to the Allied cause was probably motivated in part by fear of Nazi domination, there is no reason to doubt the African's sincere loyalty to the British connexion. In the dark days after Dunkirk the Gold Coast could easily have revolted, and yet there was no evidence, even among the most radical, of any desire to throw off the British rule.[2] On the contrary, testimonies of devotion to the empire abounded. One chief encouraged his people to greater production of needed war materials with the words:[3]

Our fathers . . . told us to be loyal to the British flag, for it was the British people who . . . put a stop to the African scourge—the slave trade. We ourselves have learned to respect the British people for their justice, fair play and wise administration, as compared to other European powers.

And Captain Balfour, the British Cabinet minister resident in West Africa during the latter part of the war, found:[4]

In the 80,000 square miles of Gold Coast territory, there is a smaller police force to keep law and order than is thought necessary to guard and patrol one single white man's camp and aerodrome. Is this a sign of a people longing to throw off the yoke of their rulers or proof of a peaceful people working in harmony with those holding authority in their land?

Though the Africans' loyalty was sincere, it did not always prevent complaints when the cost of the war effort began to be felt in the Colony itself. The illiterate peasants, for example, often found it hard to understand the complex system of controls required by modern warfare.

After the bombardment of England began, the Africans were deeply impressed by the sufferings and heroism of the British people. They responded generously to war drives, subscribing £340,715 in voluntary gifts, £205,000 in war-saving certificates, and £815,000 in interest-free

---

[1] Legislative Council, *Debates* (1939), vol. II, p. 3.
[2] M. Fortes, 'Impact of the War on British West Africa', *International Affairs*, vol. XXI (1945), p. 210; Legislative Council, *Debates* (1944), vol. I, pp. 111–13.
[3] *African World* (1 February 1941), p. 95.
[4] ibid. (6 June 1945).

loans.[1] Among the various patriotic drives, none appealed to the Gold Coast Africans more than the 'Spitfire' fund. Their contributions having financed two R.A.F. units known as the Gold Coast Bomber and Fighter Squadrons, their proud sponsors followed the exploits of these units with interest and a lively sense of satisfaction.

The Dependency's aid to the war effort, however, was not confined to financial contributions. Gold Coast Africans volunteered both for home defence and for service abroad. After the fall of France in the summer of 1940, the four British colonies were surrounded by Vichy territory. Eventually all French West Africa came under Free French control, but in the meantime local forces had to be increased. Before the war a Gold Coast naval volunteer force had been organized which was to prove invaluable in keeping coastal waters free from mines. Later, home guard and civil defence units were formed, since the Royal West African Frontier Force—the R.W.A.F.F.—would be needed for foreign service. This frontier force was an outgrowth of the early military units organized in the nineteenth century by European trading companies, and later by the British government, for the maintenance of law and order on the Guinea Coast. In 1901 the West African Frontier Force —the title 'Royal' was added in 1928—came into being as a combination of the local regiments of the four British colonies, and continued to be officered by men seconded from the British Army. Its work was twofold: to maintain internal security against the various warring tribes and to defend the colonial frontiers. As such it was a civilizing force in the life of West Africa.

During World War I the Gold Coast sent its regiment for active service in Togoland, the Cameroons, and later in East Africa. These troops fought so splendidly in the latter area that General Smuts, under whose command they were, sent the following cable: 'If you have any more troops like the Gold Coast Regiment, send them at once.'[2] In 1940 the R.W.A.F.F. was again called upon for foreign service. Along with troops from both South and East Africa, it fought in Kenya, Italian Somaliland, and Abyssinia. The Gold Coast Brigade distinguished itself for courage in these campaigns.

Once this section of East Africa was in Allied hands, the military authorities recalled the R.W.A.F.F. to West Africa for enlargement and complete reorganization. In order to provide for a larger Gold Coast unit in the force, a compulsory service ordinance was laid before the

---

[1] British Information Services, *West Africa and the War* (1945).
[2] Quoted in *Gold Coast Bulletin* (25 September 1946).

legislative council in 1941.[1] This law was not intended to establish conscription throughout the Dependency, but was only to be applied to those areas where recruiting brought insufficient numbers. The Bill caused some criticism, especially in the coastal areas where the inhabitants argued that their political status as a non-self-governing colony did not warrant such action. The African members of the legislative council finally accepted the ordinance, asking, however, that compulsion be used slowly and that a representative of the local native administration be appointed to the recruiting committee of each state. The provincial council of the Central Province took the opportunity, in giving its assent, to ask for increased self-government by passing the resolution that:[2] 'the true status of this country will be recognized and proper place given the Chiefs and their people in the administration of the country'.

During 1941–3 the R.W.A.F.F. was entirely reorganized so as to include a completely self-contained expeditionary force. Apart from the divisional troops, seventy-six different types of units, including artillery, technical, and medical sections, were prepared for action in India and Burma. While the pre-war strength of the entire West African force had been only about 6,000 to 7,000, it was now increased to 176,000. There were 1,600 commissioned and non-commissioned officers, principally from the British Army, though Africans were eligible to both types of promotion. By 1945 several Gold Coast soldiers had been thus advanced, among whom was Major Seth Anthony, who had been trained at Sandhurst Military College and who was the first West African to receive the King's Commission.

In June 1943 the 81st Division of the R.W.A.F.F. left for Burma, to be followed shortly by the 82nd Division. Both these units contained Gold Coast troops. It was the largest colonial army in the history of the British Empire ever to serve as an expeditionary force. Most of these troops fought in the Arakan province of south-western Burma, a mountainous jungle area in the control of the Japanese, and one of the most difficult fighting terrains in the world. Because of its inaccessibility, the men had to be supplied for many months entirely from the air. Yet these young Africans, accustomed as they were to tropical conditions, remained among the fittest of the jungle troops. In one campaign the West Africans, leaving all motor transport behind, carried their equipment on their heads just as the head loads of cocoa were carried at home.

[1] Legislative Council, *Debates* (1941), vol. II, p. 6.
[2] ibid., p. 8.

This enabled them to be extremely mobile, so that, often catching the Japanese off their guard, they were constantly able to cut their communication lines. The R.W.A.F.F. came out of the war, not only with a record of courage and initiative in battle, but also with a reputation for persistent cheerfulness in the most trying circumstances.[1]

In addition to the R.W.A.F.F., Gold Coast men also joined the R.A.F. when, in 1941, that section of the services decided to accept African recruits. The regular British Army and the Royal Navy, however, remained closed to them. In all, the Gold Coast gave over 65,000 men to the various services during the war.

The withdrawal of nearly 70,000 young men from a colony whose total population was under 4,000,000 did, of course, affect the economic and social life of the Dependency. Something of a labour shortage was felt at a time when increased agricultural production was vitally necessary, and the illiterate peasants found it hard to understand why their sons were needed for service abroad. The necessity of gaining full African co-operation, not only for recruiting but for every phase of the war effort, made some means of widespread propaganda essential. Consequently, in 1939 a department of information was established. Broadcasting facilities were already available for its use since Governor Hodson, in 1935, had installed the station ZOY at Accra. Later smaller stations were gradually established throughout the Dependency, and both British programmes and local ones, in the various African languages, were broadcast. In addition to the radio the Information Department made wide use of mobile motion-picture units which could go to rural areas for the showing of war and educational films. The department also published an illustrated weekly newspaper, *The Empire at War*, which was later continued under the title *Gold Coast Bulletin*. Little by little, local information centres began to appear in out-of-the-way corners of the country, where an educated member of the community would gather together war pictures and posters and read *The Empire at War* to his illiterate neighbours. Another means employed for the dissemination of correct information was the weekly news conference which the governor inaugurated for the editors of Accra. In 1943 the representatives of various local newspapers were given an opportunity to study the empire's war effort at closer range, when the British Council, a British government agency, invited eight

[1] For accounts of the R.W.A.F.F., see E. E. Saben-Clare, 'African Forces in the Far East', *African Affairs*, vol. XLIV (1945), pp. 151–6; *Gold Coast Bulletin* (5 December 1945, and 25 September 1946).

West African editors, including two from the Gold Coast, for a fort-night's visit in England. Colonel Oliver Stanley, the secretary of state for the colonies, and other colonial officials received the delegation. Its members visited parliament and the Royal Air Force, and saw much of London's war-time life. They met representatives of the British and overseas Press and were given facilities to broadcast home to West Africa.

The British Council—which has as one of its purposes the fostering of cultural contacts in the United Kingdom, the Commonwealth, and foreign countries—having made in 1941 a survey of West Africa's needs, set up a central agency in the Gold Coast and local centres in the other British colonies. It opened a library and reading room in Accra, spon-sored lectures, art courses, and other adult educational schemes for both Europeans and Africans, and inaugurated a librarians' course, the first ever given in West Africa. While the council's work was essentially of a peace-time nature, these cultural contacts between the two races were of great value in building up that sense of empire solidarity so essential to co-operative war action.[1]

With the fall of France, the strategic importance of West Africa increased, and her ports and airfields became essential in the race to get planes and supplies to the British forces in North Africa and in the Middle East. Moreover, the Nazis were using French ports as submarine bases and were planning to link Dakar with North Africa by completing the Sahara Railway. Then on 8 December 1941 the United States entered the war, and before the month was out, Churchill and Roosevelt had decided on the North African invasion. West Africa was now more fully involved than ever in the great Allied war effort.

One of its most urgent tasks was to increase transportation facilities, especially for the air service. The Allies had decided to open an African air transport for the ferrying of military planes and supplies to North Africa and the Middle East. Pan-American World Airways System was asked to develop this service, an assignment which President Roosevelt described as of an 'importance which cannot be overestimated'.[2] Impor-tant links in this African life-line were established in Liberia, Nigeria, and on the Gold Coast. At the great port and airfield of Takoradi, the R.A.F. assembled the American and British pursuit planes which were landed there by freighter. Since it was found necessary to close all the

---

[1] *British Council Report, 1943–44; 1944–45.*
[2] *Brief History of the Pan-American Airways' Service to Africa*, Exhibit No. PA-10, p. 6. See also *West Africa* (7 September 1946), p. 820.

Gold Coast surf ports, Takoradi harbour had not only to handle the regular exports and imports, but, in addition, the heavy cargoes occasioned by the R.A.F. and American bases and by the Gold Coast troop movements. It was therefore essential to increase the harbour and airfield facilities.

Large military installations were also added to the existing airfield at Accra, and when in 1941 the United States Army Air Force was established there, the air base was enlarged and became an important link in the chain of air communications between the United States and the Near East. During the peak years of 1942 and early 1943, as many as 200 to 300 American planes stopped daily at Accra for checking and refuelling, on their way north or east. A large number of installations for the Army and Pan-American personnel, for aircraft maintenance, administration, and communications, had to be provided. United States technicians, Gold Coast government contractors, and African artisans all worked together to build up at Accra a large and up-to-date base. These constructions were later sold to the British government.

All this activity, as well as the immediate preparation for the North African invasion, brought the local governments of the four British colonies in contact with American, British, and Free French military and civil officials. London, in the face of the need for some co-ordinating agency for the British interests on the coast, appointed a Cabinet minister to be resident in West Africa. The selection was Lord Swinton, the former Sir Philip Cunliffe-Lister, whose previous ministerial experience as secretary of state for the colonies, secretary of state for air, and president of the board of trade, made him admirably fitted for the post. His great task was to ensure the co-operation of the British military and civil services in West Africa. In a radio address made on his arrival in July 1942 he stated: 'I have come here with one single aim: to help everyone engaged in the war effort. We have a great effort to make, but we have great resources.'[1] To carry out this aim he immediately set up the West African War Council, which included the governors of the four British colonies and the commanders in West Africa of the Army, Navy, and Air Force. Since the outbreak of the war the governors had been meeting from time to time to discuss inter-colonial problems resulting from the conflict. The new council, however, had wider scope and power in that it represented both civil and military administration, and that its head, a Cabinet minister, could decide many problems on the spot without recourse to London.

[1] British Information Services, *West Africa and the War* (1945), p. 11.

Since the Gold Coast was the most centrally located of the four colonies, Lord Swinton made his headquarters at Achimota College.[1] From there he co-ordinated every phase of war activity, both strategic and economic, working not only with British authorities, but with the American, Free French, and Belgian as well. By air he made constant trips throughout West and North Africa and the Belgian Congo, travelling over 50,000 miles during one year. He became, as one African editor put it, 'the minister who sees for himself'.[2] The success of this co-operation between both British and non-British territories demonstrated clearly that some sort of voluntary regional association would be valuable for peace-time development of West Africa in the post-war period.

Lord Swinton remained in West Africa as resident minister for about two years until the autumn of 1944, when he was replaced by Captain Harold Balfour. While his activities during the early part of this period were principally concerned with strategic matters, he also worked at stimulating increased agricultural and mineral production. After the expulsion of the Germans and Italians from North Africa in 1943, he was freed of many military burdens and therefore was able to devote himself more completely to economic matters. Japanese successes in the Far East had cut off, as has been seen, the contact of the Allies with the natural resources of Burma, Malaya, and the Dutch East Indies, and had set a higher value on those of West Africa. War needs demanded maximum production of such vital materials as minerals, rubber, and vegetable oils. The whole area, moreover, had to achieve greater self-sufficiency in foodstuffs, since military establishments often concentrated population within urban areas, and since shipping space for imported goods was scarce.

While Swinton was in a position to integrate the economic life of West Africa, it should not be supposed that before his arrival nothing had been done by the local governors to put their colonies on a war basis. In the Gold Coast, Governor Hodson, guided by the Dependency's experience of decreased revenue in World War I, cut all unnecessary items from the budget and raised import and export taxes. During this earlier war, lack of shipping space had greatly curtailed cocoa exports. Not only had the Dependency's revenue suffered as a result, but the cocoa farms had been seriously neglected, and, the farmers' incomes being lessened, the whole economic and social life of

---

[1] Many of the college buildings were used by the government during the war while the students lodged in temporary quarters.
[2] British Information Services, *West Africa and the War*.

the Gold Coast had been affected. This time the British government, in an effort to preserve normal conditions, decided to buy the entire cocoa produce of the Gold Coast and Nigeria for the duration of the war period. In the autumn of 1939, with this end in view, a cocoa control board under the Ministry of Food was set up in London. It agreed to buy all cocoa offered, at a minimum price which would be declared at the beginning of each new season. As it would have been impossible, on such short notice, to provide government buying agents, the board decided to licence the commercial firms in each colony to buy cocoa in its name. Quotas were accordingly allocated to each company or trader on the basis of pre-war performance. The agents were to buy the cocoa at the various trading centres, to grade, bag, and ship it to the ports; they were allowed expenses and a profit margin in accord with an agreed schedule. The control board sold the cocoa to overseas buyers, usually to government agencies, such as the British Ministry of Food and the United States Commercial Corporation.[1]

While the African farmers were grateful for a guaranteed market, they objected to the quota system and to the membership of the control board. According to the quota system, there were two types of buyers —B buyers, usually Africans who had dealt with only small quantities of cocoa in the pre-war period, and A buyers, the big European firms who could now act directly as agents of the board. The A and B system was devised to permit the control to work with as small a personnel as possible, but since it gave the African or B shippers a right to buy only 11·8 per cent of the crop while the A shippers were entitled to 88·2 or 250,000 tons, it caused much local criticism. New dealers, moreover, were excluded from the industry. There were complaints also regarding the personnel of the board, chiefly because John Cadbury was its chairman, and his firm had been included in the so-called 'cocoa pool' of 1937. The Africans believed that the new government board was merely a tool of their old enemies, the traditional firms, who two years before had tried to enforce the buying agreement that had been responsible for the economic boycott of that year.[2] One African member of the legislative council expressed the general attitude when he said:[3]

. . . the farmers are firmly of the opinion that the pool which existed a few years ago came to this Colony in a frock coat suit and it is the same pool which has [now] come through the back door dressed in a double-breasted suit.

[1] *Report on Cocoa Control in West Africa, 1939–1943 and Statement on Future Policy*, Cmd. 6554.
[2] See Chapter V.   [3] Legislative Council, *Debates* (1939), vol. III, p. 70.

As dissatisfaction with the cocoa policy continued, the African members presented a resolution against the existing arrangements at the 1940 spring session of the legislative council. Their criticisms may have somewhat influenced London for, though the quota system was not changed, the British government transferred the control board from the Ministry of Food to the Colonial Office and gave it a chairman who had no connexion with the cocoa industry; it became known as the West African Cocoa Control Board, with a permanent secretary residing in one of the colonies so that he might be more closely in touch with local conditions.

The big exporting firms who held the majority of the cocoa-buying licences were also, it will be remembered, the major importers to the Gold Coast. Most of these companies belonged to the Association of West African Merchants, the AWAM, as it was popularly called. Since shipping space was limited during the war, the Gold Coast government put imports as well as the cocoa exports on a quota basis according to the principle of past performance. Such a policy, of course, gave the majority of licences to the AWAM group and this, too, became a source of irritation to the African traders. As supplies of imported goods became increasingly scarce, the local merchant found his share dwindling to almost nothing, and with it any hope of widening his business activities during the war period. It is probable, however, that if the government had not used the existing European companies with their strong commercial organization the efficient handling of both exports and imports would have broken down. This is especially true of cocoa, which requires large storage facilities while awaiting shipment. The whole problem of cocoa marketing was a vital one to Gold Coast economy, and the experience of war-time controls was to have a marked influence on post-war policy, as will be seen in a later chapter.

It has already been pointed out that Governor Hodson, fearing a long war with heavy expenses and a probable reduction of revenue, had initiated a financial policy of thrift. While he planned to give priority to war expenses and to maintain public services as near a pre-war level as possible, he believed that development projects should be delayed until the coming of peace. In the autumn of 1941, his extended term of office having been completed, he was replaced in the administration of the Gold Coast by Sir Alan Burns. The new governor shifted from Hodson's cautious financial policy to a somewhat bolder one. The acceleration of West Africa's economic life following the Japanese conquests helped to make this possible. A more fundamental reason may be found in the changed attitude which Great Britain was adopting at this time towards her colonial possessions. As this subject will be fully considered in Chapter X, it is sufficient to state here that in 1940 parliament passed a law providing that free grants up to £5,000,000 a year should be made to the dependent empire, in order to stimulate economic and social development. Each colony was to draw up its own plan for progress, and supplement its share of the imperial grant by funds from local revenue. After his first tour of the Dependency, Governor Burns decided not to wait until after the war to initiate the Gold Coast scheme, but to begin the most urgent requirements immediately. With this end in view, he determined to introduce an income tax.[1] Every previous attempt at direct taxation had aroused violent opposition from all sections of the Colony.[2] This time, however, the announcement was received with less opposition and approved by the more thoughtful sections of public opinion. The poor man was not affected, as the lower income ranges would be exempt. The rates for those actually taxed were very moderate, being the lowest, with one exception, in the entire British Empire. Of the expected tax yield of £800,000, moreover, 70 per cent would come from non-African sources, since commercial companies which had previously been taxed only in the United Kingdom would now have to pay to the Gold Coast treasury five shillings out of every pound of profit.[3]

But the finances for Gold Coast development schemes were to come not only from the new income tax and from British grants, but from the general colony revenue as well. The West African drive for maximum production urged on by Lord Swinton helped to increase this revenue by stimulating Gold Coast output. Later, speaking of this drive, the West African resident minister said:[4]

When the Japanese overran the Far East, products which we and our Allies had been accustomed to draw from there had to be replaced . . . for example, the fat ration at home—so important for health—depended now on West Africa as never before. More groundnuts, more palm oil, and more palm kernels had to be produced—far more than in the best boom years of peace.

And again note that this production had to come, not from great estates but from the little holdings of millions of Africans. . . . Then there was the demand for rubber, again not from great plantations, but largely from trees scattered over thousands of miles of forest. Timber was needed as never

[1] Legislative Council, *Debates* (1943), vol. I, p. 7.
[2] See Chapter V.
[3] Legislative Council, *Debates* (1943), vol. II, pp. 29 ff.
[4] Quoted in *West Africa and the War*, p. 7.

before, both in the Colonies and for export. Cocoa . . . was still needed. . . .
The development of mineral resources attained a new importance and
urgency—tin from Nigeria, manganese and bauxite from the Gold Coast. . . .

In response to Lord Swinton's appeal for these raw materials the
Gold Coast made greater efforts for production. The output of the large
manganese mine at Nsuta was increased. Farther north, valuable bauxite
deposits lay untouched for lack of cheap transportation to the coastal
ports. The government now built the Dunkwa-Awaso spur to the main
line of the Gold Coast railway and started mining operations. The
timber industry, a comparatively small one in pre-war days, was rapidly
built up. Other essentials mentioned by Lord Swinton were rubber and
vegetable oils. In the summer of 1942 the West African Cocoa Board
became the West African Produce Board, widening the scope of its
activities to include these needed materials as well. It took upon itself
the task of stimulating production and co-ordinating buying and
shipping processes in the British, Free French, and Belgian colonies.
Since forced quotas are against the tenets of British colonial policy, the
board used the bait of higher prices as its principal method of encouraging the African farmers to increased output. In the Gold Coast this
policy resulted in a quickening of the palm-oil, copra, and rubber
industries. One chief, for example, aroused enthusiasm in his state by
offering a silver cup and a new robe to the headman of whichever
division should produce the greatest quantity of palm-kernels. School-
children, as well as their elders, joined in Swinton's treasure-hunt for
rubber which had to be tapped, not in great plantations but from
isolated trees scattered over large forest areas. New products, such as
kapok for lifebuoys, practically untouched in the Gold Coast before,
were also gathered together in answer to war needs.

Closely allied to the great effort for the export of raw materials was
the endeavour to build up economic self-sufficiency. In order to save
shipping space, both the Africans and the Europeans had to depend on
local production for food supplies, and, to a large extent, for clothing,
household goods, and building materials as well. With regard to food,
the situation was aggravated by the presence in the urban areas of large
numbers of Allied army, navy, and air force personnel. In the Gold
Coast the Department of Agriculture encouraged an increase in vegetable farming, cattle raising, and poultry keeping. New types of
vegetables, notably the potato and the soya bean, were successfully
introduced. Pig breeding and a government bacon factory, established

for the needs of the armed forces, meant the start of a new industry which had a good future before it. Prior to the war it had been the agricultural department's aim to interest the cocoa producer in mixed farming, as a counter-balance to the Dependency's dangerous one-crop economy, so these new departures were all to the good. The situation also called for the development of several local industries, particularly those connected with building materials. Besides the lumber industry, several small brick and tile factories were also started. On the whole, great possibilities of post-war expansion were foreshadowed by these developments, both in local industry and in a balanced agricultural production. Speaking of the latter, Lord Swinton said:[1]

... we've done a great deal to improve the lot of the farmer. He will always be the backbone of the country. We've given him firm prices. We've organized seed distribution. We've established collecting stations at the most convenient points. We have encouraged improved quality and better processes. We have developed alternative crops—like rice and vegetables. We are encouraging co-operation wherever we go. And in all, the Africans themselves in the Native Administration are playing a great part, and they're getting increased experience and responsibility all the time.

While the war effort greatly stimulated the economic life of the Gold Coast, it also led to inflationary tendencies. The concentration of European and African population in the urban areas, along with a shortage of imported goods, meant sharp price rises. With the appearance of a black market, the government supply department tried to keep prices within limits, but not always successfully. Government controls could not work as efficiently in the Gold Coast as in Britain, owing to primitive conditions in outlying areas, and to the lack of widespread commercial and retail institutions through which rationing could properly function. The cost of living rose 50 to 75 per cent in some of the coastal areas and, to a lesser extent, throughout the Dependency. To meet this new situation the government set up not only price controls but also a cost-of-living commission to determine, from time to time, the amount of salary bonuses necessary for government employees. In general, wage rates increased, but certain sections of the population continued to suffer considerably from the high prices and from scarcity of goods.

If the war affected the economic life of the Gold Coast, it also made its influence felt in the political field as well. The Africans believed that

[1] *West Africa and the War*, p. 8.

their loyal support of the British Empire cause should bring them further political powers, and the demand for increased self-government, which had been growing during the 1930's, was now intensified. In certain fields the government met these demands during the war period itself, but the major changes did not come until after the peace. As a full treatment of this matter will be given in Chapter X, it is sufficient to state here that in 1942 the political offices of the central government of the Dependency were finally opened to the Africans by the appointment of two of them as assistant district commissioners. In the same year, for the first time, the governor appointed Africans to his executive council.

Then, in 1943, new municipal ordinances permitted African majorities on the various town councils. Local government was also strengthened by laws which gave increased powers to the chiefs and provided for a more efficient administration. The biggest advance, a new constitution providing for an African majority on the legislative council, while promised in 1944 did not come into force until 1946.

Looking at the results of the war period as a whole, the estimate of the future will probably be that the Gold Coast gained more than it suffered.[1] The greatest loss was in the casualties resulting from the Far Eastern campaigns, but even these were not large. Among the men serving in the army a large proportion had the opportunity of learning technical and clerical skills which proved of immense value for the Gold Coast's peace-time development. For the Africans who remained at home, war-time staff shortages gave some opportunities for administrative positions in government and commercial fields. The need for raw materials and for local self-sufficiency expanded production, stimulated local industries, and led to a more balanced agricultural output. In physical equipment the Dependency made vast gains through the war-time construction of large and up-to-date airfields, the development of Takoradi harbour, and the erection of buildings and other installations which were undertaken for military purposes but which afterwards became the property of the Gold Coast government.

To the quickening process brought about by the war in certain phases of economic and political development can also be added the psychological effect which wider contacts with world affairs had upon the West Africans. This influence, of course, made itself felt more in

[1] The results of the war on British West Africa are very ably discussed in an article by M. Fortes, an anthropologist who spent some time in this area during the war years. See 'Impact of the War on British West Africa', *International Affairs*, vol. XXI (1945), pp. 206–19.

the urban and coastal areas and among the soldiers who served overseas than in the rural districts of the hinterland. The increased opportunities for technical and administrative training gave the Africans powers which resulted in a deeper self-confidence and determination to take a more active part in their country's development. The presence of large groups of Allied service personnel in the Gold Coast, the visits of officials from the United Kingdom, the efforts of the information department and the British Council to acquaint the people, not only with the facts of the war, but with the idealism which lay behind it, all tended to increase a sense of empire solidarity and to widen the Africans' world outlook as well. The end of the war found the Gold Coast ready and impatient to make great advances in the peace era ahead.

CHAPTER X

POLITICAL DEVELOPMENT, 1945–57

World War II had a marked influence on the Gold Coast. The changes it brought were found, of course, not only in the Dependency but in all colonial areas. World opinion had become much concerned with the problem of dependent peoples and the United Nations Charter included a section in which the colonial powers agreed to promote the advancement and eventual self-government of these territories.[1] The Charter statement did not involve a fundamental change in British policy, for Britain had always aimed at the development of self-governing nations within the Commonwealth; but the post-war situation, involving an immense increase in colonial nationalism, was to force the British government to hasten the pace at which these territories advanced towards autonomy. In the Gold Coast actual steps to responsible government did not come until after the 1948 riots, but nevertheless in the immediately preceding years, there was a decided move for political advance and for a fuller social and economic welfare. Signs of this new policy were first evident during the governorship of Sir Alan Burns, who was appointed to replace Sir Arnold Hodson in 1941, but who did not go to the Gold Coast until the following year. From the outset the Africans were impressed by the resoluteness and broad outlook of the new governor, who followed up his first tour of the Dependency by a budget address which, notwithstanding war-time difficulties, promised definite plans for development. One local newspaper declared it the 'first address of action by a determined and pushful governor since the palmy days of Guggisberg'.[2] Early in his term of office (1942–7), Sir Alan proceeded to draw up a five-year development plan. Although full implementation was held up by the war, and although it was replaced in 1946 by a more comprehensive and more ambitious ten-year plan, nevertheless some important beginnings were made.

Changes were in order in the political field also. Sir Alan's first

[1] *Charter of the United Nations*, Chapter XI, 'Declaration Regarding Non-Self-Governing Territories', Article 73.
[2] *Gold Coast Observer* (12 March 1942).

attention was given to the very difficult problem of local government. It has been indicated earlier[1] that the Native Authority system, or indirect rule, as practised in Nigeria had never been fully established in the Gold Coast. Abiding by her original policy of allowing the chiefs a good measure of power in local matters, Britain had refrained from exercising adequate control in spite of the system's very evident deficiencies. Notwithstanding a slight improvement resulting from an earlier ordinance—that of 1927—the whole field of local government remained in need of overhauling. A second stage began in the late 1930's, and more fully in the 1940's, when an attempt was made to introduce a regular Native Authority system. The first step had been the 1939 Native Administrative Treasuries Ordinance,[2] which had empowered the government to compel a state to establish a native treasury and to submit it to supervision. In 1942 Sir Alan set up a committee of inquiry into the actual workings of local tribunals, the committee being composed in the main of Africans, including Sir Ofora Atta and Mr. (later Sir) Arku Korsah. Its report on the native courts amounted to an outright condemnation of the local courts system. As a result, in 1944 two further ordinances were passed which required reforms in the courts and—more important still—in the native administration as a whole. The first law (Native Courts Ordinance)[3] did much tó remove abuses which had often been connected with former African tribunals. It wisely disassociated the paramount chiefs, as they had asked, from the judicial function, and provided that each native authority should recommend to the governor a number of competent persons from which a judicial panel could be formed. The new courts thus established were graded A, B, C, D—the more important ones having increased jurisdiction. No state was allowed one of these courts unless its finances were regulated by an approved native treasury system which could then prevent the old abuse of exorbitant court fees. Regulations which gave the judicial adviser powers of review and control and which raised the standards for registrars greatly helped to improve the efficiency of the courts. By 1951 the old courts, over 300 in number, had been replaced by 135 modernized courts.

Of a more general nature than the courts ordinance was the 1944 Native Authority Ordinance, which aimed at an improvement in native administration. It made a drastic change by requiring that all organs of

[1] See pp. 45 ff.
[2] No. 16 of 1939.
[3] No. 22 of 1944. See also Hailey, *Native Administration in the British African Territories*, Part III; *African Survey* (1957), pp. 517–27.

local government must henceforth be recognized by the central government. Thus it was possible, for the first time, for the colonial authorities to have direct control over native administration. It empowered the governor in case of a prolonged 'stool' dispute or of other disorders to provide for local government by appointing a native council or group of councils, to be responsible for administration until a chief was elected. It further permitted him to group a number of chiefs into one native authority in those areas where the state divisions were so small that social and economic improvements could not easily be put into effect without a central treasury. As the Colony area of the Dependency included sixty-three different states, which states had in turn many subdivisions, the wisdom of some sort of federation was evident.

The Bill, according to custom, was first submitted to the joint provincial council which accepted it. As was to be expected, the intelligentsia opposed the Bill, reviving all the arguments of past years against increased power for chiefs. The chiefs, they insisted, might now become autocratic rather than constitutional rulers since their authority which ostensibly rested upon traditional enstoolment would in reality depend upon British support. The joint provincial council, they pointed out, had already given the chiefs a prominence in national affairs quite out of keeping with the customs of the past. The strong opposition put up by the municipal members of the legislative council plainly revealed the understandable fear that the chiefs would now become either dictatorial or subservient to government officials. Sir Alan Burns finally intervened in the legislative council debate, pointing out that he believed it to be inconsistent to want the country to develop and yet to object to allowing the chiefs the necessary power. He put the matter before the council:

> If the people of this country want to keep their Chiefs and their native customary laws as museum pieces to be put under glass cases to be looked at, then I believe this legislation is unnecessary, but if we want to make some progress in the Colony and want to see that progress maintained, then I think it is necessary to give the Chiefs power to deal with modern conditions . . . I am most anxious to see the Native Administrations take their full share in the government of this country because I believe that indirect rule by Government through the Native Authorities is the best training ground for the self-government which we are aiming at.[1]

The measure as proposed was passed over the objections of the municipal members. Now that the governor had more control over

[1] Legislative Council, *Debates*, vol. II (1944), p. 56.

local affairs, he allowed government aid to the native states, and from 1946 they received grants from central revenue equal to the amount raised by their own local taxation. Though the grants did stimulate some interest in developing local utilities, it can be said in general that these native administration ordinances came too late and did not provide for sufficient modernization of local government. As a matter of fact, the working of the new system was held up not only by opposition but by the continued existence of the old state councils over which it was difficult to exercise central government control. Many of the chiefs, as had been foreseen by the municipal representatives, ignored traditional checks and defied the wishes of their people. Destoolments increased and the former respect for traditional life and customs was lessened.[1]

The municipalities likewise underwent changes. In the years between 1943 and 1945 a new type of town council was established in Accra, Cape Coast, and Sekondi-Takoradi.[2] Each was presided over by a government official, but the majority of the members were elected Africans. Response to the town councils was disappointing, however; only a fraction of the electorate used its voting privilege and opposition to municipal taxation continued. In some of the towns the councillors had the courage to insist on high enough rates to make progress possible, but in others the old opposition was so strong that as late as 1946 the governor found it necessary to point out that there could be no true self-government if the people refused to accept its obligations as well as its privileges.[3]

The most important changes during the period of Burns's governorship were, however, those affecting central government. Frequent reference has already been made to the African demand for an increased measure of self-government. By the 1940's the Gold Coast had reached that stage in political development when, according to British policy, the next step would call for an elected African majority on the legislative council. The Africans themselves, very understandably, took every occasion to remind the British of this, as when for instance the legislative council accepted the income tax and the compulsory service ordinance, and when at the 1944 centennial celebration of the Bond Treaty the following resolution was presented to the government:

---

[1] In Ashanti, for example, an average of three out of twenty-one chiefs were destooled each year in the 1941–6 period. See K. A. Busia, *Position of the Chief in the Modern Political System of Ashanti* (London, 1951), p. 241.

[2] See pp. 41–42 for an account of an earlier attempt to improve town government.

[3] Governor's Address to Legislative Council (12 March 1946).

We the paramount chiefs of the Gold Coast . . . on the occasion of the Centenary of the Bond of 1844, signed between us and the Government of Great Britain do hereby express our sense of appreciation and gratitude for the British connection . . . and do hereby move a Vote of Confidence in the present Administration of the Gold Coast and express our good wishes for closer and more beneficient co-operation between the Government and the people of this country, hopefully looking forward immediately to a more effective voice in the affairs of the community . . .[1]

In effect the Gold Coast was ready for an increased measure of self-government for the economic, social, and political development of the inter-war years had contributed to the experience of the Dependency's leaders. The territorial councils had broadened the viewpoint of chiefs, hitherto confined to the particular interests of individual states, and service on the legislative council had taught the traditional rulers and the educated classes to work together in general with a view to the national good. As the number of educated chiefs increased, the intelligentsia found it easier to co-operate with them, though much disagreement still arose between them, especially over the narrow and autocratic tendencies of certain chiefs. In the nature of things co-operation commended itself to both groups since—from one point of view—all were members of the upper class, holding therefore many interests in common.

Among the educated chiefs of the period, Nana Sir Ofori Atta[2] had the most marked influence on political life. Recognizing early the hindrances to Gold Coast development arising from illiterate and provincial-minded chiefs, Sir Ofori Atta determined to encourage them to widen their outlook and modernize their administrative methods. He induced the various rulers in the Eastern Province to confer on inter-state problems, with such good success that the practice was later

---

[1] Legislative Council, *Debates*, vol. I (1944), pp. 111–12; see also ibid., vol. I (1940), p. 157; vol. I (1943), p. 130; vol. II (1943), pp. 37 ff.

[2] Nana Sir Ofori Atta was born in 1881 and educated at the Basel Mission in Akropong where he studied for the ministry. Giving up the ministry he worked as a clerk, then as secretary to his uncle, Omanhene of Akim Abuakwa until in 1912 he was himself elected paramount chief of this same state, the largest and one of the wealthiest in the Colony. Three years later he became a member of the legislative council, a position he held until his death in 1943. He had been knighted in 1927, one of the first African chiefs to receive this honour. See, for example, Chapters IV and V and the Legislative Council, *Debates* (1936), p. 81. For a full account of the political influence of Ofori Atta see Wight, *Gold Coast Legislative Council*, pp. 68–70 and *passim*. Other well-known chiefs during this period included Nene Mate Kole, Nana Sir Tsibu Darku IX, Togbi Sri II, Nana Amonco V, and Nana Amanfi III. See also Thomas Alicoe, *The Evolution of Gold Coast Chiefship* (Stockport, 1951), for an account by a Gold Coast African.

adopted by the government in the provincial council movement. It was he who took the major part—in collaboration with the government—in preparing the 1927 and 1944 native administration ordinances. As to his attitude towards the British, he was one of the outstanding advocates of co-operation, believing that the country's best interests lay not in independent statehood but in gradual progress towards complete self-government within the framework of the Commonwealth.

In the early years of his long career Nana Sir Ofori Atta opposed the intelligentsia on the issues of the West African National Congress, the 1925 constitution, and the native administration ordinances. From 1929 on, however, Casely Hayford having made his reconciliation with him, the municipal and provincial members of the council worked together under the leadership of these two gifted men. But Nana Sir Ofori Atta's forceful and domineering personality, and the belief, in many quarters, that he was merely the tool of the British administration, won him many enemies. Towards the end of his career, however, and especially after his death, many of the politically conscious changed their attitude, regarding his policies as having often been in the best interests of the country.

Two years before Ofori Atta's death the governor appointed him, together with Arku Korsah, the first African members of the executive council. This measure—dated 1942—marked for the Gold Coast a distinct political advance, since the governor was obliged to consult the council in the conduct of all administrative affairs. Of all the steps taken towards the goal of political autonomy during this period the most notable, however, was the 1946 constitution with its provision for a clear African majority on the legislative council and for a legislative union between the Colony and Ashanti. A suggestion for such a union was perhaps surprising in view of the ancient rivalry and wars which had separated Ashanti and the Colony until the establishment of the *Pax Britannica* at the beginning of the century.[1] Since that time Ashanti had made rapid economic and social progress and its political organization, after the 1935 restoration of the confederacy,[2] was far more closely knit than that of the sixty-three Colony states. Since the confederacy restoration there had been occasional acts of collaboration between the two areas, especially during the cocoa hold-up of 1937–8, but the former rivalry was not wholly forgotten, as future events were to reveal.[3] For the present, however, the two territories found a common bond in their political ambitions, and in 1943 Ashanti joined the Colony in signing a

[1] See Chapter II.   [2] See Chapter VI.   [3] See below p. 187.

petition for a new constitution, one of its provisions being Ashanti representation on the Gold Coast legislative council. Replying to the Gold Coast proposal in this matter of collaboration, the Asantehene (King of the Ashanti Confederacy) spoke of past enmities between the two territories and suggested a new policy in the interest of future unity:

This is not the first time that we have realized or been made to realize the need for co-operation between Ashanti and the Colony . . . if we were to trace out what has been the chief obstruction to our coming together, we would find out that it is selfishness. Selfishness, which is the outcome of a narrow and conservative way of thinking, has kept us poles apart from one another to our own disadvantage, and it is the same evil that will, if we are not careful, undermine the move that we are now contemplating. There has been lurking in the breasts of some of you in the Colony the fear that if you fall in with Ashanti, we shall seek to dominate you . . . I would like you to dispel any such uncalled for fears for the days of our imperialistic aspirations are past and forgotten. What we aim at now is not that sort of federation which in the past we tried to force on you with the aid of the sword; but one into which we all of us, of our own accord, shall freely enter. It is to be a federation based not on subjection, but on love . . . Henceforth, let our watchword be UNITY . . . If in the past we waged war against one another, let us today seek a rapprochement.[1]

Willingness of the Colony and Ashanti to seek a *rapprochement* was not without its effect in influencing the British to grant the desired increase of self-government to the Gold Coast. The governor announced the details of the new constitution in October 1944. It was not, however, until March 1946[2] that the new instrument of government was promulgated, staff shortages in the Colonial Office owing to the war having delayed its drafting. The new constitution, usually known as the Burns constitution, was actually the work of both the governor and the African leaders.

In spite of later contentions to the contrary, the constitution did mark an advance towards autonomy. The legislative council then had an elected African majority—the first colonial territory in Africa to take

[1] Asantehene's reply to joint provincial council representatives. Quoted in *Gold Coast Observer* (15 October 1943). These words are also of interest in view of the strife which reappeared in 1955 after the formation of the National Liberation Movement. See below p. 188.

[2] The constitution was published in the *Gold Coast Gazette* (23 March 1946) supplement. The texts of both the 1925 and 1946 constitutions are reproduced in Wight, *Gold Coast Legislative Council*, App. 1 and 2.

this step—and it possessed some real power in financial matters.[1] But on the other hand, it had little authority in the actual initiation or implementation of policy, and the Gold Coast still retained a non-responsible form of government.

The new legislative council numbering thirty-one members was constituted as follows: the governor as president; six *ex-officio* members and twenty-four unofficial members, eighteen of whom were elected, nine members by the joint provincial council, four members by the Asanteman or Ashanti Confederacy council, and five municipal members. There were in addition six nominated members, and it was indicated that these should be mainly Africans. Extraordinary members could be elected from time to time to give advice on technical matters, but they had no vote.

The constitution had thus provided for a political link between the Colony and Ashanti by including representatives from the Confederacy in the council. It will be noticed that neither the Northern Territories nor Togoland had direct representation, the former area being considered not yet sufficiently developed for such representation. (The establishment of the first Northern Territories council of chiefs in December 1946 pointed the way to an eventual share in the central government.) The latter area, Togoland, had been divided into two sections, north Togoland being administered as a unit with the Northern Territories and south Togoland with the Eastern Province of the Colony. South Togoland was given a territorial council in 1949, and in the following year was permitted to send one of its members to the Gold Coast legislative council.

Under the new constitution some changes were also made in the administrative divisions of the Colony. There were only two provinces, an eastern and a western, instead of three as formerly. The old office of secretary for native affairs was discontinued in favour of one chief commissioner for the entire Colony with headquarters at Cape Coast.

Public opinion, on the whole, appeared satisfied with the new constitution, although the more advanced element voiced its disappointment that it had not given the Africans greater control over government policy. The days following the inauguration of the new legislative council on 23 July 1946 were marked by national rejoicing, especially in Accra to which the Asantehene and hundreds of his followers had come for the event. On this occasion the natural hospitality and kindly spirit of the Gold Coast people were strikingly evident, leading one

[1] On the Standing Financial Committee there was a majority of Africans.

new-comer to remark: 'I have never been in such a happy and friendly country.'[1]

But beneath the goodwill which marked the celebrations were deep undercurrents of dissatisfaction and tension which were soon to become manifest. Within twenty months of the inauguration of the 1946 constitution serious popular disturbances occurred in many parts of the country. To understand the 1948 riots it must be borne in mind that the strain of war and post-war adjustments not only intensified old problems but also created many new ones. Dr. Busia points out that before the war the British had taken it for granted that the minority of educated Africans who questioned the legitimacy of colonial rule and demanded self-government did not speak for the illiterate and inarticulate body of citizens. But most of those who joined the armed services belonged to the latter class and 'when the ex-servicemen allied themselves with their literate compatriots in the agitation for self government . . . the force of the demand could not be lightly ignored'.[2] Though the number of Gold Coast servicemen was small in relation to the population their influence after demobilization was all out of proportion to their numbers. They had learnt new skills and acquired new experience and prestige and they were full of high expectations as to what post-war conditions would bring both to themselves and to their country.

Life in the Gold Coast itself was also affected by the war, for foreign troops had been quartered in many towns; new roads and airports had been built, civilians had been employed in various war-time services, farmers had increased their crops. More money was in circulation, while at the same time consumer goods were in short supply. As inflation mounted, profiteering became widespread and general discontent grew apace. And underneath these extraordinary post-war conditions were all the older problems, often intensified by the fact that the 'times were out of joint'. Everyone recognized that the native administration system was inadequate and that some modernization of local government was needed. The position of the chiefs, now resting on British authority in place of native law, made it possible for them to ignore former traditional checks and the legitimate demands of their people. Numbers of chiefs were as a consequence destooled each year and quarrels over stool property, &c., dragged out over long periods. In addition the system was not providing for the modernization of the villages. The rural

[1] Kenneth Bradley, 'Gold Coast Impressions', *Blackwood's*, vol. CCLXI (1947), pp. 1–9.
[2] K. A. Busia, 'West Africa in the Twentieth Century', *Journal of World History*, vol. IV, No. 1 (1957), p. 211.

population hoped for such comparatively simple improvements as a clean water supply, local roads, and even a primary school. In a very few cases the chiefs were sufficiently well educated to lead their people in community development projects, but in most villages there was no hope for progress until a more efficient type of local government with trained officials could be inaugurated. Discontent grew, especially in areas close to the larger towns. The comparative progress of these towns with their displays of imported goods, their cinemas, and their other modern attractions appealed to the young men of the near-by country-side. Steady increase in urban populations marked the 1940's, resulting from economic changes and from war-time needs. Gradually a wage-earning class of some size was developing—a class which was soon to take on great political significance. In this class were many young men who had received only an elementary education—the 'standard VII boys'. They considered themselves above menial work, and were unwilling to remain in the village with its agricultural economy, its backward ways, its insistence on custom, and respect for traditional authorities. Once in the towns these boys, literate but with no specialized training, got poorly paid jobs or no jobs at all. Since they still had links with their home villages, their discontent easily spread beyond the towns.[1] Despite the growing unrest, the government does not appear to have recognized the danger. The number of British officials had been drastically reduced during the depression of the 1930's, and then the war had made it difficult to replace the staff, so that in Accra and other towns officials had little time to concern themselves with sociological changes. As a result the 1948 riots came as a surprise to those who were not fully aware of the discontent and desire for better things which recent years had brought.

The seriousness of these problems was to lead henceforth to a restlessness and a hope for rapid progress in both political and economic matters. One evidence is the fact that scarcely a year after the inauguration of the 1946 constitution certain groups were already dissatisfied with it, and in August 1947 they set up a new political organization known as the United Gold Coast Convention. Its members, under the direction of Mr. George Grant[2] and Dr. Danquah, were drawn from the upper middle class, mostly lawyers and merchants.[3] Something of their discontent with the Burns constitution—which they felt they had

[1] See David Apter, *The Gold Coast in Transition* (Princeton, 1955), pp. 162ff.
[2] Mr. George Grant was one of the wealthiest African business men in the country.
[3] For a full discussion of the various classes in the Gold Coast see David Apter, *Gold Coast in Transition* Chapter 7.

already outgrown—was later expressed in the introduction to the Coussey Report,[1] which pointed out:

... what might have been ideally suited to the conditions of 1943 was wholly out of place in 1946, so rapidly had the forces released by a global war changed man's outlook and aspirations.[2]

The report goes on to speak of the inability of the government to bring down high prices, curtail profiteering, and ease other economic burdens of the country. People, it commented, were disappointed that their representatives on the new legislative council could do nothing to influence policy, and it added that to concede an African majority in the legislature without at the same time giving it some measure of responsibility was a serious defect.

Though the Coussey Report was not written until two years after the formation of the United Gold Coast Convention (U.G.C.C.), the above statement gives a fair indication of the organization's objectives. It is important at this juncture to notice certain characteristics of the U.G.C.C. Its members were largely of the *élite*, and it constantly insisted that its aim was self-government for the chiefs and the people at the earliest opportunity—but all to be achieved by legitimate and constitutional means. This emphasis on the chiefs and on constitutional procedure points up the fact that the U.G.C.C. represented a conservative type of nationalism in contrast to the popular type which later developed. It was from this same upper class, as well as from the chiefs, that the legislative councillors had been drawn in the past, and it was taken for granted that they would continue to retain their leadership as the country advanced towards independence.[3]

A new phase in the story of the U.G.C.C.—though it was not realized at the time—began in December 1947 when Mr. Kwame Nkrumah became its general secretary. Nkrumah was born in a small village of Nzima—in the western section of the Colony—in September 1909.[4] He studied at Achimota and later in the United States, where he obtained

[1] This report will be discussed below.
[2] Colonial Office, No. 248, *Report to His Excellency the Governor by the Committee on Constitutional Reform*, para. 2.
[3] Among this group were many of the men who later helped to form the Ghana Congress Party, the leading opposition during the 1951–53 Assembly. For an interesting discussion of the place of parties and movements in African nationalism see T. Hodgkin, *Nationalism in Colonial Africa* (New York, 1957), Chapter V.
[4] Nkrumah gives a full account of his life in *Ghana, the Autobiography of Kwame Nkrumah* (New York, 1957)

a Bachelor of Divinity degree from Lincoln University and a Master of Arts from the University of Pennsylvania. During his years in America and a later stay in England he had gained considerable experience in leadership by participating in various political organizations and in associations designed to promote Negro advancement or self-government in Africa. The U.G.C.C. hoped to turn this experience to good account.

When Nkrumah arrived from London late in 1947, the tension in the Gold Coast—apparent since the war—was rapidly increasing. The political agitation fostered by the U.G.C.C. created unrest, but an even greater source of disquiet and more far-reaching were certain economic troubles. Swollen shoot disease was damaging the cocoa farms at the rate of fifteen million trees a year, and in spite of much scientific research no remedy other than the drastic measure of cutting out infected trees had as yet been found. The farmers, mostly illiterate, were unwilling to destroy their diseased trees, especially at a time when cocoa prices were high. The government policy of compulsory destruction consequently was resisted in many areas. The most serious cause of complaint, however, was the scarcity of imported goods, which, coupled with the extremely high prices attached to them, caused widespread deprivation. The Africans put the blame for the high prices on the European importing firms, alleging that these were out to make excessive profits. The government in the meantime maintained a non-committal attitude and allowed discontent to grow, instead of taking a stand in the matter and ordering a public investigation.

Late in 1947 one of the Accra subchiefs, Nii Bonne, in an effort to force the lowering of prices, began to organize a boycott campaign. It was actually started in January 1948, but it was difficult, of course, to get the people to obey its regulations. It was later described in the report of an investigating committee in the following terms:

A system of fines, which in our view were quite illegal, and a general intimidation of offenders against the boycott quickly grew up. . . . The difficulties of the Authorities in effectively restraining this form of intimidation . . . are manifest and considerable lawlessness resulted.[1]

Finally, at the end of February, the Accra Chamber of Commerce agreed to reduce prices, and on the twenty-eighth retail buying was to be resumed. On the same day a group of ex-servicemen planned to hold

[1] Colonial Office No. 231, *Report of the Commission of Enquiry into Disturbances in the Gold Coast, 1948* (London, 1948), p. 34. Hereafter cited as *Watson Report.*

a parade for which they had been given governmental permission, on condition that it followed a prescribed route. In the event the marchers attempted to change the route and to force their way to Government House at Christianborg. When the police were ordered to fire, two men were killed and four or five wounded before the parade could be turned back.

At the same time other disorders had broken out in the business district of Accra. Crowds, dissatisfied with the new prices resulting from the boycott agreement, and incited by agitators, began to riot and loot and burn both European and Syrian owned stores. The turmoil increased when a mob gathered round the prison and succeeded in freeing some prisoners who also joined in the looting. These disturbances continued through 28 and 29 February and quickly spread to other Gold Coast cities and towns. In all, 29 persons were killed, 237 injured, and the property damage amounted to over £2,000,000.[1] The government arrested six of the U.G.C.C. leaders, including Nkrumah and Dr. Danquah,[2] and removed them to various isolated areas in the Northern Territories. These men became popular heroes widely acclaimed as the 'Big Six'.

As the cause of the riots lay evidently far below the surface, Sir Gerald Creasy,[3] the recently appointed governor, made arrangements with the secretary of state for the colonies for an independent commission to be sent out from the United Kingdom to undertake a thorough investigation of the matter. This commission, under the chairmanship of Mr. A. K. Watson, Recorder of Bury St. Edmunds, was given very wide terms of reference to investigate the reasons for the disturbances and to make recommendations. The commission remained in the Gold Coast for about a month, and not only conducted hearings on the riots but also looked into the general problems of the country. The six U.G.C.C. leaders, who were released on the arrival of the commission, had secured the services of a British lawyer, Mr. Dingle Foot, K.C., so that their case was fully heard. The findings of the commission, often referred to as the Watson Report, were released in August 1948.

The Watson Report, attempting to discuss the general situation of the country, began by stating that the most serious problem of the Gold

[1] ibid., p. 85.

[2] The other men were William Ofori Atta, Akufo Addo, Ako Adjei and E. Obetsebi Lamptey.

[3] Sir Alan Burns's term as governor ended in August 1947. His successor, Sir Gerald Creasy, did not come to the Gold Coast until January 1948. Though he assumed office at an unfortunate time it appears that a more energetic policy might have been followed. Sir Charles Arden-Clarke replaced him in 1949.

Coast was the suspicion which surrounded government activity of every sort. It affirmed that the causes of the riots were not only political but economic and social, and recommended far-reaching and positive remedies in all of these areas. Other conditions singled out as causes of African discontent were the frustration of the educated classes because of insufficient opportunities to participate in government and the need for further industrial and educational development. With regard to the chiefs it stated that the population looked upon them with suspicion as mere instruments of British policy, and that the more advanced Africans were firm in their belief that the chiefs should take no part in political life, but should confine themselves to their traditional rôle. The section of the report dealing with recommendations for the future advanced the opinion that the 1946 constitution had been 'outmoded at birth'[1] because it had been planned in the light of pre-war conditions. It suggested a real beginning of African responsible government by creating an enlarged legislative assembly and, most significant of all, an executive council including five African ministers who would be charged with departments and responsible to the legislature.

The publication of the Watson Report was of considerable importance in the development of post-war British colonial policy. Certain conservative sections of British opinion strongly criticized the commissioners for having recommended so substantial an increase in Gold Coast autonomy. The Colonial Office itself accepted the report in its main features, but was careful to point out that it did not agree with all its statements.[2] It strongly condemned, for example, the view that the chiefs' influence was on the wane, holding that they still had an essential and beneficial part to play, through modernized local government, in the development of the Gold Coast. As far as changes in the 1946 constitution were concerned the British government agreed to a further advance towards autonomy, but considered that no step should be made until a local African committee, fully representative of the people, had had an opportunity to study the Watson proposals. In January 1949 the government appointed an all-African committee under the chairmanship of the late Sir Henley Coussey, then a fifty-five-year-old African judge. The thirty-eight members included chiefs and people from all parts of the country, among them all of the 'Big Six' except Nkrumah. The group represented all sections of public opinion except the most radical. If

[1] *Watson Report*, p. 24.
[2] Colonial Office, No. 232, *Statement by His Majesty's Government on the Report of the Commission of Enquiry into Disturbances in the Gold Coast, 1948* (London 1948).

Nkrumah had been included then, public opinion would have been more fully considered and future results might have been quite different.

The Coussey Committee's report which was published in October 1949[1] covered the whole field of government—central, regional, and local. It recommended a further step in applying the British type of representative government to the Gold Coast, but it sought to blend Western institutions with the Gold Coast's traditional ones, since it found no intrinsic disharmony between the two systems. As its suggestions were largely those embodied in the 1951 constitution, it suffices to remark here that it advised an enlarged legislative assembly consisting principally of members elected directly or indirectly by popular vote; and an executive council with a majority of African ministers who would formulate policy and would be responsible to the assembly. Local and regional government proposals provided for efficient and modern techniques, but at the same time the commission showed its respect for tradition by leaving a place for the chief in both the local councils and in the assembly.

The Coussey Committee had faced an arduous task, made all the more difficult by the unsettled political condition of the country. The wisdom and moderation of its proposals attracted attention not only in the Gold Coast itself but farther afield, and it received high praise in the British Press.[2] The British government accepted the main proposals as a workable plan for carrying out its promise to give the Gold Coast the beginnings of responsible government, and they became the basis of the 1951 constitution. According to the new instrument a cabinet included 3 ex-officio ministers and 8 African ministers drawn from the legislative assembly. The 11 ministers were to introduce and defend 'government' measures in the assembly which comprised a speaker, the 3 ex-officio ministers, 6 special members representing mining and commercial interests, and 75 African elected members (37 from the Colony, 19 from Ashanti, and 19 from the Northern Territories). Of the 75 elected members, only the 5 municipal members were directly elected; in the Colony and Ashanti 33 rural members were elected by colleges of directly elected representatives, and the remaining 37 were territorial members elected by the various regional councils. This constitution, then, provided for the principal Coussey proposals with the significant exception that the Colonial Office required the cabinet to be responsible

[1] Colonial Office, No. 248, *Report to His Excellency the Governor by the Committee on Constitutional Reform, 1949* (London, 1949), para. 2 (hereafter cited as *Coussey Report*).
[2] See *West Africa* (5 and 19 November 1949) for discussion of the various Press comments on the *Coussey Report*.

to both the governor and assembly rather than to the assembly alone as the Coussey Report had asked.[1]

In the Gold Coast the Coussey Report had been well received by all the moderates, even though the Colonial Office change caused disappointment. Press comment by all but the most radical papers was favourable. The *Ghana Statesman* expressed the belief that the Coussey Committee's work 'will go down in history as the real turning point in British relations with the peoples of the Gold Coast'. This comment emphasizes a most significant event. It had always been British policy to grant the Gold Coast eventual self-government, but most officials thought it would be many years before the country would be ready. This step, then, represented a major decision and British acceptance of the Coussey Report and its demand for semi-responsible government can be considered a dividing-line in Gold Coast history.

While the Coussey Report was welcomed by moderate public opinion, it was criticized by radicals, especially by the *Accra Evening News* (Kwame Nkrumah's paper). In one issue the statement is made:

As for us, we have already declared our stand with regard to the new constitution that only full Dominion status . . . will satisfy us and by this demand we shall stand and face all storms however strong they are. Ghana[2] must be free and free now.[3]

The stand taken by Nkrumah against the Coussey Report had a very great influence upon the less privileged sections of the people, as his power had steadily increased since the 1948 riots. After his release from detention in the Northern Territories, he had begun to organize youth groups with the assistance of K. A. Gbedemah and Kojo Botsio—men who were later to rank only second in importance to Nkrumah, both in his party and in his government. These youth groups eventually supplied other influential followers as, for example, Krobo Edusei, Kofi Baako, J. E. Jantuah, and Bediako Poku. The Asante Youth Organization, the Accra Youth Study Group, and many groups in other parts of the country were later federated as the Committee of Youth Organizations

[1] Colonial Office, No. 250, *Statement by H.M. Government on the Report of the Committee on Constitutional Reform* (London, 1949).

[2] 'Ghana' is the name which was adopted by the Gold Coast when it became independent in 1957. It refers to a traditional empire (Ghana) oldest known state of Western Africa which supposedly flourished from the third to the seventeenth century, and whose tribes, driven southward by the Almoravid conquest, are believed to have been ancestors of the Akan group of the Gold Coast. See R. A. Maury, 'The question of Ghana,' *Africa*, vol. XXIV (1954), pp. 200–13.

[3] *Accra Evening News* (17 December 1949).

(C.Y.O.). In the beginning these groups were intended to act as vanguards for the U.G.C.C., and thus attract the younger elements of the Gold Coast population to the parent organization. Nkrumah holds, however, that the U.G.C.C. executive committee resented the C.Y.O. because it was composed of 'the less privileged, or radical, section of the people and voiced the economic, social and political aspirations of the rank and file. It went completely against their more conservative outlook.'[1]

Nkrumah remained with the U.G.C.C. until the middle of 1949, but it was increasingly evident that its executive committee following the leadership of Dr. Danquah was completely out of sympathy with his policies. They felt that Nkrumah had betrayed the trust they had given him in his appointment as secretary of the U.G.C.C., and that he had used his opportunity to build up a personal following rather than remaining loyal to the organization which he represented. In view of their conservative attitude Nkrumah, together with his closest followers, Botsio and Gbedemah, came to the conclusion that a separate political party was called for. The account of his break with the U.G.C.C. in July 1949 is told in his own words. Upon leaving the U.G.C.C. conference room he relates:

I was confronted by an excited crowd.

'Resign!' they shouted, as soon as they saw me, 'resign and lead us and we shall complete the struggle together!'

I realized at once that they were sincere and determined. Above all I knew that they needed me to lead them. I had stirred their deepest feelings and they had shown their confidence in me; I could never fail them now. Quickly I made my mind up.

'I will lead you!' I said. 'This very day I will lead you!'

Hurriedly I returned to the conference room and announced that I had decided to resign, not only from the general secretaryship, but also from membership of the U.G.C.C. The delegates were then as jubilant as the crowds outside.

Standing on the platform surrounded by an expectant crowd, I asked for a pen and a piece of paper and, using somebody's back as a support, I wrote out my official resignation and then read it to the people. The reaction was immediate and their cheers were deafening. . . . Standing before my supporters I pledged myself, my very life blood, if need be, to the cause of Ghana.[2]

This decision marked the beginning of a new type of nationalist movement in the Gold Coast, one which would appeal to the politically awakened masses. Henceforth Nkrumah used his outstanding gifts of

[1] Nkrumah, *Ghana*, p. 97.   [2] ibid., p. 107.

leadership and his very considerable powers of oratory to build up the
Convention People's Party (C.P.P.). Soon its influence was widespread
in both the Colony and Ashanti.

Shortly before the publication of the Coussey Report, the C.P.P. had
begun to prepare the ground for a campaign of so-called 'Positive
Action'. The new constitution, it had foreseen, would not grant complete self-government and dominion status; the C.P.P. planned to force
the British to concede it. In October, Nkrumah published a pamphlet
threatening as a last resort 'strikes, boycotts, and non-co-operation
based on the principle of absolute non-violence',[1] if the government
did not give independence by the end of 1949. The legislative council's
acceptance of the Coussey Report in December 1949, with its implicit
rejection of Nkrumah's demand for immediate and complete self-
government, was met, as had been threatened, by the C.P.P.'s campaign
of Positive Action. In spite of the government's warning that political
strikes were illegal, the party declared a nation-wide strike and boycott
effective at midnight, 8 January 1950. Its non-violent character was
difficult to maintain and it soon degenerated into lawlessness. On
20 January, Nkrumah and other C.P.P. leaders were arrested[2] and the
Accra Evening News banned. While Nkrumah was serving his term in
prison, the C.P.P., under the very efficient leadership of his lieutenant,
Mr. Gbedemah, increased its adherents throughout the country. Elections for the new constitution were to be held in February 1951 and the
C.P.P. was determined to win at the polls. In July 1950 the legislative
council had decided to lower the voting age to twenty-one. During the
following months an intensive campaign to prepare a largely illiterate
population for its first general election was skilfully carried on.[3] While
the government left no stone unturned to secure an efficient and secret
election procedure, the C.P.P. continued its work of political organization[4] in the urban and rural areas of the Gold Coast. Electioneering was
planned with an insight into the aspirations of the common people.
Slogans, banners, a popularly worded manifesto, these had a far wider
appeal than the staid procedure of the United Gold Coast Convention.
The very fact that Nkrumah was in prison because he had campaigned
for self-government strengthened the party's position. His picture was

---

[1] Nkrumah, Kwame, *What I Mean by Positive Action* (Accra, 1949).
[2] Nkrumah, however, was not arrested for organizing *Positive Action*, but for writing
seditious articles.
[3] *G.C. An. Report, 1951*, Appendix 1.
[4] The C.P.P. constitution is given in K. Nkrumah, *Ghana*, Appendix A. See *West
Africa* (20 January 1951) for an account of the C.P.P. electioneering.

on display, his words quoted—words which would 'conquer a man's heart'.[1] Nkrumah kept in touch with his party and managed to give some guidance through messages smuggled out from his prison cell to Gbedemah, who with great skill was continuing the work of party organization and propaganda. But it is also necessary to stress that the conception and eventual success of the C.P.P. can only be fully explained in terms of Nkrumah's leadership.[2]

The C.P.P. manifesto made sweeping promises—industrialization, jobs for all, free primary education, national health service, the equal opportunities of a socialist state. True, the realization of these things would mean hard work, but with imperialism out of the way the people of Ghana could do it. Stress was laid on materialistic advantages and there was no mistaking the secular spirit embodied in the slogan, 'Seek ye first the political kingdom and all things will be added unto it.' Actually the proposals bearing upon the development of the country were not greatly different from those envisaged by the 1946 Ten Year Plan, but the C.P.P. promised to get results in far less time because self-government, it claimed, would release the energies of the people and act as a spur to greater effort.

Throughout the months immediately preceding the election, the C.P.P. leaders toured the country with the result that when the polling took place in February 1951 the C.P.P. carried off a sweeping victory. Final count showed that 34 of the 38 seats contested on a party basis were won by the C.P.P.; 3 by the U.G.C.C., and 1 by an independent. Nkrumah, though still in prison, was elected as one of the members for Accra. At this point, Sir Charles Arden-Clarke was faced with the momentous choice of releasing Nkrumah or requiring that he complete his prison term. His decision is best related in his own words:

Nkrumah and his party had the mass of the people behind them and there was no other party with appreciable public support to which one could turn. Without Nkrumah, the Constitution would be still-born and nothing come of all the hopes, aspirations and concrete proposals for a greater measure of self-government, there would no longer be any faith in the good intentions of the British Government, and the Gold Coast would be plunged into disorders, violence and bloodshed.[3]

[1] *West Africa* (20 and 27 January 1951).
[2] James Coleman, 'Emergence of African Political Parties', *Africa Today*, edited by C. Grove Haines (Baltimore, 1955), p. 234; David Apter, *Gold Coast in Transition*, Chapter 10.
[3] Charles Arden-Clarke, *African Affairs*, vol. LVII (January 1958).

With the news of his release, Nkrumah's followers massed at the prison gate, and lifting him shoulder high, carried him in triumph through the streets of Accra. Later he gave a Press conference to journalists, many of whom had come to Accra to report on the Gold Coast's first general election. He told them:

I desire for the Gold Coast dominion status within the Commonwealth. I am a Marxian socialist and an undenominational Christian. The places I know in Europe are London and Paris. I am no communist and have never been one. I come out of gaol and into the assembly without the slightest feeling of bitterness to Britain. I stand for no racialism, no discrimination against any race or individual, but I am unalterably opposed to imperialism in any form.[1]

Later in February the names of the first Gold Coast ministers were announced. In addition to Kwame Nkrumah, who was given the title of leader of government business, five other C.P.P. members were appointed to ministries—K. A. Gbedemah, Kojo Botsio, Dr. Ansah Koi, A. Casely-Hayford, and T. Hutton-Mills. Nkrumah had at first demanded that all eight ministries reserved for Africans be given to members of his party; later, he agreed to giving the two remaining ministries to E. Asafu-Adjaye of Ashanti and to J. Braimah of the Northern Territories. The executive council still included, of course, three European *ex-officio* members responsible for defence and external affairs, finance, and justice. The governor, as has been seen, retained extensive powers and the legal framework was still that of a colonial constitution. In actual practice, however, a high proportion of the governor's authority was delegated and he never made use of his reserve powers, so that both the council and the assembly went a long way during the 1951–4 period toward a more fully responsible government.

Before his election Nkrumah had characterized the 1951 constitution as 'bogus and fraudulent' because it did not give the Gold Coast complete responsible government. Now, however, he determined to make a success of it during the period which must necessarily elapse before a new instrument of government could be demanded of the British, and so prove to the world that the Gold Coast was ready for independence. In the event the intervening years provided a valuable training for the assuming of the full responsibility which autonomy would bring. Both Sir Charles Arden-Clarke and Nkrumah have given frank accounts of the first few months under the new constitution. The former recalled his first meeting when he invited Nkrumah to form a government:

[1] *The Times* (14 February 1951).

That meeting was redolent with mutual suspicion and mistrust. We were like two dogs meeting for the first time, sniffing at each other with hackles half raised trying to decide whether to bite or wag our tails. Soon afterwards, Nkrumah came to see me alone and we were able to get to know each other. This time the hackles were down . . . and before the end the tails were wagging.[1]

And again in describing the first cabinet meetings:

It was interesting to watch how that Cabinet began to work. At first there was mutual suspicion and mistrust between the group of three ex-officio Cabinet Ministers—whose suspicions, incidentally, were shared by the Governor— and the group of eight elected African Cabinet Ministers . . . The problem was how to improve the atmosphere and make the Cabinet work as a team; this was a question of human relationships, and I am glad to say that within three months, the Cabinet was like one happy family all quarrelling and arguing among themselves irrespective of whether one was ex-officio and the other an elected member, and loyally abiding by the decision of the majority in every case.[2]

The first regular meeting of the new legislative assembly opened on 20 March with messages of congratulations from the United Kingdom and with the address of the governor given for the first time in Gold Coast history 'in the terms advised by my Ministers and approved by my Executive Council'.[3] The Speaker, in opening the debates on the following day, remarked that 'the eyes of the whole world are set upon this country and its new Assembly; our success will not reflect credit on this country only, but it may influence the destiny of others who are similarly situated'.[4] While the level of debate compared unfavourably with that of more mature countries during the first year, in time much progress was made in mastering the difficult rules and in acquiring the necessary self-discipline required for parliamentary government. The standing orders of the assembly provided for rules of debate, motions, and a question period modelled after the British House of Commons. The function of the assembly differed sharply from that of the old legislative council in that it provided a government, i.e. it actually elected the eight African ministers and thus was in a position to control rather than merely to advise the executive council (the cabinet). Moreover, the

[1] Arden-Clarke, ibid.; Nkrumah's account is given in *Ghana*, p. 136.
[2] Arden-Clarke, 'Gold Coast into Ghana', *International Affairs*, vol. XXXIV (January 1958), p. 52.
[3] Legislative Assembly, *Debates*, Issue No. 2, vol. I, 1951, p. 8.
[4] ibid., p. 18.

assembly now legislated for the Northern Territories as well as for the Colony and Ashanti; of the African elected members 37 came from the Colony, 19 from Ashanti, and 19 from the Northern Territories.

In view of the 1951 constitution the governor had, in the previous year, divided the central secretariat into the separate departments which would become the future ministries, ensuring thus a smooth administration before the new ministers took office. In addition, he appointed British secretaries to act as permanent officials under the authority of the various African ministers once the new constitution was in force. This policy, at first criticized by the Africans, was later appreciated in view of the valuable co-operation it entailed between the Africans and the British or expatriate officers.[1] Many British civil servants showed that they were willing to give faithful and disinterested service as readily to an African as to a British minister. Goodwill and confidence between the European and African resulted. Gold Coast history can be regarded as an example—not only of successful advance to independence but of genuine racial understanding as well. A tribute must be paid to the men and women of the present generation and to their forebears—a long line of Africans and Europeans of the stamp of Aggrey and Guggisberg who built up a tradition of mutual respect and racial co-operation.

It was clear to the Nkrumah government in 1951 that as soon as the new development plans got under way, more civil servants would be needed. For this purpose a Public Service Commission was established, but with the policy of recruiting from overseas only in those cases where no suitable African candidate was available. Because the previous colonial government had made insufficient efforts to train African officials, or as the term goes, to Africanize the civil service—the Gold Coast was faced with a serious shortage of properly qualified Africans, and it was therefore necessary to continue the appointment of overseas officers. In July 1953, Dr. Nkrumah[2] announced in the assembly that the country would have to rely on expatriates for some years to come. Every appropriate means, he assured, for expediting Africanization would be adopted, yet not at a speed harmful to efficiency or to the interests of overseas officers. Actually the number of Africans holding posts in a variety of positions which had been formerly classified as 'senior' and held by Europeans rose from 171 in 1949 to 916 in 1954.

[1] R. Saloway, 'The New Gold Coast', *International Affairs*, vol. XXXI (Oct. 1955), p. 471.
[2] In June 1951, Nkrumah was invited to America where he received the honorary degree, Doctor of Laws, from his alma mater, Lincoln University in Pennsylvania.

By 1957 when the Gold Coast became independent, there were still 1,100 expatriates, but the number of Africans had risen to over 3,000, largely in class 4 of the administrative service. Thus it is evident that rapid Africanization has taken place, not so much by the termination of European positions as by expansion.[1]

The years following the introduction of the 1951 constitution were marked by much social and economic development. Such activity was possible because surplus revenue had been accumulated during the war and because of the high price of cocoa in the world market. This dynamism in Gold Coast affairs came also from the optimism generated by the spirit of nationalism and by the satisfaction consequent on the increased self-government. Such interest in social change has been characteristic, not only of the Gold Coast but of many other African areas in recent years. Nevertheless the Gold Coast inhabitants have shown themselves to be among the most alert of the continent, and they have made the most of their educational opportunities. But, in spite of the people's enthusiasm and the country's sound financial position, the new government faced serious problems. The Gold Coast was still very much an underdeveloped country, although the colonial government had already made important advances in the economic and social fields. In addition to such fundamental handicaps as a debilitating climate and widespread incidence of tropical disease, the country's economy was dangerously narrow in its dependence on cocoa and limited mineral exports. Basic public services of all kinds needed to be initiated or expanded. In such circumstances it was understandable that the central government would take a greater share of the responsibility than would be the case with more advanced areas.[2] In short, one of the principal tasks before the Nkrumah government in 1951 was to continue and expand the development plans already initiated by the colonial government. The 1946 plan had envisaged an expenditure of £11,500,000

[1] G.C. Govt., *A Statement on the Programme of the Africanization of the Public Service, 1954*, p. 10. After August, 1955 all civil servants became members of the local Gold Coast service, indirectly responsible to the Prime Minister through the Public Service Commission. At that time all pensionable officers were given the choice of leaving the Gold Coast service with a compensation for loss of career, or of joining the new local service. Of the 771 officers entitled to leave, 142 did so. See *Despatches on the Gold Coast Government's Proposals for the Constitutional Reform exchanged between the Secretary of State for the Colonies and H.E. the Governor*, Col. No. 302, 1954.

[2] Interesting discussions of the Gold Coast's development problem, but from quite different points of view are to be found in Barbara Ward Jackson, 'The Gold Coast, an Experiment in Partnership', *Foreign Affairs*, vol. XXXII (1954), pp. 608-16; R. B. Davison, 'Must Nkrumah Rely on State "Socialism" to Speed the Development of Ghana?', *Africa Special Report*, vol. II (September 1957). The latter article refers in large part to the period after independence.

over a ten-year period, but, owing to a better financial position after 1951, it was possible to compress the plan into a six-year period and to set its goal to nearly £100,000,000. By 1955 over £50,000,000[1] had already been spent on such enterprises as agricultural services, road systems, railway and harbour modernization, power and water supplies, while in the field of social service the beginning of a universal free primary education system had been initiated in the Colony and Ashanti, and health services had been extended. A detailed discussion of these developments will be reserved for the next chapter, but already it may be pointed out here that the government, by its conservative financial policy, was able to control the inflationary tendency which the high export price of cocoa might well have occasioned, to undertake an ambitious development programme, and at the same time to keep the cost of living at a steady rate. Nkrumah and his ministers thus showed great maturity when they could have easily fallen into the temptation —so common to young nations—to give in to the electorate's demand for a larger share of the cocoa profits and a more immediate taste of the fruits of prosperity.

Unfortunately, the handling of such large sums of money in the interests of the country opened the door to temptation, and it was not long before the opposition parties demanded that certain accusations of political corruption be investigated. In 1953 an investigating commission was appointed which found some evidence of misuse of funds, but which reported that 'allegations of general misconduct among those holding high office in the Gold Coast were not substantiated'.[2] Again in 1956 a more serious state of affairs was brought to light by the Jibowu Commission,[3] whose report stated that the Cocoa Purchasing Company had not only misused public funds but had done so for political purposes. It concluded that:

most of the irregularities which we have had to investigate would have been prevented if the Government had taken a firm stand to check and punish irregularities of the type complained about . . . as far back as 1953.[4]

The Cocoa Purchasing Company had been established by the government in 1952 as a statutory company to function as a subsidiary of the

[1] *G.C. An. Report, 1954*, pp. 8 and 170.
[2] *Report of the Commission of Enquiry into Mr. Braimah's Resignation and Allegations Arising Therefrom* (Accra, 1954).
[3] *Report of the Commission of Enquiry into the Affairs of the Cocoa Purchasing Company Limited, Accra, 1956* (known as the Jibowu Report).
[4] ibid., para. 214.

Cocoa Marketing Board. It was to buy cocoa for the Board and in 1953 it was made the Board's agent for issuing loans to cocoa farmers. The investigating committee further discovered that the Cocoa Purchasing Company was, in fact, controlled by the Convention People's Party and used 'for the purpose of winning adherents for the C.P.P.', giving loans out of government-provided funds mainly to party sympathizers.

Simultaneously with the issue of the Jibowu Report, the government published its own proposals for the future prevention of the irregularities in question, advising that the assembly be given a wider control over all public boards and statutory bodies.[1]

Another issue brought to the fore in the 1951-3 period was that of local government. The Coussey Committee had recognized, as has been seen, that the success of parliamentary government in the Gold Coast depended on a sound and democratic local government system. The type of local authority it recommended[2] carried with it a direct threat to not a few features of the traditional system, but since at that time the C.P.P. was not yet in power, little protest was then made. Besides, the middle-class *élite* who supported the Coussey Report expected to be in positions of authority when the new local organs were established and to co-operate with the chiefs in their functions. But with the C.P.P.'s success in the 1951 elections, it was that party's leaders who were to prepare and, more important still, to put the new ordinance in force.[3] The Bill they presented provided for councils in which two-thirds of the members would be chosen by popular vote and one-third would be appointed by the chiefs. The council chairman, chosen from among the elected members, would have the real power in local affairs. Once the Bill was published the chiefs and their supporters were quick to recognize that the new set-up would give the C.P.P. an opportunity to dominate local as well as national politics. Further, for most of the chiefs it also meant loss of revenue and influence and, indeed, of their very position as leaders of their people. Because of the vital issues involved, the Bill was strongly opposed by conservative opinion both within and without the assembly.[4] It was recognized that in the final analysis the

[1] G.C. Govt., Part 1, *Government Proposals in regard to the future constitution and control of Statutory Boards and Corporations in the Gold Coast*. (The Jibowu Report is Part 2 of this publication.) For comment on the Jibowu Report, see *West Africa* (8 and 15 September 1956).

[2] *Coussey Report*, Part III; Legislative Council, *Debates*, Issue No. 4 (1949), pp. 99-137.

[3] *Local Government Reform in Outline* (Accra, 1951); *Local Government Ordinance of 1951*, No. 29.

[4] Legislative Assembly, *Debates* (1951), Issue No. 4 (vol. 1), pp. 52-73, 93-121, 180-201, 219-45, 261-85, 302-30, 341-93. See also Apter, *Gold Coast in Transition*, Chapter 11.

issue at stake was whether local and regional authority in the Gold Coast was to be based on secular[1] or traditional authority.[2]

But there was nothing the conservatives could do about it. The C.P.P. majority ensured a safe passage for the Bill, and it became law in November 1951. It replaced the old native authorities by some 250 local and urban councils. The chief, who was to be council president, would preside—except in the Northern Territories—only on ceremonial occasions; power and the conduct of day-to-day business was to lie with the elected chairman and the council. The ordinance also allowed for some thirty-one district councils which would take the responsibility of wider areas. The Bill further required that every local council appoint a finance and staff committee and other committees if necessary. Councils were to be responsible for the good government of the area and were, in general, to provide for such local needs as minor roads, water supply, markets, certain education services, &c. Funds were to be obtained through rates, and the councils were required to levy an annual *per capita* basic rate. Further revenue was to be obtained from special rates, fees, and grants from the central government. In the Colony and Ashanti, the council could collect the revenues from the stool lands and could receive a share of this revenue by agreement with the stool concerned. In a word, the ordinance did away with the local authority system then in force and removed all administration from the old state councils, leaving them ceremonial functions only. The chief was to remain, the government declared, and was to be provided for, but by the new law the traditional character of local administration was to be discarded in favour of the popularly elected council.

Finally to supervise the new councils, the central government set up a Ministry of Local Government which would exercise its functions through government agents who would replace the district commissioner. The powers associated with the former office were, however, substantially diminished.

[1] The office of chief and other customary practices are considered to be partly sacred in origin and it is in this sense that the terms 'secular' and 'traditional' can be distinguished.

[2] Authorities on African administration consider that one of the most difficult problems of rapidly developing African areas is to discover the correct rôle of the chief—a rôle which will command the respect of both the educated, politically conscious younger generation and those who prefer the traditional ways of the past. Though the chief loses power as political advance takes place, if he has the respect of his people and keeps himself abreast of the times, there seems to be no reason why he should not continue to exercise much influence in rural areas. The villages, by and large, have as yet had little share in Ghana's developmental projects. If local councils and the chiefs co-operate, a tremendous work can be done to relieve the central government and to stimulate the people to self-help projects. *The Journal of African Administration* from time to time has articles on this problem of the chiefs.

By the end of 1954 most of the new councils had been organized, but the transition from the old system was not an easy one. In several areas opposition to the raising of funds by means of the annual rate led to severe rioting,[1] but the most serious difficulties besetting the new régime, besides the insufficiency of funds, were the lack of trained staff, the very poor quality of many of the councillors, and the grip of party politics in certain areas.[2] To remedy the staff problem, the government set up a school in Accra for the training of local government clerks,[3] and in 1954 inaugurated an intensive publicity campaign to create a more enlightened public opinion with regard to the new system.

In general it can be said that the local government reform was begun too late. If it had been started as soon as the Coussey Report had recommended it, political struggles would have been avoided and some provision could have been made for more harmonious co-operation between the traditional and elected members. Some few local authorities have been successful, but it remains to be seen whether, with experience, a more general success will obtain.

To turn again from local to central government. In March 1952, Nkrumah was accorded the title of Prime Minister—the first African in any British colonial territory to receive such an appointment. But the title did not carry with it any further measure of power, and Gold Coast public opinion, the Convention People's Party in particular, was pressing for further advance. When Mr. Oliver Lyttelton, the secretary of state for the colonies, visited the Gold Coast in 1952, Nkrumah took the opportunity to discuss the matter with him. Mr. Lyttelton intimated that the Colonial Office would be willing to consider proposals for further self-government if the chiefs and other groups in the Gold Coast were first given an opportunity to express their opinions. Accordingly, Nkrumah in October 1952, speaking in the legislative assembly, invited the territorial councils, political parties, and other groups to submit their views on certain specific questions regarding possible changes in the constitution. The response bore witness to keen public interest, and over 100 groups submitted memoranda. In addition the Prime Minister

[1] *G.C. An. Report, 1953*, pp. 6–7.

[2] *West Africa* has recently published three illuminating series of articles on the new ocal governments. See *West Africa* series entitled 'Local Government Democracy' by R. E. Wraith (September and October 1955); 'Local Government in Practice' by George Bennett (September 1954); and 'Local Government in Ghana' by M. E. Paul (September and October 1957); see also A. Hannigan, 'Local Government in the Gold Coast', *Journal of African Administration*, vol. VII (July 1955).

[3] E. B. S. Alton, 'Local Government Training School in the Gold Coast', *Journal of African Administration*, vol. IV, No. 3 (1952), p. 108; C. A. McLaren, 'Local Government Training in the Gold Coast', ibid., vol. IX, No. 2 (1957), pp. 63–71.

held meetings with the regional councils and with the opposition parties, and public opinion was thus given a wide opportunity to express itself. Several weeks before the opening of the July session of the legislative assembly the government published a White Paper containing its own proposals on the matter of self-government, together with those of the more important groups which had submitted reports.

The government proposals did not yet provide for complete independence. Nkrumah and his associates had learned by the experience of two years in office that the coveted independence should be requested of the British through constitutional channels rather than forced by unilateral action. Further, he and his party were now realistic enough to see that changes could not be rushed, that many administrative adjustments had yet to be made, and that the Africanization programme was not sufficiently advanced for the country to stand alone. What they suggested therefore in the 1953 proposals was, in fact, an interim constitution which would carry them through the present period of transition. The discussions which Nkrumah had held with the territorial councils had revealed, in addition, that many people felt that the chiefs and the traditional life of the Gold Coast were not being sufficiently respected and safeguarded. The 1953 reports submitted to the government by the territorial councils had all suggested in fact that arrangements for a second chamber be included in the new constitution. Those who favoured an upper house made up of chiefs argued that such a body would serve as a check on too hasty legislation, 'abolish the present uneasy relationship between traditional rulers and representative members'[1] in the single chamber, and enable the chiefs and elders to add their wisdom and experience to what many considered the irresponsible and immature policies of the party in power. There were, however, serious arguments against a bicameral legislature; among them the considerable expense, the danger of constant friction between the two houses; the risk of involving the chiefs in political controversy thereby weakening the very position that the upper house sought to preserve. In short, the suitability of a second house for the Gold Coast was held to be by no means certain; accordingly no provision was made for it in the 1954 constitution, although the government proposals laid it down that should there be a new demand it could be referred to a later assembly for re-examination.[2]

These proposals for the new constitution were published in June 1953;

---

[1] *Government's Proposals for Constitutional Reform, 1953*, para. 37.
[2] ibid., para. 42.

they having been accepted by the assembly and the British government, the new instrument came into force in April 1954.[1] It called for an all-African cabinet—from which the European ministers had been withdrawn—responsible for the internal government of the country. The legislative assembly of 104 members was to be chosen entirely by direct election.

Thenceforth the tie with Britain was tenuous—intentionally. The governor still kept certain reserve powers and was responsible for external affairs and defence, but the British government made it clear that it was retaining only the minimum powers and that this 1954 constitution represented the last stage before complete independence. To critics who expressed fears that the British government was allowing the Gold Coast to advance too fast towards independence, it was pointed out that Dr. Nkrumah's government had gained much experience during its three years in office, and that this growth of capacity to govern justified further constitutional advance.[2]

The first election under the new constitution was held on 15 June 1954, the country having been divided into 104 electoral districts. It is important to emphasize that this was the first time the Gold Coast people directly elected all members of the assembly, since the 1951 constitution had provided for indirect election in the Northern Territories and in the rural areas of the Colony and Ashanti. As in 1951, the Conventional People's Party won with a majority of 71 out of 104 seats. Shortly before the polling, a new party, the Northern People's Party (N.P.P.), had been organized in the Northern Territories with a programme aimed at safeguarding Northern culture and at securing for the North 'a progressively increasing share in the administrative and other services of the country'.[3] It was frankly a regional party, born of fear of the anti-traditional and over-centralized activities of the C.P.P., and holding the development of its own backward area to be more pressing than the winning of immediate self-government. One of its assembly members was reported as saying 'we are proud of our chiefs and these C.P.P. boys show them no respect'.[4]

The other opposition groups which contested the 1954 election were: the Ghana Congress Party which had been the leading opposition party under the 1951 constitution and which represented the conservative

---

[1] *Despatches on the Gold Coast Government's Proposals for Constitutional Reform, 1954*, Colonial No. 302.
[2] British Information Services; *Background Note 404*, 3 April 1954.
[3] *West Africa* (8 and 15 May 1954).
[4] Quoted by Apter, *Gold Coast in Transition*, p. 228.

position of the chiefs and older intelligentsia which had predominated in the Gold Coast under indirect rule; the Moslem Association Party (M.A.P.);[1] and the Togoland Congress Party (T.C.P.).[2] The opposition groups were defeated in the election, winning only 33 seats as compared with the 71 controlled by the C.P.P. The voting results were as follows: Northern People's Party, 12 (a surprising success to win 12 seats out of 17 since it was so recently organized); Togoland Congress Party, 2; Ghana Congress Party, 1; Moslem Association, 1; Anlo Youth Organization, 1; Independents, 16. Of the registered electors 58 per cent voted. To sum up: of all votes cast, the C.P.P. received 391,817 and the others all together 314,903.[3] The strength of the latter vote was, it should be noted, significant in view of the stronger opposition to the C.P.P., which was to develop in the future.[4] The C.P.P. had also to contend with a number of rebels, especially in Ashanti, who were eventually expelled for opposing official C.P.P. candidates.[5]

In the former assembly under the 1951 constitution, most opposition members had supported the Ghana Congress Party with which the

---

[1] The Moslem Association was founded shortly before the 1954 elections. It was based on religious, and to some extent, regional interests since the largest groups of Gold Coast Muslims were to be found in the Northern Territories and Ashanti.

[2] The Togoland Congress Party was organized in 1951 with a view to campaigning for the unification of British and French Togoland. For further discussion, see p. 192.

[3] *G.C. An. Report, 1954*, p. 7.

[4] Bennett, George, 'The Gold Coast General Election of 1954', in *Parliamentary Affairs*, vol. VII (1954) No. 4 has a detailed account of the election.

[5] For a detailed treatment of the organization and functioning of the C.P.P., see Apter, *Gold Coast in Transition*, Ch. 10. It can be indicated briefly here that it was at first a mass political party—a sort of mixture of a Tammany machine and a radical evangelical movement, with Nkrumah as its symbol and binding force. He is the life chairman of the party and up to the date of writing no one approaches him in power and influence. The figures closest to him in public esteem are Kojo Botsio, who has held a number of ministries and is now Minister of Economic Affairs, and K. A. Gbedemah, who has been an outstandingly successful Minister of Finance since 1954. To quote Apter, 'These two are in somewhat "jealous" competition for the position of second-in-command. Apparently, as observed both in interview and from a wide range of local experience, Botsio is a close confidante of Nkrumah, but Gbedemah is the organizational leader under Nkrumah. Worthy of some note is the fact that Gbedemah, the least ideologically oriented, is considered ambitious, and loyal to the groups who worked with him when Nkrumah was in jail and when the party was first effectively organized. Most of these groups consist of the extreme left-wing of the party. On the other hand, Botsio, considered far more left-wing than Gbedemah, does not seem to have a large personal following in the party, but rather receives his support from Nkrumah as a kind of ideological mentor of the party. There is little doubt that only the presence of Nkrumah has kept the left-wing from exerting overt and hasty actions, and a controversy between Gbedemah and Botsio from breaking out openly.' Ibid., p. 206.

For the constitution of the C.P.P. which gives the aims of the party and an outline of its organization, see Nkrumah, *Ghana*, Appendix A. Developments in Ghana since independence have, of course, affected the party. See, for example, *The Times* (16 December, 1957); *Africa, Special Report* (November 1957 and March 1958).

chiefs—representing the territorial councils—often identified themselves. In the 1954 assembly however, the Ghana Congress Party
counted but one member, Dr. Busia; the opposition strength now lay
with the Northern People's Party. At first Nkrumah was unwilling to
recognize a party organized on a regional basis as an official opposition.
He feared such recognition would establish a precedent and encourage
regionalism. Mr. S. D. Dombo, Douri-na, chairman of the Northern
People's Party, however, appealed to the speaker of the assembly who
ruled that he should be recognized as official opposition leader. As such
he was entitled to receive a salary.

In September 1954 a new political group, the National Liberation
Movement (N.L.M.), emerged in Ashanti. Dissatisfaction with C.P.P.
policy was brought to a head by an economic issue—the government's
decision to raise the export duty on cocoa, while at the same time it
froze the price paid to the farmer at 72 shillings a load, even though the
world price was sharply increasing.[1] The extra revenue thus gained was
to be applied to general development. While some of the Ashanti farmers
who own the richest cocoa lands in the country accepted the government
policy, others objected, claiming that a larger share of the added revenue
should be apportioned to them, instead of the sum being applied to
general needs. It was not easy for the farmers to see matters in terms of
an ultimate goal—whereas it was precisely with a view to giving both
Ashanti and the whole nation a more balanced and soundly based
development that the government, fearing inflation, determined to
concentrate on capital expenditure.[2]

But the question of the cocoa price before long receded in importance
as the discussion widened to embrace more fundamental issues. In a few
weeks the National Liberation Movement[3] was demanding a federal
form of government which would give autonomy to the several regions,
considerable control over their own finances; in short, lessen dependence
on Accra. It also demanded a bicameral legislature in order that the
chiefs and more conservative members of the community might be in
a position to exercise some influence in the national government and
thus check what the opposition termed 'the creeping dictatorship' of the
South. Eventually some support for the N.L.M. was won from the

[1] For the question of the cocoa price set by the Cocoa Marketing Board, see p. 204.
[2] See P. T. Bauer, *West African Trade: A Study of Competition, Oligopoly and Monopoly in a Changing Economy* (Cambridge, 1954) for a criticism of this view of the
benefits of price fixing.
[3] The National Liberation Movement was started by Baffuor Atto, the Asantehene's
Chief Linguist. In October 1957 the N.L.M. and other opposition parties in Ghana
merged under the leadership of K. A. Busia and took the name of United Party.

Northern Territories and Togoland to whom the idea of regional liberty
was attractive.

In October 1954 the movement took on a far more serious aspect when
the Asantehene, who commanded wide respect throughout Ashanti, and
fifty paramount and divisional chiefs of the Asanteman Council gave the
movement their approval and signed a petition to the Queen of England
asking for a commission of inquiry into the question of a federal form
of government for the Gold Coast. In his reply of January 1955, the
secretary of state for the colonies observed that the 'use of an outside
body like a Royal Commission to weigh the various points of view could
only be taken to mean that the people of the Gold Coast were unable
to settle their own affairs',[1] and that a failure to resolve the question
peacefully among themselves would necessarily retard their progress
towards independence.

In the meantime violent clashes had broken out in and around Kumasi
between the supporters of the N.L.M. and the C.P.P. Attempts at
bombings and several political murders ensued. This violence was to
continue throughout the years of increasing disagreement which lay
ahead. The Gold Coast government appears to have been slow to
recognize the seriousness of the situation. Looking back from the
vantage-point of time, it seems clear that its unwillingness to give a
generous consideration to the opposition viewpoint at an early date only
deepened the rift between the N.L.M. and the C.P.P. and gave the
former time to draw malcontents into its camp. Perhaps if Nkrumah
had gone to Ashanti in the first weeks of manifest discontent and had
then made the offers of increased regional power to which he later
agreed, he might have prevented the federal movement. At any rate,
late in 1954, the government finally made an attempt at reconciliation
when several C.P.P. members of the assembly invited the N.L.M.
leaders to a round-table conference. The invitation, however, was
rejected on the ground that it was not official, whereupon, on 30 December, Nkrumah took up the matter on a radio broadcast[2] in which he
explained the government's position with reference to a federal constitution. He pointed out that the present constitution for a unitary state
rested on a mandate of the people as expressed in national elections, and
that the Gold Coast was too small an area to support four federated
governments. With regard to a second chamber for chiefs, he still
believed that this question should not be decided until after independence for fear of delaying the achievement of that goal. He concluded

[1] *Gold Coast Weekly Review* (12 January 1955).   [2] ibid.

his broadcast with an official invitation to the N.L.M. leaders to confer with the government on the subject of regional devolution, but the invitation was again refused.

It is important to stress the fact that there was much bitterness between the two groups. Many of the N.L.M. leaders were dissident C.P.P. members. In addition they considered that the Ashanti assembly members were not truly representative of that area, but their request for a re-election had been refused by the Nkrumah government.

In April 1955 the government made another attempt at settlement by appointing a select committee composed of members of the national assembly to discuss the issue, but the opposition members pointed out —as they were to do again in the future—that it was useless to sit on committees or join conferences since the C.P.P. so planned them that their own party would always have the majority representation.

In order to break the deadlock, the government now invited Sir Frederick Bourne to come out from England as a constitutional adviser and requested him to make a detailed study of means whereby additional power might be given to the regions, in a manner less drastic than those proposed by the federalists. Sir Frederick had had great experience in constitutional matters in India and Pakistan, and it did not take him long to acquire a wide understanding of the situation and a deep affection for the people of the Gold Coast. Unfortunately the leaders of the N.L.M. and the Asanteman Council did not take part in any of the consultations, for shortly after Sir Frederick Bourne's arrival the government had passed a Bill[1] allowing lesser chiefs to appeal to the governor-in-council in traditional law disputes rather than to the Asanteman Council. This Bill the N.L.M. leaders considered a direct attack on traditional usages and, as such, a proof that the government was not sincere in its offers to consider the N.L.M. position.[2]

Sir Frederick Bourne's report[3] advised against federation as being unsuitable for so small a country, but recommended a diffusion of power to regional assemblies which would have large responsibility for

[1] State Councils (Ashanti) Amendment, 1955. Nkrumah states in *Ghana*, p. 240, that the purpose of the bill was to protect those C.P.P. chiefs who had been destooled for refusing to support the N.L.M.

[2] Mr. Amponsah of the N.L.M. later explained this action in the assembly. 'The Opposition agreed to meet Sir Frederick Bourne when he arrived. But as *The Times* of London put it: "The very Government that invited Sir Frederick Bourne chose to bedevil the very issue at the very moment the Constitutional Expert was about to begin his work!" And so the Government made it impossible for the Opposition to meet Sir Frederick Bourne.' Legislative Assembly, *Debates*, November 1956, col. 93.

[3] *Report of the Constitutional Adviser* [Bourne Report] (Accra, 1955).

local matters and which would receive grants-in-aid from the central government. He held that the chiefs still had an important part to play in local government, that their position should be safeguarded, and their experience utilized for the general good of the regions. Matters concerned with their traditional functions should not be brought before the legislative assembly until the appropriate council of chiefs had been consulted.

While the N.L.M. considered the Bourne suggestions to be in harmony with their policy, they did not think the report went far enough because, among other things, the regional assemblies were merely consultative and had neither legislative nor tax powers. They therefore continued to demand a constituent assembly as the only means of securing their goal. On his side, the Prime Minister then called an inter-party conference at Achimota to consider the Bourne Report and related matters. But the N.L.M. and Asanteman Council still refused to attend, giving among their principal reasons the fact that the government had invited to the conference

bodies which did not exist and which had been created by the party in power in order that they might have majority support at that Conference . . . Some of those bodies were the Moslem Council and the Brong/Kyempen Council; these bodies did not exist either in law or in fact . . . The Government also invited rival bodies and left out those which did not agree with the Government.[1]

The Achimota Conference, after a month's session, adjourned on 16 March. It had discussed in detail the practical application of the Bourne proposals to the Gold Coast situation, indicating its general acceptance of his report, and had also recommended a House of Chiefs for each region to discuss social and cultural legislation.[2]

The refusal of the N.L.M. to co-operate with the Achimota Conference found the Prime Minister in a difficult position. Many sections of public opinion, especially his own C.P.P. followers, were now demanding that the period of preparation based on the interim constitution of 1954 should be brought to a close and that the Gold Coast ask the British for a definite date for independence. It had been with the hope of securing all-party approval for a unitary constitution in an independent Gold Coast that he had called the Achimota Conference. With the failure to secure this unanimity, he now decided to prepare a White

[1] Legislative Assembly, *Debates* (November 1956), col. 93–94.
[2] *Report of the Achimota Conference* (Accra, 1956).

Paper on his constitutional proposals and have it debated in the assembly. The paper which was published on 20 April 1956 set out the government's plans for an early achievement of independence for the Gold Coast under the name 'Ghana'.[1] The paper stated that this change in status probably could be made by certain modifications in the existing constitution and the adaptation of conventions which had come into use in the United Kingdom. With reference to regional government, it announced its general agreement with the Achimota application of the Bourne Report.

But with the publication of these April proposals, the constitutional dispute became even more serious for the Asanteman Council now announced that, while it welcomed independence which was not a constitutional issue, the matter of a unitary or federal form of government must be settled before the departure of the British. Fear that this departure would leave Ashanti and the Northern Territories under the control of southern politicians tended to stiffen the opposition's determination that satisfactory safeguards would be set up before it was too late.[2]

The issue was now up to the British government for obviously it could not accept the Gold Coast government's independence proposals in view of so fundamental a difference of opinion as to what form the new constitution should take. The only solution seemed to be a general election, even though the existing assembly had still two years to run. In a statement to the House of Commons on 11 May 1956 the secretary of state for the colonies, Mr. Lennox Boyd, announced that

because of the failure to resolve the constitutional dispute we can achieve our common aim of the early independence of that country within the Commonwealth in one way and in one way alone; that is, to demonstrate to the world that the peoples of the Gold Coast have had a full and free opportunity to consider their constitution and to express their views on it in a general election.[3]

He added that if the election resulted in a reasonable majority supporting the independence proposals, he would set a 'firm date' for this event. As for Ghana's membership in the Commonwealth, that was not a matter for the British government alone, but for all the existing members of the Commonwealth to decide.

The actual elections were delayed until after May 1956 because of the

[1] *Constitutional Proposals for Gold Coast Independence* (Accra, 1956).
[2] *West Africa* (12 May 1956).
[3] *Parliamentary Debates*, Commons, vol. DLII, col. 1557.

Togoland plebiscite—scheduled for 9 May—by which the inhabitants of that area were to choose between integration with an independent Gold Coast or the continuance of the United Nations trusteeship. To summarize briefly Togoland events since 1952:[1] in that year the Gold Coast government had set up the Trans-Volta-Togoland region (T.V.T.) as one of its administrative divisions. The government had also taken substantial measures to see that the people of Togoland participated with those of the Gold Coast in every level of government under the increased representation provided by the 1951 and 1954 constitutions. Such changes had affected the various political groups. A large number of Ewes in both Togoland and the Trans-Volta area were attracted by the dynamic programme of the Convention People's Party, which used its strong position to gain support for the 'integration' of British Togoland with the Gold Coast when it should become independent. At the same time the Togoland Congress Party (T.C.P.) was advocating the unification of British and French Togoland as an independent state. The object of this party had always been the reunification of the Ewe tribe, split between British and French Togoland, and they feared that, if British Togoland were united with Ghana, France would annex French Togoland, and the Ewes would be permanently divided. This policy was strongly supported by those in South Togo who resented the C.P.P. methods as tending to excessive centralization of power at Accra in contrast to a federal system which would have assured Togoland a fuller share in political activities.[2] (In the Northern Territories, on the other hand, the N.P.P.—although opposed to the C.P.P. on domestic issues—supported it on the integration question because of the close cultural and historic bonds between the Northern Territories and north Togoland.) A new phase opened in Togoland history as the Gold Coast approached more closely to independence through the inauguration of the 1954 constitution. In June of that year the British government informed the United Nations that it would not be in a position to administer the Togoland trusteeship after the Gold Coast had become independent. While the majority of the United Nations members had previously opposed integration, the new situation led them to recognize that such a move would not mean 'colonial annexation', but rather the

---

[1] See p. 111 for an account of Togoland in the period before 1952.

[2] It is necessary to point out that the groups which supported the unification of British and French Togoland apparently had in mind an ultimate union of some kind with the Gold Coast. They seem to have been seeking an independent state only temporarily in order to be in a better bargaining position to demand a federal form of government before agreeing to join the Gold Coast.

sharing of Togoland in an independent African government. The General Assembly therefore agreed in December 1955[1] to a British Togoland plebiscite to determine whether the population preferred (1) integration with the Gold Coast after its independence or (2) the establishment of British Togoland as a separate entity from the Gold Coast pending the ultimate determination of its political future.[2]

The plebiscite which was held on 9 May 1956 under United Nations auspices resulted in an overall majority of 58 per cent for the integration of Togoland with the Gold Coast. (In south Togoland, however, where the Togoland Congress Party was organized, 55 per cent voted against integration.) To conclude the account of the Togoland issue, though somewhat ahead of our narrative, the United Nations General Assembly in December 1956, in view of the plebiscite result, gave its approval to the union of Togoland with the Gold Coast as soon as the latter became independent.[3]

After the Togoland problem was settled, the crucial general election—required by Mr. Lennox Boyd to ascertain if the Nkrumah independence proposals were supported by a reasonable majority—was announced for 12 and 17 July 1956. Shortly before the polling, Dr. Busia was persuaded to accept the parliamentary leadership of the N.L.M. and its allies.[4] Dr. Busia comes from the royal house of Wenchi, where his brother is paramount chief.[5] As he is interested in scholarship rather than in politics, it appears to have been a sense of civic need which led him to take an active part in political affairs. In 1951 he was the Ashanti Confederacy representative and again in 1954 he was elected, this time by the Wenchi constituency, as a representative of the Ghana Congress Party, which later merged with the National Liberation Movement.

The N.L.M. seemed at first to have no definite party policy beyond

[1] United Nations General Assembly Resolution, 944 (X) of December 1955. This action was unique in the annals of the United Nations for British Togoland was the first territory to achieve self-government—as had been envisaged by the United Nations Charter, article 76.

[2] See James S. Coleman, 'Togoland', *International Conciliation*, No. 509 (September 1956) for a detailed account of the Togoland problem from 1946 to 1956.

[3] United Nations General Assembly Resolution, 425 of December 1956.

[4] *West Africa* (2 and 9 June 1956). S. D. Dombo of the N.P.P. was appointed deputy opposition leader.

[5] Dr. Busia was born in 1913 and educated at Mfantsipim, Wesley College and Achimota. He later went to Oxford as an Achimota scholar where he was elected Carnegie Research fellow. In 1941–42 he did field work in Ashanti for his thesis which was later expanded into the book *The Position of the Chief in the Modern Political System of Ashanti*. After several years experience as an Assistant District Commissioner in the Gold Coast, he returned to Oxford for his doctorate. In 1949 he was appointed lecturer in African Studies at the Gold Coast University College and Head of the Department of Sociology in 1951, with the title of Professor in 1954.

a deep distrust of the C.P.P. so that the movement was a sort of 'catch-all' for various persons and groups who were dissatisfied with government policy—traditionalists, intellectuals, farmers discontented with the cocoa price, Muslim groups,[1] and C.P.P. rebels. But the most serious opposition eventually came from the Asanteman Council. Deprived of their former influence by the 1954 constitution and by the new form of local government, many of the chiefs were embittered—sensing that the country was coming under the control of the Convention People's Party and doomed to be a prey to the irresponsibility, the corruption, the juggling of party politics, and anti-traditional spirit they associated with it.

Nor was the C.P.P. distrusted by the chiefs only. Antagonism was developing in the various regions, based on the conflict between sectional and national interests. Ashanti, it will be remembered, was once a highly organized, militaristic state often at war with the South, and the fiery spirit of the past had been revived, to some extent, by the fear that an independent Gold Coast would mean domination from the coastal area. As Dr. Busia wrote:

> Any constitution which fails to recognize the identity of the Ashanti nation will arouse violent feelings against it. The demand for a federal union arises from this consideration. It is no secret that the strength of feeling is so strong that for nearly two years the Prime Minister of the Gold Coast has not visited Ashanti.[2]

Feeling also ran high in the Northern Territories. Far less developed than the South, its leaders believed it should receive special consideration in order that it come to approximate more closely the general level of progress found in the Colony and Ashanti. On the other hand, tribal loyalties were still strong and the conservative chiefs looked askance at the possibility of Southern control. They clung to the treaties of friendship, trade, and protection which former chiefs had signed in the late nineteenth century with the representatives of Queen Victoria.[3] They would have preferred to remain British 'protected persons' and only agreed to accept independence on condition that the British government see to it that their regional rights be strongly protected by the new constitution.[4]

Yet there was much to be said in favour of a unitary constitution for

---

[1] The Muslims formed the Moslem Association Party (M.A.P.) in 1954 and allied themselves with the N.L.M.   [2] From a letter to *The Times* (18 September 1956).
        [3] See Chapter 7.   [4] Letter to *The Times* (18 September 1956).

the Gold Coast, as opposed to the federal union proposed by the N.L.M. Nkrumah had pointed out constantly in his speeches and writings[1] the importance of fostering a spirit of national consciousness in a newly emergent country, and regional nationalism could not but hinder such a development. The experience of Nigeria whose national movement had been split by regional rivalries, he feared, would be repeated in the Gold Coast. The country was not only too small, with less than five million inhabitants, to divide into separate states; it was too poor in trained personnel to staff four different governments. Holding such views it appeared imperative to Nkrumah to set up a strong government before independence became a fact in order to forestall the conflict between North and South and East and West which was sure to ensue after the British administration no longer held power in the country.

In addition it should be recalled that the conflict between national and sectional interests was complicated by the closely related disagreement as to the type of government best suited to the Gold Coast. The C.P.P. stood for a modern, highly concentrated parliamentary state and as a consequence for reducing the position of the chiefs whom they regarded as remnants of an outmoded feudalism; while the opposition groups were inclined, more or less consciously, to protest against excessive centralization and to favour that diffusion of power, and that respect for traditional institutions which have characterized conservative bodies at all times and in all parts of the world. There is danger, of course, in placing the above groups into the neat categories familiar to political scientists. Dr. Busia warns that such labels as 'right wing' and 'left wing' are inappropriate in the Gold Coast where differences are

mainly in internal policies, such as the approach to the reorganization of local government, the position of the chiefs, the rate of development of a particular region, behaviour and interpersonal relations, or the details of the manner of implementation of plans of development.[2]

Disagreements notwithstanding, the C.P.P. and the N.L.M.—the two main groups in Gold Coast politics—did not seem to hold out for policies which are absolutely irreconcilable. It would be possible, given political wisdom, to adapt traditional institutions to modern requirements and so integrate African and Western life. Nationalism at its best has room for,

[1] See for example K. Nkrumah, *Ghana*, chapters 19 and 21 and his speeches in the assembly.
[2] K. A. Busia, 'The Gold Coast and Nigeria on the Road to Self-Government', *Africa Today*, edited by C. Grove Haines (Baltimore, 1955), p. 298.

indeed is enriched by, regional differences in the form of various ancient customs and institutions, however much in the interest of a common fatherland, it must enforce, by means of a centralized government that unity of purpose and procedure which make for a common patriotism. But to weld together into a harmonious whole regional and national purposes is, in the nature of things, a slow process and the Gold Coast leaders, in mid-1956, were in no frame of mind for the patience, tolerance, and wise foresightedness indispensable to a satisfactory settlement of the constitutional crisis. Two years of strife among a people with scant experience of modern government and little practice of the restraints implied in parliamentary procedures had so inflamed passions and deepened fears that it was becoming increasingly difficult for each party to enter into the other's point of view. Nevertheless some means of agreement had to be found, and it was hoped that the general elections, required by the British government before the date of independence was set, would clear the atmosphere. They were held on 12 and 17 July 1956 and resulted in a larger majority for the C.P.P. than many had expected. It won all 44 seats in the Colony; 8 out of 21 in Ashanti; 8 out of 13 in Trans-Volta Togoland; and 11 out of 26 in the Northern Territories. Of the opposition groups, the Northern People's Party won 15 seats; the National Liberation Movement, 12; the Togoland Congress Party, 2; the Moslem Association Party, 1; the Federation of Youth Organizations, 2; and Independents, 2. Since one Independent later joined the C.P.P., that party controlled 72 seats in all, while those of the combined opposition groups numbered 32.

The election results were of extreme significance in that they satisfied the British government's requirement that a 'reasonable majority' must agree on the form of Ghana's constitution before an actual independence date would be set. Although the C.P.P. had won a majority only in the Colony and Trans-Volta Togoland, the Accra government considered its all-over total of 72 seats against 32 as decisive, and in August 1956 Nkrumah introduced the necessary motion in the assembly, asking the British government to enact the proper legislation for the independence of Ghana.[1] The motion was approved by 72 in favour; no votes were cast against it, since the opposition was not in attendance at the debate. The British government announced in September that it considered the election results as sufficient evidence of a reasonable majority and that 'subject to parliamentary approval, Her Majesty's Government intends that Independence should come about on March 6, 1957'.[2]

[1] *Gold Coast Weekly* (15 August 1956).   [2] ibid. (26 September 1956).

But many difficulties still stood in the way, since the opposition leaders, while declaring that they welcomed independence, continued to insist on the constitutional safeguards they considered essential for the protection of the regions. Their determination had been recently strengthened by the publication of the Jibowu Report[1] which, as has been seen, revealed the existence of serious corruption and malpractice among several C.P.P. members of the Cocoa Purchasing Company staff.

In August the opposition had sent a delegation to London[2] to petition again for a federal form of government, but when, on 15 September, the colonial secretary announced the exact date for independence, the opposition leaders withdrew their petition for a federation and demanded only that adequate safeguards be written into the constitution before 6 March 1957. Busia, who was with the London delegation, summed up their aim as 'an agreed Constitution that safeguards the minority rights of the Northern Territories, respects the identity of the Ashanti nation, provides for an independent judiciary, and secures the legal freedom of every citizen'.[3]

In October, Nkrumah made another attempt to get the opposition to accept his constitutional plans by holding a series of discussions outside the assembly at which representatives of the four territorial councils were also consulted.[4] But, in spite of the discussions, the government proposals as published in the November White Paper[5] differed only in minor matters from previous plans and revealed that Nkrumah had actually agreed to none of the opposition's key demands. These demands, meant to preserve an independent Ghana from the possible dictatorship of a single chamber government, were as follows: a second chamber for chiefs; a council of state formed of the Prime Minister, the leader of the opposition, the Attorney-General, and the heads of the four regions which should advise the Governor-General on the exercise of his prerogative powers on the public service and judicial appointments, and should act as a final court of appeal on local constitutional matters; increased powers for the regional assemblies; and further safeguards to prevent any unduly easy amendment of the constitution.

[1] See p. 180.
[2] *West Africa* (15 September 1956).
[3] Busia in a letter to *The Times* (22 September 1956).
[4] *Gold Coast Weekly* (31 October and 7 November 1956).
[5] *The Government's Revised Constitutional Proposals for Gold Coast Independence* (Accra, 1956). See also speech delivered by the Prime Minister in the Legislative Assembly, 12 November 1956 reprinted as Supplement to *Gold Coast Today* (5 December 1956).

Nkrumah's November proposals, in spite of their having been rejected by the opposition, were submitted to the assembly on 15 November 1956 and passed by a vote of 70 to 25. They were then presented to the British government as a foundation for the new Ghana constitution.[1] Thereupon the constitutional dispute reached its climax as the N.L.M. and the N.P.P. sent a joint resolution to London threatening to secede from the new state of Ghana.[2] With Dr. Nkrumah on the one hand and the opposition on the other hand refusing to yield in any respect almost on the very eve of independence, it looked as if civil strife might accompany or even delay the birth of the new nation. In the end the wisdom and statesmanship of Mr. Lennox Boyd, the secretary of state for the colonies, saved the situation.[3] Together with Sir Charles Arden-Clarke, he made a last effort to adjust differences. At the end of January 1957, interrupting the tour of Africa upon which he was engaged, he visited the Gold Coast, and having given a full hearing to the spokesmen of both the N.L.M. and the C.P.P. he led each party to face the fact, finally, that their differences notwithstanding, there was in reality unanimity of opinion as to what they desired for Ghana. Concluding his parting speech, he said:

I . . . am confident that, given goodwill and trust on all sides, your contrasting political threads can be closely and lastingly woven together, like one of your beautiful Kente Cloths into a rich and colourful pattern of independent nationhood.[4]

While each party yielded on certain points, in the interest of the whole country, it was the government party that made the greatest concessions. On the face of it Nkrumah, Botsio, and Gbedemah took no small risk in agreeing to certain modifications in the proposed constitution in view of the fact that the new provisions were not at all popular with their party. On their side the opposition likewise made concessions, but they received substantial safeguards as is indicated by Dr. Busia's remark

[1] The Ghana Independence Bill which was passed by the House of Commons, 18 December 1956, was merely an enabling bill conferring on Ghana the power necessary to have the status of an independent country and therefore clearing the way for the British Government to grant her a constitution as a sovereign state. See *G.C. Weekly Review Supplement* (26 December 1956).

[2] *West Africa* (24 November and December 1956). The secession movement was supported by the Asanteman Council but not by Dr. Busia.

[3] Sir Gordon Hadow who was acting governor during the most trying weeks of the secession threat also deserves a place of honour among those who helped solve the constitutional crisis. He had long lived with the Ashanti, and therefore understood their viewpoint.

[4] *Gold Coast Weekly Review* (6 February 1957).

that they had made it very difficult for anyone to establish a dictatorship in the Gold Coast.

The final draft of the constitution, while maintaining the unitary state, conceded a greater measure of power to the several regions, and, above all, tried to protect the constitution by making amendments to certain basic clauses dependent not merely on a two-thirds vote of the entire national assembly but on the agreement of two-thirds of the regional assemblies. In his explanatory White Paper[1] Mr. Lennox Boyd noted that the amended constitution now offered 'reasonable safeguards against abuse, and a fair and workmanlike foundation on which to build nationhood within the Commonwealth'.

The new constitution, which had been born with so much travail, was signed by Her Majesty the Queen, in council on 22 February 1957.[2] It provides for a system of government broadly similar to that of other commonwealth states.[3]

Executive and Legislative Power: Executive power is vested in the Queen as represented by a Governor-General in Ghana. There will be a Cabinet of Ministers, being members of Parliament, who will be charged with the general government of Ghana and who will be collectively responsible to Parliament. Ministers will be appointed and removed on the advice of the Prime Minister. The Governor-General must terminate the Prime Minister's appointment if the National Assembly passes a motion of no confidence in his Government, unless within three days of such a motion the Prime Minister decides on dissolution of the National Assembly.

Supreme legislative power will be vested in Parliament. The Assembly will have a Speaker and 104 members. Its maximum life is to be increased from four years, as at present, to five years. Members are elected by universal adult suffrage and secret ballot.

Public Service and Judiciary: A Public Service Commission will

[1] *Proposed Constitution of Ghana*, Cmd. 71, 1957. The Ghana Assembly has since made constitutional change dependent merely upon a simple majority vote.

[2] *The Ghana (Constitution) Order in Council, 1957*, Statutory Instruments 1957 published in supplement to *Gold Coast Gazette*, no. 13, Accra, 1957.

[3] The 1959 constitution made the position of the sovereign in Ghana, as in the United Kingdom, that of a constitutional monarch dependent for her policies upon the Government of the day—the Ministry which commands a majority in the national assembly. A Governor-General was to be the Queen's representative in Ghana as in other Commonwealth countries. Sir Charles Arden-Clarke held this position until May 1957, when he was replaced by the Earl of Listowel, a Labour peer. Since 1959, however, there has been discussion of changing Ghana's form of government to that of a republic, though still remaining within the Commonwealth. Ghana's position would then be somewhat like that of India.

continue to advise the Governor-General on the appointment of public officers, except that in a limited class of posts, the Governor-General will act on the advice of the Prime Minister.

The Judicial Service Commission will have similar functions in connexion with the judiciary. The Chief Justice and Justices of Appeal will be appointed on the advice of the Prime Minister, and Puisne Judges and other judicial officers will be appointed on the advice of the Judicial Service Commission. Judges may be removed by a two-thirds vote of the whole National Assembly.

The Regions: Ghana will be divided into five regions: Eastern, Western, Trans-Volta Togoland, Ashanti, and Northern, the boundaries of which shall not be altered except with the consent of the regions concerned. A Regional Assembly will be established in each region with functions and powers relating to local government, agriculture, animal health and forestry, communications, medical and health services, public works, town and country planning, housing, police, education and such other matters as the Parliament of Ghana may determine. The maximum life of a Regional Assembly is three years. Details of the composition and powers of the Assemblies are to be worked out by a regional constitutional commission which will be appointed as soon as possible. (Meanwhile Interim Assemblies will be formed consisting of the members of parliament for each region.)

Houses of Chiefs: The constitution guarantees the office of Chief in Ghana as existing by customary law and usage. A House of Chiefs will be established by Act of Parliament in each Region. There will be a head of each Region; in Ashanti it will be the Asantehene, and in the other Regions a person chosen by the House of Chiefs. The constitution contains provision for dealing with appeals from traditional councils in matters of a local constitutional nature such as the election, installation, or deposition of any Chief.

Appeals from State Councils will be made to the House of Chiefs of the Region concerned, who will be obliged to refer the appeal to an Appeal Commissioner appointed for the Judicial Service Commission. The ultimate decision on appeals will be with the Appeal Commissioner.

When any Bill affecting the traditional functions or privileges of a Chief is introduced into the National Assembly, the Speaker must refer it to the House of Chiefs of the region in which the Chief exercises his functions and no motion can be moved for the second reading of the Bill until three months after its introduction into the National Assembly.

Amendment of the Constitution: Any Bill to amend the Constitution must be passed by a two-thirds majority of the whole National Assembly; amendments to certain basic clauses, including those concerning the public service, the regions, the Houses of Chiefs, elections, suffrage, racial discrimination and freedom of conscience, require in addition the prior consent of two-thirds of the Regional Assemblies. Any Bill to abolish a Regional Assembly or diminish its powers requires the consent of the region concerned.

The final step immediately preceding independence was taken when the British Prime Minister announced in the House of Commons on 21 February 1957 that all the Commonwealth Prime Ministers had agreed that Ghana should be recognized on 6 March as a full member of the Commonwealth.[1] After this announcement and the publication of the new constitution on 22 February, there was relative peace in the Gold Coast and the opposition leaders agreed to take part in the independence celebrations.

Before ending this survey, a brief account is in order tracing the economic and social developments of the 1946–57 period. But first a word about Independence Day. The festivities brought to Ghana the greatest international gathering that West Africa had ever seen, with representatives of over seventy nations sharing in the solemnity of the day. To all it was a deeply significant occasion and to none more so than to those men and women of both races who had toiled and co-operated to bring about this day when an African people could at last have the full and final responsibility for their own nation. To Sir Charles Arden-Clarke in his address to the country it marked 'the culminating point in a memorable partnership between you and those of us who have come from the United Kingdom and other parts of the Commonwealth to help you create the new Ghana'.[2]

To Busia, leader of the opposition, it was a fitting occasion to recall Ghana's debt to Great Britain. He concluded:

We have also benefited from British administration and law to which we owe our conception of nationhood, democracy and individual freedom. . . . To the people of Britain and to the Queen we would say again simply but with heart-felt sincerity, thank you; we are glad that our ties are to continue in the domain where human ties are most enduring—in the devotion and goodwill of the human heart freely given and reciprocated.[3]

[1] *Parliamentary Debates*, Commons (21 February 1957), vol. DLXV, col. 605.
[2] *Ghana Weekly Review* (6 March 1957).
[3] *Journal of the Parliaments of the Commonwealth*, vol. XXXVIII (April 1957).

To Nkrumah above all, it was a deeply significant event. On the eve of Independence Day, at the last meeting of the old legislative assembly he had made an important speech in which he outlined the policy which the new state of Ghana would pursue in domestic and foreign affairs. On Independence Day itself, at the opening of the Ghana Parliament, he spoke movingly of the new nation and then, looking beyond Ghana to the influence which its freedom would have on the rest of Africa he reminded his fellow citizens that:

we have a duty to prove to the world that Africans can conduct their own affairs with efficiency and tolerance and through the exercise of democracy. We must set an example to all Africa.[1]

[1] *Ghana Weekly Review* (6 March 1957).

CHAPTER XI

ECONOMIC AND SOCIAL PROGRESS
IN THE POST-WAR ERA

Ghana entered upon her new life as an independent state in March 1957, with a foundation of economic and social services somewhat above that of most African territories. It has been shown in previous chapters that this development began in the first decades of the century, when the growth of cocoa farms and the spread of mission schools helped to provide the material and human elements on which later progress was to be built. During the 1920's Sir Gordon Guggisberg gave the Gold Coast its first experience of planned development when he inaugurated the Ten Year Development Plan which specialized, above all, in transport, education, and health facilities. Following the depression years of the 1930's, World War II brought a certain stimulus to economic and social life as the Gold Coast made every effort to provide both the urgently needed raw materials and the increased internal communications which the allied war activities demanded. At the beginning of the war, in 1940, the British government had passed the first Colonial Development and Welfare Act which promised financial aid for the various needs of the British colonies. This new programme was an additional stimulus to the interest which the war had already created in further economic development.

Early in the conflict Sir Alan Burns had begun his term (1941-7) as governor of the Gold Coast with a tour of the entire Dependency for the purpose of determining its most urgent needs. In spite of war-time dislocations, he did not delay the preparation of a definite scheme, and in 1944 he published a sessional paper outlining a five-year development plan.[1] Post-war shortages hampered its full completion, but the plan did succeed in providing for certain pressing agricultural and social needs and it made a first attempt at encouraging industry by setting up the Industrial Development Board—forerunner of the subsequent Industrial Development Corporation.

Since Gold Coast progress depended to such a large extent on cocoa

[1] *General Plan for the Development of the Gold Coast*, Sessional Paper No. 2 of 1944.

203

earnings, however, it is wise to examine that industry before undertaking a further discussion of the general economic development. An
earlier chapter[1] pointed out that improper marketing conditions had led
to a serious boycott in 1937-8 and to a recommendation from a parliamentary commission that a co-operative selling organization be established. Such action was prevented by the war, and during those years
all marketing was in the hands of the West African Produce Control
Board. While the Africans appreciated the government's guarantee to
buy the entire crop, there was much criticism of the low price paid by
the board and of the buying system which allocated the majority of
licences to European firms. In 1944 and again in 1946 the British
government presented command papers to parliament outlining plans
for the new organization which would control cocoa marketing in the
post-war period.[2] The scheme, which did not greatly differ from that
of the war period except that the board would be under the colonial
rather than the British government, envisaged the establishment of
machinery in the Gold Coast and Nigeria to purchase the entire cocoa
crop, to prescribe prices to be paid to producers, and to be responsible
for sales. Its main objective was to protect the African producers from
the unfair competition and fluctuating prices which had characterized
the pre-war market. A Gold Coast Cocoa Marketing Board[3] was therefore set up in 1947; it still retains its original powers as sole exporter
and sole buyer of all Gold Coast cocoa for export, and it is also responsible for grading. Cocoa sales overseas are arranged by the board's
subsidiary marketing company in London. The board's greatest influence lies in its power to fix the price which shall be paid to the farmer.
By limiting this price within a narrow range, no matter how high the
world price may go, the board has been able to accumulate very substantial reserves which amounted to over £53,000,000 in 1958. Originally
these reserves were set aside for two main funds—one for price stabilization to enable the board to pay the farmers a fairly steady price no
matter how low the world price may drop; the other fund for the
rehabilitation of the cocoa industry, including aid to diseased farms and
expenditure on research. Some time later the board also began to give
grants for various purposes of general benefit to the cocoa farmers or to

---

[1] See pp. 68 ff.

[2] *Report on Cocoa Control in West Africa, 1939–1943 and Statement of Future Policy*,
Cmd. 6554 (1944); *Statement on Future Marketing of West African Cocoa*, Cmd. 6950
(1946).

[3] For a recent summary of the Gold Coast cocoa situation, see Royal Institute of
International Affairs, *Ghana, A Brief Political and Economic Survey* (London, 1957),
pp. 41–48. See also *Gold Coast Annual Reports* for the years concerned.

the industry as a whole. Thus, for example, the board gave nearly £3,000,000 to the Gold Coast University College, and it has supplied scholarship funds for the children of the farmers.

Up to 1951 the greater portion of the cocoa earnings accrued to the Cocoa Marketing Board, and it was during those years that the bulk of its reserves were accumulated. Later, however, the Gold Coast government inaugurated a new policy by which it absorbed a large part of the cocoa profits through a higher export tax. Most of the money obtained from this export duty—it was as high as £38,000,000 in the 1954-5 peak year—was earmarked for the country's development plans. The government justified such action on the grounds that by making use of the current prosperity of the cocoa industry, it could build up the economic resources of the country and thus reduce its dependence on the vagaries of one crop.[1] It believed that such a policy of enforced savings was in the best interests of the cocoa farmer as well as of all the other citizens.[2]

The most urgent cocoa problem over the last two decades, however, has been concerned with the conquest of plant diseases. Swollen shoot, black pod, and capsid all attack cocoa trees. Swollen shoot, the most serious of the diseases, was first detected in the 1930's,[3] but it was nearly ten years before the scientists finally discovered that it is a virus spread by mealy bugs. Though much research has been done, the only certain remedy so far discovered for swollen shoot is the complete cutting out of the infected tree.[4] A large-scale campaign for its eradication was started by the government in 1946, but so drastic a remedy was fiercely resented by the farmers since trees continue to bear for some years after being infected. It was difficult to make illiterate farmers understand the

[1] The Marketing Board system has been the subject of some controversy, much of it of a very technical nature. One common criticism is that the farmer should be given the stimulus of a higher price as an incentive to greater production. Those who support the system point out that the farmer is guaranteed a steady price, inflation is controlled and the government is supplied with a surplus fund for the general development of the country. Lord Hailey, *An African Survey Revised, 1956* (London, 1957), pp. 1349–50, has a general discussion of the problem. See also C. Leubuscher, *Bulk Buying from the Colonies* (London, 1956). P. T. Bauer, author of *West African Trade* (Cambridge, 1955) has sharply criticized the statutory marketing system.

In September 1957, the U.N. Food and Agriculture Organization's Cocoa Study Group held an international conference at Ibadan in Nigeria. Various problems including world cocoa price stabilization were discussed. See *West Africa* (28 September and 5 October 1957).

[2] For the political repercussions of this policy, see p. 187.

[3] G.C. Govt., *Swollen Shoot of Cacao: Report on Mr. H. A. Dade's Visit to the Gold Coast* (Accra, 1937); *Report on the Commission of Enquiry into the Swollen Shoot Disease of Cacao in the Gold Coast*, col. no. 236, 1948.

[4] The West African Cocoa Research Institute at Tafo in the Gold Coast employs a large staff of technical experts to study cocoa disease and rehabilitation.

danger to the entire Gold Coast industry, but with swollen shoot spreading at the rate of some fifteen million trees a year, the government believed it essential to hold to its policy of forced destruction. The cutting-out campaign soon became a major political issue and was partly responsible for the riots of 1948 and for the general unrest which eventually led to the 1951 constitutional reforms. During the 1951 electioneering, the Convention People's Party had promised that the compulsory destruction of cocoa trees would stop, and this promise they felt they had to carry out once they were in office. Nkrumah tried to win the voluntary co-operation of the farmers by a 'New Deal for Cocoa' campaign.[1] He used the mass appeal propaganda tactics which had won him political success and increased the government compensation for each tree destroyed. A few farmers were won over, but obviously total co-operation was essential. Fortunately the new C.P.P. ministers realized the danger of the course they had adopted, and some fifteen months later the compulsory arrangement was readopted; since then much progress has been made.

In the ten years from 1946 to 1956 a total of fifty-four million trees were cut out, and in most parts of the country the disease is now under control, though constant inspection—a costly process—must be maintained. The devastated farms of the Eastern region have been replaced by new ones, largely in Ashanti, and about half the crop now comes from that area.

The spread of cocoa disease has, of course, affected the amount of production. Annual yields have dropped from the 310,000 ton pre-war peak to an average of some 228,000 tons over the last decade.[2] In spite of this crop reduction, actual cocoa earnings have risen steeply—thanks to favourable prices—from an export value of £34,000,000 in 1949 to £84,000,000 in the 1954 peak year. In 1955–6 the drop in world prices lowered the figure so substantially that the Cocoa Marketing Board had to support the price paid to farmers, but since 1957 the cocoa prices have again risen.

This discussion has shown the importance of cocoa to Gold Coast economy. Since the war, cocoa earnings have provided for nearly 70 per cent of the total value of the country's exports, and it has been possible to inaugurate development plans—far more ambitious than in most areas of Africa—supported almost entirely from this sector of the

[1] K. Nkrumah, *Ghana*, pp. 151–3.
[2] Ghana production accounts for some 30 per cent of the world crop. See Appendix for crop statistics.

economy. The first post-war plan, that of 1948, envisaged an expenditure of £11,500,000 to be spent over a ten-year period. Fortunately for the Gold Coast, boom conditions made it possible in 1951 to enlarge its scope and to aim at such widespread development that the outlay was nearly £80,000,000. The original ten-year span was compressed to five years in 1952, although various problems later making it necessary to add another year, the plan was not completed until 1957.[1]

This multi-purpose development plan aimed in general at improving the basic services of the country rather than at revenue-producing projects. The main estimates included agriculture, transport and communications, electricity, water supplies, educational and medical services, and housing. The entire country was enthusiastic over the plan, although in the nature of things its achievements proved disappointing to those areas which received less than they had expected.[2]

In the field of agricultural progress the government put much stress on the improvement of food crops for local consumption and—to avoid undue reliance on cocoa—it has been experimenting with the development of alternative export crops. One of the chief objectives of the 1951 Development Plan has been the setting up of a chain of twenty-one agricultural stations throughout the country for demonstrating better methods of husbandry. Their work has included pest and disease control, testing new crops, experiments with irrigation, and mechanized farming as well as general advice and assistance to farmers. In the Northern Territories important projects to check soil erosion and to develop mixed farming and rice production are under way. In the South experimentation has been going on for some time with possible export crops. The results obtained with bananas, oil-palm, and coffee are promising and it is hoped that the latter two can be grown successfully on the derelict cocoa farms of the Eastern region.[3]

[1] *Digest of Statistics, November 1957* (Accra, 1957). The original 1951 plan provided for an expenditure of £74,000,000, but since then some schemes have been altered and others added. By June 1957 £93,613,700 had been spent for development since 1951, but this included the Tema Harbour, etc. See Appendix for statistics of the various plans.

[2] The 1951–7 Development Plan was only able to make a start at raising the Gold Coast above the category of an underdeveloped country and there is still much poverty. If the economic situation should deteriorate there is grave danger that the C.P.P. left wing would try to replace the present democratic constitution with a more authoritarian form of government. It appears important that Ghana continue to receive aid from the more fully developed countries.

[3] *Development Progress Report 1955*, para. 33–58.

In 1949 a statutory board, the Agricultural Development Corporation, was set up to assist with all kinds of agricultural undertakings, especially those connected with large-scale production. In 1955 it was combined with the Agricultural Marketing Board as a single body responsible for both development and marketing activities. Among its experimental projects, it is directing a palm-oil estate, poultry, pineapple, and tobacco development schemes, and in its fisheries division it is supporting the gradual introduction of power craft to replace the dug-out canoe in sea-fishing.

Mining exports continue to rank next in importance to cocoa in Ghana's external trade. Their value in 1958 was 28·4 million pounds, 27 per cent of total exports. In 1954 the various mining companies were employing about 36,000 Africans, but it was estimated that about 12,000 small-scale diamond diggers were working on their own.

The timber industry has grown so rapidly in recent years that it now ranks next in value to cocoa and gold in export trade. While the total value was £77,000 in 1938, it had risen to £11,000,000 in 1958. But the rate of timber extraction has risen so rapidly that a permanent decline in the volume of timber exports is officially expected within the next two or three years. The country's timber consists of hardwoods, and exports include mahogany, obeche, sapele, and utile.

Industry in Ghana is still in its infancy. The government has long realized that any major improvement of the standard of living could be eventually obtained only through some measure of industrial development. In 1953 Professor W. A. Lewis of the Manchester University, at the request of the government, undertook an investigation into the possibility of starting successful industries in the Gold Coast. After a careful study of the resources of the country and the problems involved, his report concluded that the Gold Coast was not yet ready for any major experiments in industrial expansion.[1] 'A small programme is justified but a major programme in this sphere should wait until the country is better prepared to carry it.' He recommended that the first priority should be given to improving agriculture. 'This is the way to provide the market, the capital and the labour for industrialization.' The second priority was to extend the basic services of the country, 'adequate and cheap supplies of electricity, water, gas, transport facilities, etc., so that factories could function efficiently'. A start in the domestic

---

[1] W. A. Lewis, *Report on Industrialization and the Gold Coast* (Accra, 1953). Professor Lewis accepted a two-year appointment as economic adviser to the Ghana government in 1957.

production of certain common imports might be tried, and he listed those industries which he considered favourable for experimentation—oil expressing, canning, salt-making, beer brewing, bricks and tiles, cement, &c. He stressed the necessity for the government to provide a favourable environment for private capital and to announce its willingness to welcome foreign enterprise. The Lewis Report has evidently had much influence on government policy.[1] Since then Dr. Nkrumah has made repeated statements that the government desires to attract projects of overseas firms to Ghana for industrial development and that it is prepared to give all possible assistance to overseas businessmen interested in exploring the potentialities of the country, particularly those who would be willing to train Africans for managerial responsibility. Such skill is far more important than scientific knowledge for industrial success and it can be learned only by experience. The government can send trainees abroad, but the firms themselves are in a better position to train satisfactory managers. Dr. Nkrumah has also stressed the government's willingness to give generous tax relief and other forms of special assistance to pioneer industries. He has reiterated his assurance that there will be continued freedom of transfer of profits and capital for overseas firms. The present government has no plans for nationalization, but in case a future government should consider the nationalization of a particular industry essential, the constitution guarantees adequate compensation.[2]

In line with the Lewis Report's stress on the necessity of creating a favourable environment for industry, the government has accelerated its earlier efforts at extending the country's basic services. This has been particularly striking in the field of communications. In his 1956 budget speech, Mr. Gbedemah, the minister of finance, said, 'Of all the economic developments undertaken the most spectacular has been, perhaps, the expansion of our communications.' Since the war, more than 1,000 miles of all-weather roads have been constructed, so that the country now has altogether over 1,645 miles of excellent tarred roads, including the Accra–Kumasi–Tamale–Bolgatanga route, the main artery of the country. The completion of the 805-foot Volta Bridge at Adomi, one of the largest bridges in Africa, has greatly improved communications between Accra and Togoland. In the line of railway construction, the new Achiasi–Kotoku link reduces the journey between Accra and

[1] The Industrial Development Corporation, established in 1947, has considerably enlarged its activities since 1953, placing increased emphasis on the encouragement of industries under the management of subsidiary companies.

[2] The Ghana (Constitution) Order in Council, 1957, para. 54.

Takoradi by 163 miles, while two short lines have been built in connexion with the Tema harbour project. In addition to new construction, the government has spent large sums on the improvement of existing railways with a gradual conversion to the use of new diesel-electric locomotives.

The expansion of harbour facilities is one of Ghana's most pressing needs. With the post-war increase in trade, Takoradi harbour became seriously inadequate, and it has been necessary to extend its capacity by the construction of five new shallow-water wharves for handling logs and sawn timber, a new double log quay, a new tanker berth, and a new bauxite berth. The need of a new port on the eastern side of Ghana has long been felt necessary, and after careful investigation of possible sites, Tema, seventeen miles east of Accra, was chosen and work was begun in 1954. At present it is planned to enclose about 500 acres of deep water between two breakwaters and to include a finger quay to accommodate four ocean-going ships; a fishing harbour and ancillary services will be included.[1]

Increased international and intercolonial air service extended the activities of the Accra and Takoradi airports. In 1947 the West African Airways Corporation (W.A.A.C.) came into service financed by the four British West African territories. It provided internal transport within the country as well as links from Ghana to Nigeria, Sierra Leone, Gambia, Senegal, and the Sudan. The training of African air traffic personnel was given assistance by the British government which provided advanced courses for a selected staff sent from the Gold Coast.

In addition to these road, rail, and harbour improvements, the govern-also endeavoured to extend the basic services essential to industry by the provision of further water and power supplies. A new electricity department, established in 1947, extended services so that by 1958 public electricity generating capacity had increased to 34,000 kilowatts, while the mines had a further generating capacity of 54,500 kilowatts. Major schemes for water development in both urban and rural areas were also included in recent plans. The problem of rural water supply is an acute one, especially in the Northern Territories where serious water shortage is by no means unknown. While much has been done to provide wells, boreholes, dams, or piped water—the 1951 plan

[1] Tema was chosen, in part, because of its relevance to the needs of the Volta Scheme. A model town is now being built there to support the harbour. If the Volta Scheme materializes, the harbour can readily be expanded to ten berths by the addition of a second finger quay, and to eighteen or twenty berths if ultimately necessary.

included nearly £2·5 million for this purpose—a great deal still remains to be done in a field of such basic concern to the health and progress of the areas concerned.[1]

No account of Ghana's plans for economic development would be complete without a discussion of the great Volta River Project, undoubtedly the most far reaching of all her schemes for future industrialization. Indeed if the project is carried to completion, it will not only reduce the country's dependence on cocoa, but will bring into existence a great new source of power and industry which will be of great significance in the future of Ghana. Briefly the project envisages the building of a dam and hydro-electric power station capable of generating about 600,000 kilowatts at Ajena on the Volta River. This would provide electricity for a large-scale aluminium industry and for other purposes. Local bauxite from a vast deposit some 200 miles away would be used to feed an aluminium smelter which would aim at an eventual production of 210,000 tons a year. Earlier investigations into the project led to discussions in 1952 between the British and Gold Coast governments and two aluminium companies: Aluminium Limited of Canada and the British Aluminium Company in Great Britain. It was agreed then that the magnitude and complexity of the project was so great that a preparatory commission should be set up by the British and Gold Coast governments to make further detailed investigations into the wisdom of the undertaking.[2] The Commission, which started work in 1953 headed by Commander R. G. A. Jackson (now Sir Robert Jackson), published its findings in 1956.[3] The following general conclusions were made:[4]

1. The project can be regarded as technically sound and could be carried out successfully.
2. From the evidence available, it is considered that the project as conceived in the earlier technical reports, cannot be improved from an economic point of view.

[1] The National Liberation Movement, later consolidated with other opposition groups to form the United Party, has criticized certain phases of the economic planning as handled by the C.P.P. government. It held that funds spent on elaborate buildings, &c., would have been more wisely applied to such basic needs as clean water in areas where disease is widespread because of this lack. It suggested also that larger amounts should be applied to agricultural development, housing and health services. See K. A. Busia, *Judge for Yourself* (Accra, 1956), a political pamphlet circulated just before the 1956 elections.
[2] *Volta River Aluminium Scheme*, Cmd. 8702, 1952.
[3] Volta River Preparatory Commission, *The Volta River Project*, 3 volumes (London, H.M.S.O.), 1956.
[4] ibid., vol. I, p. 3.

3. Since the cost of power and rail freight would diminish rapidly with increasing aluminium production, the greatest return from the project would be derived by achieving maximum production as soon as possible.

4. The project should be competitive in relation to other schemes, provided that:

    (a) it was completed according to the timetable of construction;

    (b) a sound policy was adopted in the employment and provision of living conditions for the labour force;

    (c) economic stability in the country was maintained;

    (d) the aluminium companies were satisfied that the internal cost of operating the smelter would be acceptable.

5. The local effects of the dam and lake could be dealt with satisfactorily.

6. The Commission considers that the other factors enumerated in the report which might influence the Volta Project should not affect it adversely, provided that the future development plans of the Gold Coast Government were effectively co-ordinated with the Project . . . and provided that the climate for investment in the Gold Coast was attractive; and assuming that the level of future world demand for aluminium and future developments in the generation of power from nuclear energy did not make the Project uneconomic.

The Commission estimated the cost of the Volta River Project at about £231 million with prices as they were in September 1955. It recommended that an overall increase of 40 to 50 per cent should be allowed as a safe margin, which would bring the figure to a possible £309 million.[1] It reported that it would take about eight years or more to complete the project which, if eventually carried out, would bring Ghana, through the production of aluminium, new exports roughly comparable to all its present exports, cocoa excepted. But, in addition, the huge artificial lake which would be formed—over 3,000 square miles —would open up new possibilities for fisheries and inland transport and could provide water for the irrigation of the dry plains near Accra. Other industries requiring water and cheap power could, of course, be beneficial by-products of the scheme. The project has been studied, not only by the companies involved in the Preparatory Commission but also

---

[1] Following Dr. Nkrumah's visit to the U.S.A. early in 1959, the Kaiser Corporation made a reassessment of the project, and found that by moving the dam about one mile south of the proposed site, and using new methods of construction, it was possible to reduce substantially the cost of building the dam, and at the same time increase its power generating capacity. It is now probable that the Volta River Project will be carried out by a predominantly U.S.A.–Canadian consortium; that the smelter will be at Tema, and not at Kpong, and that instead of smelting Ghana bauxite it will smelt imported aluminium, at least in the first few years.

by a group of American interests.[1] The large amount of capital required and new aluminium developments in other parts of the world have made its execution somewhat problematic. Moreover, since the execution of the Volta project would temporarily divert resources (men, materials, &c.) from other development projects, it has been criticized on these grounds, although many believe that ultimate benefits would make it worth while. In any case the Ghana government continues to look on the project as the best means of diversifying and strengthening its economy and is making every effort to secure its implementation.

In summing up this section on Ghana's economy, it is clear that the post-war years were marked by an outstanding development in basic services, but that little was accomplished in the field of revenue-producing projects. Funds for the 1951–7 development plans came almost entirely from within the country.[2] Because of the lack of private capital and managerial skill it was necessary—and probably will be for some time to come—that the central government take the initiative for increased productivity, but private enterprise and a more active participation of the farming population are also desirable. Even if the Volta project is implemented, it is still important that agricultural output be diversified and increased; and that the nation's public services be expanded in such a way as to attract foreign enterprise to the country.[3]

SOCIAL DEVELOPMENT

One of the most significant phases of Gold Coast development in the post-war years was in the field of education. Marked advances were made between 1944 and 1951, but the more spectacular changes came

[1] *West Africa* (3 and 24 August 1957).

[2] The Colonial Development and Welfare Fund also contributed over £4 million to the Gold Coast in the post-war years. With the attainment of independence, Ghana is no longer eligible for this help. Until foreign investors gain confidence in the new nation it seems important that Ghana continue to receive assistance from Britain. See *United Kingdom's Role in Commonwealth*, Cmd. 237, 1957 for a discussion of British assistance to young Commonwealth nations.

In addition to help from British funds the Gold Coast also received, before its independence, about £500,000 from the United States Foreign Operations Administration. Since March 1957 the U.S.A. has given additional aid, but this matter lies beyond the scope of this survey. *Africa Special Report* (October 1957) discusses the matter of a possible U.S. policy towards Ghana.

[3] For a discussion of the problems involved in West African industrial development see F. J. Pedler, 'Foreign Investment in West Africa', *International Affairs*, vol. XXXI (1955); Barbara Ward Jackson, 'The Gold Coast, an Experiment in Partnership', *Foreign Affairs*, vol. XXXII (1954), pp. 608–16.

with the advent of the Nkrumah government. The 1944 Plan, following a report submitted by the 1937–41 educational survey committee, proposed to expand primary and secondary school facilities, to provide for more teacher training colleges, and to consider an adult education programme.[1] In the primary field the need for expansion was especially acute as only 15 per cent of the country's children were actually in school. In order to stimulate the various native administrations to take greater interest and responsibility in the development of primary and middle school education, and eventually to develop their own schools, the government began to give grants to the native authorities. District education committees (on which the four leading mission educational units were represented) were organized to advise and assist the native authorities in this development. The Akim Abuakwa District Education Committee was the first to begin to function in 1942 and set the pattern for others to follow. At first all financial aid went to mission schools, since all government schools were already assisted direct from central government and no native authority school had as yet been founded. In this same period the government opened the first teacher training establishment in the Northern Territories.

The 1944 Plan made no provision for expansion of higher education, since in the preceding year the British government had appointed a commission to study the whole question of college and university education in West Africa. This body, generally known as the Elliot Commission, included in its membership educationists, members of parliament, and Africans from the three colonies of Sierra Leone, Nigeria, and the Gold Coast. After having made a survey of West Africa, it prepared a general report which appeared in 1945 and which stated that 'the extension of higher education, and of university development, in West Africa, is urgent'.[2] There was a division of opinion among the members of the Elliot Commission, the majority advocating that the existing colleges in Sierra Leone, the Gold Coast, and Nigeria should be developed to university standing, whereas the minority favoured concentration of resources, for some years at least, on a single West African university to be located in Nigeria. Mr. Korsah, the Gold Coast member of the Commission, stood with the majority group and in this he was supported by local opinion, as there is a very marked appreciation of higher education in the country. The British colonial secretary at first preferred the minority opinion for a single West African university, but

[1] *Gold Coast Education Committee Report, 1937–41* (Accra, 1941).
[2] *Report of the Commission on Higher Education in West Africa*, Cmd. 6655.

later agreed to a separate Gold Coast establishment on the under-standing that it should be endowed largely from local resources.[1] In 1948 university classes were begun, using Achimota buildings until the new campus at Legon, near Achimota, would be ready. The teaching staff, with Mr. D. M. Balme as principal, was drawn largely from the British universities. The campus at Legon has been very attractively planned and many of the buildings were completed by 1957. Though very new, it has already something of the traditional atmosphere of a long-established university. Unfortunately, owing to inadequate secondary school facilities, there have been an insufficient number of properly prepared candidates in recent years to take advantage of the university's full student capacity. The number of students will, however, reach over 600 in 1959-60.

As a result of the 1944-50 planning, there was a substantial increase in educational facilities in the immediate post-war years. In addition to the university college, the teachers in training doubled in number; and the total of children in the primary schools rose from 80,000 in 1946 to 235,000 in 1951.

But in spite of these developments, there was still a widespread demand for further educational opportunities and when the Convention Peoples' Party came into office it was determined to accelerate the pace of the pre-1951 schemes. As the governor, Sir Charles Arden-Clarke, later put it, the new ministers brought 'a much more imaginative approach to these problems, an attitude also governed by the estimated popularity and vote-catching capacity of any particular plan'.[2] The previous plan had called for a steady increase in primary schools with a proportional increase of middle schools, teacher training institutions, and so on up to the university level. But the C.P.P. ministers thought it politically advantageous to go in for immediate fee-free primary education which would eventually be made compulsory. 'That was regarded as the most popular measure that could be enacted, but it threw the whole educational programme out of balance.'[3] The Accelerated

---

[1] The cost of establishing the Gold Coast University College was borne largely by local revenue including an initial grant of £3,765,000 from the Gold Coast Government and £1,897,000 for the Cocoa Marketing Board reserves. The Colonial Welfare and Development Funds also contributed £400,000. Advances were also made for current expenses by the government at the rate of £500,000 a year and in 1954 it promised a £2,000,000 endowment fund. The second Hall at the college has been named 'Akuafo' (Farmers) Hall to commemorate the benefactions of the Cocoa Marketing Board which have been generously added to since the original grant. Though largely supported by government funds the university is an autonomous institution.

[2] Sir Charles Arden-Clarke, 'Gold Coast into Ghana; some Problems of Transition', op. cit.   [3] ibid.

Plan,[1] as it was called, opened the primary classes to all children without requiring the tuition fees which had formerly been charged. The enrolment jumped from 235,000 in 1951 to 468,000 in 1957,[2] a greater increase than had been estimated, and the country found both its school buildings and teacher training resources extremely inadequate.

Besides enlarging the primary classes, the Accelerated Development for Education Plan aimed at speeding up the Africanization of public life by the provision of secondary and higher educational facilities.[3] Out of a capital expenditure of some £8,000,000, to be extended over a six-year period, about three-quarters of the amount was to be devoted to secondary schools, technical schools, and teacher training institutes. Since the training of teachers was the key to the rest of the plan, several new training colleges were opened and existing ones were enlarged. The annual output of teachers rose from 791 in 1951 to 1,680 in 1955.[4] Nevertheless this increase was well below the numbers needed for the Accelerated Plan, and many schools have had to depend on untrained or pupil teachers with a resultant lowering of quality in primary work.[5] This same lack of staff has made it impossible, for the present at least, to assure universal primary education as was at first hoped. In spite of these rather discouraging aspects, the Accelerated Plan has been responsible for many improvements and the government is now working at changes which will help to get the programme back in balance.

Recognized secondary schools in receipt of various forms of government aid rose from 13 in 1951 to 31 in 1955. Achimota now confines its classes to the secondary level since the opening of the university college in 1948. Several of the older secondary schools such as Mfantsipim and Wesley Girls' High School have added new buildings. But in spite of the new or enlarged secondary schools, the need for further expansion is very great, as the present output of sixth-form pupils is barely half

---

[1] *Accelerated Development Plan for Education, 1951* (Accra, 1951). The plan also required that, outside of government schools, no new primary or middle school could be opened after 1951 except as a private, unrecognized and unaided school. Local Authorities, however, if they are unable to manage new schools themselves, may hand over management to a missionary body, or private person. But the school remains a Local Authority school and it may assume management at any time. Para. 6, 26, 38.

[2] *Education Statistics, 1957* (Accra, 1957).

[3] *Development Progress Report, 1955*, para. 165.

[4] ibid.

[5] The total number of teachers in 1955 was 18,000 and of them 11,090 or 61 per cent were uncertificated. Assembly members and the general public have been concerned about the lowered standards which resulted from the Accelerated Education Plan. See, for example, *West Africa* (2 April 1955) and *Universitas* (March 1955), p. 30.

the number which could be accommodated by the University College and the Kumasi College of Technology.[1]

Technical education is of marked importance in the newly independent Ghana with its rapidly growing public services and its hopes for industrial development. Four new technical institutes were recently opened. The Kumasi College of Technology is of special importance for it plans to train large numbers of students for the economic and educational needs of the country. A total student body of 2,000 is envisaged. Work has gone ahead rapidly on its buildings and by March 1955, 750 students were in residence. The college has departments of agriculture, commerce, engineering, pharmacy, science, and general studies.

In addition to its regular schools, the Gold Coast developed widespread and very successful organizations for adult education. The programme of Extra-Mural Studies was first begun on a trial basis when a tutor from the Oxford University Delegacy for Extra-Mural Studies gave a series of lectures in mid-1947 on 'Economic History and Problems'. Gradually the work was expanded, and in 1949 the University College took over the responsibility with David Kimble as Director of the Department. Since then a splendid organization has been developed with regular weekly classes held in towns and villages all over the country in such subjects as politics, economics, English, and international affairs. There are also short residential courses at the university college during holiday periods. A voluntary democratic organization, the People's Educational Association, has also grown up to assist in the organization of these classes and to foster the practical community action which results from class study.[2]

The idea of community self-help has also been successfully encouraged through mass-education teams which have visited many of the remoter parts of the country and have conducted courses in literacy, public health, and community leadership. This movement was given a new impetus when the government assigned additional funds to the Department of Social Welfare and Community Development in 1951 for intensified literacy campaigns and for rural development schemes. In the urban areas the Department has encouraged all kinds of welfare services, day nurseries, youth clubs, and community centres.

---

[1] The university college, however, is not *entirely* dependent on students entering directly from secondary schools, as members of an older age group sometimes take private courses to prepare for college entrance examinations.

[2] D. Kimble, *Progress in Adult Education* (Achimota, 1950) gives the account of this successful experiment in adult education and community development.

It is also responsible for work with juvenile delinquents and the handicapped.

Another form of social development that has received much attention in the post-war years has been concerned with the health services. In 1954 there were thirty government hospitals, three of which have nursing training schools attached to them, and a total of 2,630 hospital beds. The outstanding addition under the 1951 development plan was the erection of a £2,800,000 central hospital at Kumasi, the largest in the country, and possessing the most up-to-date medical equipment. The decision to spend so large a sum on one hospital has been criticized by some who believed that it would have been wiser to build a number of smaller hospitals in areas which still lack regular medical service. There has also been some recent discussion of enlarging and modernizing the Accra Hospital at Korle Bu so that it could function as a training hospital for the projected medical department at the University College.

In 1951 the government appointed a commission to study the health needs of the country. Its report underlined the urgent necessity of preventive medicine, especially in the Northern Territories where the problem of endemic disease is most serious. Malaria, yaws, leprosy, onchocerciasis, tuberculosis, bilharzia, and guinea worm are widespread. Medical field units, originally formed to treat sleeping sickness in the affected areas of Ashanti and the Northern Territories, have now extended their activities to these other diseases, but there still remains very much to be done. The 1955 Development Progress Report pointed out that preventive medicine would yield greater improvement in public health in relation to the money spent, than would the provision of hospitals, but because of the urgent demand for the latter, the bulk of available funds had been allocated to that purpose.

The account of social development would not be complete without a consideration of the Christian missions. They take a major part in the educational work of the country. In 1957, for example, of the 4,882 primary and middle schools there were 2,189 under the larger Protestant Mission bodies (Presbyterian, Methodist, Anglican) and 1,162 under Catholic auspices.[1] On the secondary and teacher training level the same high proportion of missionary-directed schools obtains. Actually, then, only a small percentage of the country's schools is under full government control, but the education department grants substantial sums to all approved schools, and thus bears a good proportion of the expense. The missions also share to a great extent in the work of the hospitals and

[1] *Education Statistics, 1957.*

medical dispensaries and assist in the other social services of the country.[1] Among the people of Ghana there is much appreciation of the missions, especially among those who realize that the early missionary pioneers started most of the social services long before the government entered the field, and who appreciate the beneficent influence of Christianity in preserving spiritual values in face of the many materialistic influences affecting Africa today.

The cost of these social services was heavy, especially during the 1955–7 period when cocoa prices dropped and led, in 1956, to the first experience of an unfavourable trade balance. Thus Ghana entered upon its first year of independence with a weaker financial position than it had known in the early 1950's. The nation had strong reserves, but the government was determined, nevertheless, to be realistic about the new situation and to postpone certain large development projects until a later date. On 5 March 1957, the eve of independence, the Prime Minister gave a speech at the last session of the legislative assembly in which he spoke very frankly of the economic situation of the country. The government had hoped to begin its second development plan in July 1957, but as a consequence of lessened revenue it had decided to replace it with a Consolidated Plan which would extend for only two years and would involve a much smaller financial outlay than the original plan.[2]

The Prime Minister, in this same independence eve speech, went on to discuss other phases of Ghana's future policy. With reference to the Commonwealth he pointed out that his country's desire to be within it was inspired by the belief that the Commonwealth countries were dedicated to seeking a solution to their common problems by democratic and peaceful means and he wished to add that as long as the Commonwealth as a whole stood by that policy that Ghana's continued association with it was assured.

This desire of Ghana to remain within the Commonwealth rather than to break all ties with the former mother country is a tribute to those aspects of British colonial policy which are concerned with guiding the progress of colonies in a democratic manner towards eventual

[1] Nkrumah has several times paid tribute to the missions. A Press conference summary during the independence celebrations quoted him as saying: 'European missionaries in Ghana can rest assured that they are safe in independent Ghana. They are welcome, according to Dr. Nkrumah, who gratefully acknowledged his gratitude to missionary education.' *Daily Graphic* (9 March 1957).

[2] The recovery of cocoa prices at the end of 1957 made it possible to go ahead with preparations for the 1959–64 development plan which calls for a very marked expansion at the cost of £300 million. See *Ghana Today* (1 April 1959).

self-government. Ghana could have demanded its independence by means of violent revolt. That its leaders and its people preferred to use constitutional means is, in its turn, a tribute to that political and social maturity which has made it possible for their country to take its place among the autonomous nations of the world.

As the first British colony in tropical Africa to attain independence, the Prime Minister recognized that Ghana has a challenging responsibility, since the success or failure of the new state will have far-reaching consequences 'for other African territories striving towards independence'. He has often emphasized the fact that an African way of doing things will undoubtedly emerge, and that the peoples of his race will have a true contribution to make to world culture and peace. Then turning to foreign policy he stated:

As Ghana achieves independence it observes a world torn and divided in its political relationships. The Government of Ghana therefore feels at this stage the country should not be aligned with any particular group of powers or political blocs.

The Government of Ghana does not intend to follow a neutralist policy in its foreign relations but it does intend to preserve its independence to act as it seems best at any particular time.[1]

The Gold Coast, then, had come to the end of the road leading to independence, but everyone knows that independence does not solve all of a nation's problems. Given Ghana's lack of political experience and the tribal and sectional rivalries still existent, the government would indeed be faced with the difficult question of how to preserve democratic processes and at the same time achieve rapid economic development. An account of the manner in which the new state has met this challenge lies beyond the scope of this book, but it can be reiterated in conclusion that the solution concerns not only the new-born state of Ghana, but beyond it, those other areas still under colonial rule which also look forward to national autonomy. The supreme task for all of them will be to find a national consciousness based on moral and spiritual ties which will bind their citizens into nations which have a true African personality but which are, at the same time, capable of entering into an international viewpoint with the other nations of the world.

[1] *Ghana Weekly Review* (13 March 1957).

BIBLIOGRAPHY

BIBLIOGRAPHICAL GUIDES

Bibliography of African Bibliographies. (Capetown, 1948.)

Books for Africa. The Quarterly Bulletin of the International Committee on Christian Literature for Africa. (London, 1944.)

CARDINALL, ALLEN. *A Bibliography of the Gold Coast*. (Accra, 1931.)

COLEMAN, JAMES S. 'A Survey of Selected Literature on the Government and Politics of British West Africa', *American Political Science Review*, vol. XLIX (1955), pp. 1130–50.

KLINGBERG, FRANK. 'A Survey of Recent Books on British Africa with Special Reference to the Native Problem', *Journal of Modern History*, vol. X (1938), pp. 77–93.

LANGER, WILLIAM and ARMSTRONG, HAMILTON. *Foreign Affairs Bibliography, 1919–1932*. (New York, 1933.)

LEWIN, PERCY EVANS, ed. *Annotated Bibliography of Recent Publications on Africa, South of the Sahara, with Special Reference to Administrative, Political, Economic and Sociological Problems*. Royal Empire Society. (London, 1943.)

————. Royal Empire Society, Library. *A Select List of Recent Publications Contained in the Library of the Royal Institute Illustrating the Constitutional Relations between the Various Parts of the British Empire*. (London, 1930.)

————. *Subject Catalogue of the Royal Empire Society*, vol. I. (London, 1930.)

LIBRARY OF CONGRESS. *Africa South of the Sahara*. (Washington, 1957.)

————. *British West Africa: A Selected List of References*. (Washington, 1942.)

————. *Introduction to Africa: A Selective Guide to Background Reading*. (Washington, 1952.)

————. *Non-self-governing areas with Special Emphasis on Mandates and Trusteeships: a Selected List of References*. (Washington, 1947.)

PERHAM, MARGERY. *Colonial Government, Annotated Reading List on British Colonial Government*. (London, 1950.)

RAGATZ, LOWELL J., ed. *Bibliography for the Study of African History in the Nineteenth and Twentieth Centuries*. (Washington, 1943.)

ROBERTS, HENRY. *Foreign Affairs Bibliography, 1942–1952*. (New York, 1955.)

WOOLBERT, ROBERT. *Foreign Affairs Bibliography, 1932–1942.* (New York, 1945.)

WORK, MONROE T., ed. *Bibliography of the Negro in Africa and America.* (New York, 1928.)

DOCUMENTS
PUBLISHED BY THE UNITED NATIONS

TRUSTEESHIP COUNCIL. *The Ewe Problem.* U.N. Doc. T.L. 131 (21 February 1951).

———. *Trusteeship Agreements; Texts of the Eight Trusteeship Agreements Approved by the General Assembly at the Sixty-second Meeting of its First Session, 13 December 1946.* U.N. Doc. T/8 (25 March 1947).

PUBLISHED BY THE BRITISH GOVERNMENT

COLONIAL OFFICE. *Annual Report on the Social and Economic Progress of the People of the Gold Coast, 1920–1955.*

———. *Report of the British Mandated Sphere of Togoland (1920–1938).* 18 vols. [title varies] (London, 1922–39.)

———. No. 186. *Mass Education in African Society.* (London, 1944.)

———. No. 197. *Organization of the Colonial Service.* (London, 1946.)

———. No. 199. *The Co-operative Movement in the Colonies.* (London, 1946.)

———. No. 209. *Report of the Commission on the Civil Service of British West Africa.* (London, 1946.)

———. *Report by His Majesty's Government in the United Kingdom of Great Britain and North Ireland to the Trusteeship Council of the United Nations on the Administration of Togoland for the year 1947–54.* (London, 1948–55.) [Title varies.]

———. No. 231. *Report of the Commission of Enquiry into Disturbances in the Gold Coast, 1948.* (London, 1948.)

———. No. 232. *Statement by His Majesty's Government on the Report of the Commission of Enquiry into the Disturbances in the Gold Coast, 1948.* (London, 1948.)

———. No. 248. *Gold Coast Report to His Excellency the Governor by the Committee on Constitutional Reform, 1949.* (London, 1949.)

———. No. 250. *Gold Coast Statement by His Majesty's Government on the Report of the Committee on Constitutional Reform.* (London, 1949.)

———. No. 302. *Dispatches on the Gold Coast Government's Proposals for Constitutional Reform Exchanged between the Secretary of State for the Colonies and H.E. the Governor, 24 August 1953 to 15 April 1954.* (London, 1954.)

FOREIGN OFFICE. *British and Foreign State Papers, 1842[–1910].* (London, 1858–1920.)

———. Historical Section. *British West Africa.* Peace Handbook, No. 90. (London, 1920.)

COLONIAL OFFICE. *Gold Coast*. Peace Handbook, No. 93. (London, 1920.)
———. *Togoland*. Peace Handbook, No. 110. (London, 1920.)
PARLIAMENT. *The Parliamentary Debates. House of Lords*. (London, 1919–57.)
———. *The Parliamentary Debates. House of Commons*. (London, 1919–57.)
———. *The Parliamentary Papers, 1843[–1945]*. (London, 1843–1945.)
    1910, Cd. 4993. '*Reports of Gold Coast Forests*, by H. Thompson.'
    1911, Cd. 5743. '*Correspondence Relating to Alienation of Tribal Lands*.'
    1912, Cd. 6278. '*Report on the Legislation Governing the Alienation of Native Lands in the Gold Coast Colony and Ashanti; with Some Observations on the "Forest Ordinance", 1911*, by H. Conway Belfield.'
    1922, Cmd. 1600. '*Report of a Committee on Trade and Taxation for British West Africa*.'
    1926, Cmd. 2744. '*Report by the Hon. W. G. Ormsby-Gore on his Visit to West Africa during the year 1926*.'
    1938, Cmd. 5845. '*Report of the Commission on the Marketing of West African Cocoa*.'
    1941. Cmd. 6277. '*Report by Major G. St. J. Orde-Browne, O.B.E., on Labour Conditions in West Africa*.'
    1944, Cmd. 6554. '*Report on Cocoa Control in West Africa, 1939–1943, and Statement on Future Policy*.'
    1945. Cmd. 6655. '*Report of the Commission on Higher Education in West Africa*.'
    1946, Cmd. 6935. '*Trusteeship. Territories in Africa under United Kingdom Mandate* (revised texts).'
    1946, Cmd. 6950. '*Statement on Future Marketing of West African Cocoa*.'
    1952, Cmd. 8702. '*Volta River Aluminium Scheme*.'
    1957, Cmd. 71. '*The Proposed Constitution of Ghana*.'
STATUTORY INSTRUMENTS. 1950. No. 2094. *The Gold Coast (Constitution) Order-in-Council, 1950*.
———. 1957. No. 277. *The Ghana (Constitution) Order-in-Council, 1957*.
VOLTA RIVER PREPARATORY COMMISSION. *The Volta River Project*. 3 vols. (London, 1956.)
BRITISH INFORMATION SERVICES. *Weekly War Notes, 1944–45*. (New York, 1944–5.)
———. *West Africa and the War*. (London, 1945.)
———. *The Making of Ghana*. (New York, 1956.)

PUBLISHED BY THE GOLD COAST GOVERNMENT

Blue Book, 1919, 1921, 1922–1923, 1925–1927. (Accra, 1920–38.)
Gold Coast Gazette, 1919, 1923–1937, 1946–1957. (Accra, 1919–57.)
Departmental Reports of the Gold Coast Government, 1919–1948.

Law, Statutes of the Gold Coast Government: 1937. (Accra, 1937.)

LEGISLATIVE COUNCIL. *Debates, 1919–1941, 1943–1950.* (Accra, 1919–50.)

LEGISLATIVE ASSEMBLY. *Debates, 1951–56.* (Accra, 1951–6.)

Sessional Papers of the Gold Coast Government: 1934–1947.

SURVEY DEPARTMENT. *Atlas of the Gold Coast,* 4th ed. (Accra, 1945.)

CARDINALL, ALLEN. *A Bibliography of the Gold Coast.* (Accra, 1931.)

Development Progress Reports, 1951–1955. (Accra, 1951–6.)

Economic Survey 1954–1955. (Accra, 1955–6.)

The Government Proposals for Constitutional Reform. (Accra, 1953.)

GUGGISBERG, GORDON. *The Gold Coast: A Review of Events of 1920–1926 and the Prospects of 1927–1928.* (Accra, 1927.)

Local Government Ordinance of 1951. Supplement to the *Gold Coast Gazette,* No. 16, 16 January 1952. (Accra, 1952.)

Local Government Reform in Outline, Ministry of Local Government. (Accra, 1951.)

Regional Administrations. Report of the Commissioner (Phillipson Report). (Accra, 1951.)

Report of the Achimota Conference. (Accra, 1956.)

Report of the Commission of Enquiry into the Affairs of the Cocoa Purchasing Co. Ltd. (Jibowu Report). (Accra, 1956.)

Report of the Commission of Enquiry into Mr. Braimah's Resignation and Allegations Arising Therefrom. (Accra, 1954.)

Report of the Constitutional Adviser (Bourne Report). (Accra, 1955.)

Report of the Select Committee on Africanization of the Public Service. (Accra, 1950.)

Report on Finance and Physical Problems of Development in the Gold Coast. Seers, Dudley, and Ross, C. R., Office of the Government Statistician. (Accra, 1953.)

Report on Industrialization of the Gold Coast. W. A. Lewis. (Accra, 1953.)

Statement on the Programme of the Africanization of the Public Service. (Accra, 1954.)

PUBLICATIONS OF SOCIETIES, POLITICAL PARTIES, AND OTHER SPECIAL GROUPS

AFRICAN SOCIETIES IN THE GOLD COAST

ACHIMOTA DISCUSSION GROUP. *Pointers to Progress; the Gold Coast in the Next Five Years.* Edited by C. T. Shaw. (Achimota, 1942.)

———. *Quo Vadimus or Gold Coast Future.* Edited by C. S. Deakin. (Achimota, 1940.)

ACHIMOTA AND KUMASI DISCUSSION GROUPS. *Towards National Development; Post-War Gold Coast.* Edited by M. Ribeiro. (Achimota, 1945.)

COMMITTEE ON YOUTH ORGANIZATION. *The Ghana Youth Manifesto, Towards Self-Government.* (Kumasi, 1948.)

CONVENTION PEOPLES' PARTY. *What I Mean by Positive Action*, by Kwame Nkrumah. (Accra, 1949.)

GOLD COAST ABORIGINES' RIGHTS PROTECTION SOCIETY. *Memorandum of the Case of the Gold Coast for a Memorial to be Presented to His Majesty the King Emperor in Council through the Right Honourable the Secretary of State for the Colonies, for the Amendment of the Gold Coast Colony (Legislative Council) Order in Council, 1925.* (London, n.d.)

——. *Petition for Amendment of the Gold Coast Colony (Legislative Council) Order in Council, 1925.* (London, n.d.)

——. *Petition to the House of Commons.* (London, 1935.)

GOLD COAST YOUTH CONFERENCE. *Are We to Sit Down?* (Accra, 1942.)

——. *First Steps towards a National Fund. Better Education and Health: Trade and Commerce: Marriage and Inheritance: Funeral Customs: and the Syrian.* (Accra, 1938.)

——. *Something to Hate.* (Accra, 1940.)

DANQUAH, J. B. *Self-Help and Expansion: A Review of the Works and Aims of the Youth Conference, with a Statement of its Policy for 1943, and the Action Consequent upon that Policy.* (Accra, n.d.)

NATIONAL DEMOCRATIC PARTY. *The Road to Sure, Solid Self-Government. The Manifesto of the National Democratic Party.* (Gold Coast, 1951.)

UNITED GOLD COAST CONVENTION (THE PEOPLES' ORGANIZATION). *Letter to Nananom in Council Touching the Controversial Issues in the Coussey Report.* (Saltpond, 1950.)

SOCIETIES IN GREAT BRITAIN

THE LABOUR PARTY. *The Colonies; The Labour Party's Post-War Policy for the African and Pacific Colonies.* (London, 1943.)

FABIAN COLONIAL BUREAU. *Downing Street and the Colonies.* (London, 1942.)

——. *International Action and the Colonies; Report of a Committee of the Fabian Colonial Bureau.* (London, 1943.)

HINDEN, RITA. *Socialists and the Empire.* (Fabian Pamphlet, London, 1946.)

LABOUR PARTY PUBLICATIONS. *The Empire in Africa; Labour's Policy.* (1920.)

ROYAL INSTITUTE OF INTERNATIONAL AFFAIRS. *The Colonial Problem; A Report by a Study Group of Members of the Royal Institute of International Affairs.* (London, 1937.)

SAMUEL, HERBERT LOUIS. *The British Colonial System and Its Future; An Address to the Anti-Slavery and Aborigines' Protection Society.* (London, [1943].)

UNIVERSITY OF OXFORD DELEGACY FOR EXTRA-MURAL STUDIES. *Adult Education in the Gold Coast; A Report for the Year 1948–1949 by the Resident Tutor.* (Achimota.)

PERIODICALS

Africa: Journal of the International Institute of African Languages and Culture; African Affairs; African World; Anti-Slavery Reporter and Aborigines' Friend; Crown Colonist; Empire, Journal of the Fabian Colonial Bureau; Foreign Affairs; Journal of African Administration; Transactions of the Gold Coast and Togoland Historical Society; West Africa; West African Review; World Mission.

NEWSPAPERS

Accra Evening News; African Morning Post; Ashanti Pioneer; Ewe News-Letter; The Daily Echo; Daily Graphic; Ghana Statesman; Ghana Today; Gold Coast Bulletin; Gold Coast Express; The Gold Observer; The Gold Coast Today; The Gold Coast Weekly Review; The Spectator Daily.

BOOKS AND PAMPHLETS

AMAMOO, J. C. *The New Ghana: the Birth of a Nation.* (London, 1958.)

APTER, DAVID E. *The Gold Coast in Transition.* (Princeton, 1955.)

BAUER, P. T. *West African Trade; a Study of Competition, Oligopoly and Monopoly in a Changing Economy.* (Cambridge, 1954.)

BEER, GEORGE: *African Questions at the Paris Peace Conference.* (New York, 1923.)

BENTWICH, NORMAN. *The Mandates System.* (London, 1930.)

BUELL, RAYMOND. *The Native Problem in Africa.* 2 vols. (New York, 1931.)

BURNS, SIR ALAN. *Colonial Civil Servant.* (London, 1950.)

BUSIA, K. A. *Judge for Yourself.* (Accra, 1956.)

———. *The Position of the Chief in the Modern Political System of Ashanti.* (London, 1951.)

———. *Social Survey Sekondi-Takoradi.* (Accra, 1950.)

CAMERON, SIR DONALD. *My Tanganyika Service and Some Nigeria.* (London, 1939.)

CARBON . FERRIERE, JACQUES DE. *La Gold Coast; administration, finances, économie.* (Paris, 1937.)

CARDINALL, ALLEN. *In Ashanti and Beyond.* (London, 1927.)

———. *The Natives of the Northern Territories of the Gold Coast, Their Customs, Religion, and Folklore.* (London, n.d.)

CASELY HAYFORD, JOSEPH. *Gold Coast Native Institutions.* (London, 1903.)

CHAPMAN, DANIEL A. *The Natural Resources of the Gold Coast.* (Achimota, 1940.)

CLARIDGE, W. WALTON. *A History of the Gold Coast and Ashanti from Earliest Times to the Commencement of the 20th Century.* 2 vols. (London, 1915).

CLOUGH, OWEN, ed. *Report on African Affairs, 1929–1933.* 5 vols. (London, 1930–4.)

CONSIDINE, JOHN J. *Africa, World of New Men.* (New York, 1954.)

COOKSEY, J. J. and McLEISH, ALEX. *Religion and Civilization in West Africa. A Missionary Survey of French, British, Spanish and Portuguese West Africa, with Liberia.* (London, 1931.)

DANQUAH, J. B. *Ancestors, Heroes and God. The Principles of Akan-Ashanti Ancestor-Worship and European Hero-Worship.* (Kibi, Gold Coast, 1938.)

———. *Liberty of the Subject; A Monograph on the Gold Coast Cocoa Hold-up and Boycott of Foreign Goods (1937–38) with Prolegomena on the Historical Motives behind the Farmers' Movement.* (Kibi, Gold Coast, n.d.)

———. *An Objectivied [sic.] History of Akim-Abuakwa. A Lecture.* (Kibi, n.d.)

DAVIS, JACKSON, CAMPBELL, T., and WRONG, MARGARET. *Africa Advancing; A Study of Rural Education and Agriculture in West Africa and the Belgian Congo.* (New York, 1945.)

DEKAT, ANGELINO. *Colonial Policy.* 2 vols. (The Hague, 1931.)

EDU, JOHN E. *Dangerous Delays in Gold Coast Mass Education.* (Accra, 1949.)

ELLIS, ALFRED B. *A History of the Gold Coast of West Africa.* (London, 1893).

FAGE, J. D. *Ghana: a historical interpretation.* (Madison, 1959.)

FIELD, M. J. *Religion and Medicine of the Ga People.* (London, 1937.)

FORTES, M. *Dynamics of Clanship among the Tallensi.* (London, 1945.)

FRANKEL, HERBERT S. *Capital Investment in Africa; Its Course and Effects.* (New York, 1938.)

FULLER, SIR FRANCIS. *A Vanished Dynasty.* (London, 1921.)

GERIG, BENJAMIN. *The Open Door and the Mandates System; A Study of Economic Equality before and since the Establishment of the Mandates System.* (London, 1930.)

HAILEY, BARON WILLIAM MALCOLM. *African Survey; A Study of Problems arising in Africa, South of the Sahara.* Issued by the Committee of the African Research Survey under The Auspices of the Royal Institute of International Affairs. (London, 1938.)

———. *African Survey: Revised 1956.* (London, 1957.)

———. *Future of Colonial Peoples.* (Princeton, 1944.)

———. *Native Administration in the British African Territories.* Parts III and IV. (London, 1952.)

———. *The Position of Colonies in a British Commonwealth of Nations.* (New York, 1941.)

HANCOCK, W. K. *Survey of British Commonwealth Affairs*, vol. II. *Problems of Economic Policy 1918–1939*, Part 2. (New York, 1942.)

HODGKIN, THOMAS. *Nationalism in Colonial Africa.* (New York, 1957.)

JOHNSON, J. W. DE GRAFT. *Historical Geography of the Gold Coast.* (London, 1929.)

———. *Towards Nationhood in West Africa.* (London, 1928.)

JONES, THOMAS JESSE. African Education Commission. *Education in Africa; A Study of West, South and Equatorial Africa by the African Education Commission under the Auspices of the Phelps-Stokes Fund and Foreign Mission Societies of North America and Europe; Report prepared by Thomas Jesse Jones*. (New York, 1922.)

KELLER, ALBERT. *Colonization; A Study of the Founding of New Societies.* (Boston, 1908.)

KIMBLE, DAVID. *The Machinery of Self-Government.* (London, 1953.)

KINGSLEY, MARY H. *West African Studies.* (London, 1899.)

KUCZYNSKI, ROBERT. *The Cameroons and Togoland; A Demographic Study.* (London, 1937.)

LUCAS, SIR C. E. *The Gold Coast and the War.* (London, 1920.)

———. *Historical Geography of the British Colonies. West Africa*, vol. III. (Oxford, 1894.)

LUGARD, F. D. *Dual Mandate in British Tropical Africa.* (Edinburgh, 1926.)

McCARTHY, J. C. *The 'Trials of Ghana' [Towards Self-Government].* (Gold Coast, 1950.)

MacMILLAN, WILLIAM M. *Democratize the Empire; A Policy of Colonial Reform.* (London, 1941.)

McPHEE, ALLAN. *The Economic Revolution in British West Africa.* (London, 1926.)

MAIR, LUCY PHILIP. *Native Policies in Africa.* (London, 1936.)

———. *Welfare in the British Colonies.* (London, 1944.)

MANOUKIAN, M. *Akan and Ga Adangme Peoples of the Gold Coast.* (London, 1950.)

MARTIN, E. C. *British West African Settlements, 1750–1821.* (London, 1927.)

MEEK, CHARLES K., HUSSEY, E. R. and MACMILLAN, W. M. *Europe and West Africa; Some Problems and Adjustments.* (London, 1940.)

NEWLAND, H. O. *West Africa: A Handbook of Practical Information for the Official, Planter, Miner, Financier and Trader.* Edited by P. E. Lewin. (London, 1922.)

NKRUMAH, KWAME. *Ghana, the Autobiography of Kwame Nkrumah.* (New York, 1957.)

ORIZU, A. A. NWAFOR. *Without Bitterness; Western Nations in Post-War Africa.* (New York, 1944.)

PADMORE, GEORGE. *Gold Coast Revolution.* (London, 1953.)

PAX, ROMANA. *All African Seminar [Ghana].* (Fribourg, 1957.)

PIM, ALAN. *The Financial and Economic History of the African Tropical Territories.* (Oxford, 1940.)

RATTRAY, R. S. *Ashanti.* (Oxford, 1923.)

———. *Ashanti Law and Constitution.* (Oxford, 1929.)

———. *Religion and Art in Ashanti.* (Oxford, 1927.)

———. *Tribes of the Ashanti Hinterland.* (Oxford, 1932.)

ROYAL INSTITUTE OF INTERNATIONAL AFFAIRS. *Ghana, A Brief Political and Economic Survey.* (London, 1957.)

SMITH, EDWIN W. *Aggrey of Africa.* (New York, 1929.)

———. *The Church Conference on African Affairs; The Indigenous African Church.* (Westerville, Ohio, 1942.)

———. *The Golden Stool: Some Aspects of the Conflict of Cultures in Modern Africa.* (New York, 1923.)

STRICKLAND, CLAUDE. *Co-operation for Africa.* (Oxford, 1933.)

TIMOTHY, BANKOLE. *Kwame Nkrumah.* (London, 1955.)

TOWNSEND, MARY. *Rise and Fall of Germany's Colonial Empire, 1884–1918.* (New York, 1930.)

WARD, W. E. *A Short History of the Gold Coast.* (London, 1935.)

WEST AFRICAN CACAO RESEARCH INSTITUTE. *W.A.C.R.I., 1944–1949.* (Tafo, Gold Coast, 1950.)

WIGHT, MARTIN. *The Gold Coast Legislative Council.* (London, 1947.)

WILTGEN, RALPH. *Gold Coast Mission History, 1471–1880.* (Techny, Illinois, 1956.)

WOLFSON, FREDA. *Pageant of Ghana.* (London, 1958.)

WORTHINGTON, EDGAR B. *Science in Africa; A Review of Scientific Research Relating to Tropical and Southern Africa.* (Oxford, 1938.)

WRIGHT, QUINCY. *Mandates under the League of Nations.* (Chicago, 1930.)

ARTICLES

ALTON, E. B. S. 'The Local Government Training School in the Gold Coast', *Journal of African Administration*, vol. IV (1952), pp. 108–13.

APTER, DAVID E. 'British West Africa', *Annals of the American Academy of Political and Social Science*, vol. CCXCVIII (March 1955), pp. 117–29.

ARDEN-CLARKE, SIR CHARLES. 'Gold Coast into Ghana: Some Problems of Transition', *International Affairs*, vol. XXXIV (1958), pp. 49–56.

BENNETT, GEORGE. 'Gold Coast General Election of 1954', *Parliamentary Affairs*, vol. VII (1955), pp. 430–9.

BRADLEY, KENNETH. 'Gold Coast Impressions', *Blackwood's*, vol. CCLXI (1947), pp. 1–9.

BUELL, RAYMOND. 'The Mandates System after Ten Years', *Current History*, vol. XXXI (1929), pp. 545–50.

BUSIA, K. A. 'West Africa in the Twentieth Century', *Journal of World History*, vol. IV (1957), pp. 201–17.

C.R.A.S. 'The R.W.A.F.F. Highway', *Blackwood's*, vol. CCLXI (1947), pp. 238–46.

CARR-GREGG, JOHN. 'Self-rule in Africa: recent advances in the Gold Coast', *International Conciliation*, No. 473 (1951).

CARTLAND, G. B. 'The Gold Coast, an Historical Approach', *African Affairs*, vol. XLVI (1947), pp. 89–97.

CLIFFORD, SIR HUGH. 'The Gold Coast', *Blackwood's*, vol. CCIII (1918), pp. 51–68.

COLEMAN, JAMES S. 'Current Political Movements in Africa', *Annals of the American Academy of Political and Social Science*, vol. CCXCVIII (March 1955), pp. 95–108.

———. 'Togoland', *International Conciliation*, No. 509 (September 1956).

DAVISON, R. B. 'Must Nkrumah Rely on State "Socialism" to Speed Development of Ghana?', *Africa Special Report*, vol. II (September 1957.)

DUBOIS, W. E. 'Black Africa Tomorrow', *Foreign Affairs*, vol. XVII (1938), pp. 100–10.

———. 'The Realities in Africa', *Foreign Affairs*, vol. XXI (1943), pp. 721–32.

FORTES, M. 'Impact of the War on British West Africa', *International Affairs*, vol. XXI (1945), pp. 206–19.

FRY, MAXWELL. 'Town Planning in West Africa', *African Affairs*, vol. XLV (1946), pp. 197–204.

'Ghana Souvenir Number', *West African Review*, vol. XXVIII (March 1957).

HAILEY, BARON WILLIAM MALCOLM. 'Colonies in World Organization', *African Affairs*, vol. XLIV (1945), pp. 54–58.

———. 'Native Administration in Africa', *International Affairs*, vol. XXIII (1947), pp. 336–42.

———. 'Trusteeship in Africa; How the New System Differs from the Old', *African World* (May 1946), pp. 16–18.

HANNIGAN, A. 'Local Government in the Gold Coast', *Journal of African Administration*, vol. VII (1955), pp. 116–23.

HERSKOVITS, MELVILLE. 'Native Self-Government', *Foreign Affairs*, vol. XXII (1944), pp. 413–23.

HUXLEY, ELSPETH. 'British Aims in Africa', *Foreign Affairs*, vol. XXVIII (1949), pp. 43–55.

HUXLEY, JULIAN. 'West African Possibilities', *Yale Review*, vol. XXXIV (1944), pp. 255–69.

JACKSON, BARBARA WARD. 'The Gold Coast, An Experiment in Partnership', *Foreign Affairs*, vol. XXXII (1954), pp. 608–16.

K.G. 'The Gold Coast. Background to the Coussey Report', *The World Today*, vol. VI (1950), pp. 110–19.

McKAY, VERNON. 'British Rule in West Africa', *Foreign Policy Report*, vol. XXIV (June 1948).

———. 'Nationalism in British West Africa', *Foreign Policy Report*, vol. XXIV (March 1948).

MAIR, LUCY PHILIP. 'Chieftainship in Modern Africa', *Africa*, vol. IX (1936), pp. 305–16.

MALINOWSKI, B. 'Pan-African Problem of Culture Contact', *American Journal of Sociology*, vol. XLVIII (1943), pp. 649–65.

MAURY, R. A. 'The Question of Ghana', *Africa*, vol. XXIV (1954), pp. 200–212.

OLLIVIER, BARON SYDNEY. 'Guggisberg', *National Dictionary of Biography*, 1922–30. (London, 1930.)

PAUL, M. E. 'Local Government in Ghana', *West Africa* (September–October 1957.)

PERHAM, MARGERY. 'African Facts and American Criticisms', *Foreign Affairs*, vol. XXII (1944), pp. 44–57.

———. 'The British Problem in Africa', *Foreign Affairs*, vol. XXIX (1951), pp. 637–50.

———. 'Education for Self-Government', *Foreign Affairs*, vol. XXIV (1945), pp. 130–42.

———. 'A Restatement of Indirect Rule', *Africa*, vol. VII (1934), pp. 221–34.

PICKARD-CAMBRIDGE, A. W. 'The Place of Achimota in West African Education', *Journal of the Royal African Society*, vol. XXIX (1940), pp. 143–53.

QUARTEY, P. D. 'Indirect Rule from a Native Viewpoint', *Negro Year-Book, An Annual Encyclopedia of the Negro, 1937–38*. (Tuskegee Institute, Alabama, 1937.)

SALOWAY, SIR REGINALD. 'The New Gold Coast', *International Affairs*, vol. XXXI (1955), pp. 471–80.

SIMNETT, W. E. 'Britain's Colonies in the War', *Foreign Affairs*, vol. XIX (1941), pp. 655–64.

SOUTHON, ARTHUR. 'Gold Coast Methodism: The First Hundred Years, 1835–1935', *Africa*, vol. VIII (1935), pp. 239–40.

'Survey of Local Government in the Gold Coast Since 1947', *Journal of African Administration* (Supplement), vol. IV (1952).

TAGART, E. S. 'The African Chief under European Rule', *Africa*, vol. IV (1931), pp. 63–76.

UNITED AFRICA COMPANY. 'What Cocoa Means to the Economy of the Gold Coast', *Statistical and Economic Review* (September 1948), pp. 1–28.

VITON, ALBERT. 'Postwar Imperialism; A Democratic Solution', *Asia*, vol. LXI (1941), pp. 437–41.

WHITTLESEY, DERWENT. 'British and French Colonial Technique in West Africa', *Foreign Affairs*, vol. XV (1937), pp. 362–73.

WRAITH, RONALD E. 'Local Government Democracy', *West Africa* (September–October 1955).

APPENDIX

Summary of Annual Statistics (selected excerpts) Source: *Digest of Statistics, November 1957* (Accra, 1957)

	Unit	1938	1951	1952	1953	1954	1955	1956	1957
PRODUCTION									
Cocoa: Purchases by crop year[1]	Tons	232,000	262,223	210,663	246,982	210,693	220,198	228,789	264,375
EXTERNAL TRADE									
Imports:									
Total value	£'000	7,867	63,793	66,611	73,803	71,050	87,877	88,920	—
Sterling Area:									
United Kingdom	£'000	4,289	33,951	37,882	42,568	35,990	43,132	43,442	—
Other	£'000	458	4,253	3,618	3,742	4,138	5,725	5,520	—
Non-Sterling Area:									
North America	£'000	835	4,023	5,064	4,535	3,880	4,083	4,305	—
O.E.E.C. Countries and possessions	£'000	1,677	15,759	15,387	17,102	19,264	21,934	22,934	—
Other	£'000	608	5,808	4,659	5,857	7,779	13,003	12,719	—
Volume Index	1948=100	—	168	167	205	208	—	—	—
Volume Index	1954=100	—	—	—	—	100	127	123	—
Exports, includ. re-exports									
Total value	£'000	11,429	91,990	86,377	89,943	114,595	95,661	86,599	—
Sterling Area:									
United Kingdom	£'000	7,505	38,236	34,903	37,648	46,172	38,532	29,948	—
Other	£'000	238	3,268	2,615	3,617	5,019	5,392	5,243	—
Non-Sterling Area:									
North America	£'000	1,417	30,036	25,532	25,398	20,002	17,785	16,843	—
O.E.E.C. Countries and possessions	£'000	2,176	16,648	18,435	19,291	36,009	29,611	32,368	—
Other	£'000	92	3,803	4,892	3,989	7,393	4,341	2,198	—

Volume index	1948 = 100	—	111	108	118	108	—	—	—
Volume index	1954 = 100	—	—	—	—	100	98	111	—
Re-exports	£'000	266	1,990	2,090	1,949	1,363	503	666	—
Balance of visible trade	£'000	3,562	28,197	19,766	16,140	43,519	8,364	2,320	—
Cocoa exports	Th. tons	253·2	229·5	212·0	236·6	214·1	205·9	234·4	—
	£'000	4,541	60,310	52,533	56,143	84,599	65,559	51,063	—
Gold Exports	Th. f.o.t.	677·5	692·3	704·6	732·6	787·9	723·8	599·3	—
	£'000	4,842	8,562	9,238	9,458	9,822	9,052	7,489	—
FINANCE[2]									
Public revenue:									
Total, including extra-ordinary	£'000	3,792	25,455	34,174	42,510	49,942	80,568	64,132	52,456
Indirect taxation	£'000	2,792	16,878	24,841	26,478	31,362	62,388	43,277	29,740
Direct taxation	£'000	—	4,564	5,295	8,522	8,035	7,306	7,617	7,370
Other	£'000	1,000	4,013	4,038	7,511	10,545	10,874	13,239	15,346
Public expenditure:									
Expenditure other than development	£'000	3,637	18,669	36,375	38,481	56,894	79,860	62,208	43,819
Development from surplus assets	£'000	—	3,759	61	—	—	—	—	—
Expenditure from Development Funds	£'000	—	—	6,668	13,765	15,470	14,977	25,269	17,466
Railway Harbour and Port Services[3]									
Revenue	£'000	1,150	3,266	3,598	4,180	4,395	4,560	5,901	5,292
Expenditure, including loan charges	£'000	1,145	2,788	3,614	4,393	4,741	5,173	5,672	4,919

[1] Crop years (October–September) ending in calendar year stated.

[2] With effect from 1956–7 the financial year covers the period 1 July to 30 June. The 1955–6 financial years covers the fifteenth month period 1 April 1955 to 30 June 1956. Prior to 1955–6 financial year figures relate to the period 1 April to 31 March.

[3] Ghana Railway and Takoradi Harbour only until March 1950.

EXPENDITURE OUT OF DEVELOPMENT FUNDS[1]
(£ thousand)

	Plan total	Expenditure to 31 March 1955[2]	1955–6 Actual[3]	1956–7 Actual	Expenditure to 30 June 1957	1957–8	
						July–June Estimates	July–Aug. Actual
Total Expenditure out of Development Funds	127,012·7	50,879·1	25,268·6	17,466·0	93,613·7	17,948·1	2,055·4
Development Fund	84,741·4	46,694·0	20,088·9	12,664·7	79,447·6	5,293·8	870·2
First Plan	79,447·6	46,694·0	20,088·9	12,664·7	79,447·6	—	—
Consolidation Plan[4]	5,293·8	—	—	—	—	5,293·8	870·2
Second Development Fund[5]	13,309·7	29·3	14·9	301·5	345·7	6,631·4	—
Reserve Development Fund	28,961·6	4,155·8	5,164·8	4,499·8	13,820·3	6,022·8	1,185·2
Development Fund and Second Development Fund:							
Ministry of Agriculture	5,832·1	2,447·7	1,423·7	949·1	4,820·4	640·7	46·4
Ministry of Trade	3,461·9	1,470·8	683·1	875·1	3,029·0	388·0	3·8
Ministry of Communications	29,709·7	15,027·7	6,041·2	3,713·6	24,782·6	2,844·8	278·2
Ministry of Works	18,167·0	8,491·4	4,109·5	3,305·3	15,906·2	2,046·5	163·9
Ministry of Defence and External Affairs	3,400·4	1,716·0	666·1	307·4	2,689·5	624·5	7·8
Ministry of Education	17,376·4	9,078·3	2,840·9	985·5	12,904·7	2,313·0	207·9
Ministry of Finance	635·5	—	—	—	—	635·5	41·2
Ministry of Health	5,669·0	3,034·4	1,140·0	498·0	4,672·4	700·0	33·5
Ministries of Interior and Justice	3,394·0	1,728·0	845·2	359·9	2,933·2	452·0	20·3
Ministry of Housing	5,315·1	3,136·3	976·6	637·5	4,750·4	298·0	29·2
Ministry of Local Government	4,813·7	537·8	1,349·1	1,145·6	3,032·5	981·2	37·8
Development Commission	191·5	—	—	187·6	187·6	1·1	0·1
Prime Minister's Office	—	—	—	—	—	—	—
Ministry of Labour and Co-operatives	84·8	54·9	28·4	1·6	84·8	—	0·1

Reserve Development Fund:

Tema Harbour	16,045·6	2,539·8	3,575·4	2,080·0	8,195·2	3,300·0	1,070·0
Tema Township	10,354·2	713·8	1,100·0	1,607·9	3,421·7	2,667·7	108·0
Volta River Project	1,661·8	902·2	489·4	166·9	1,558·5	55·1	7·2
Housing Corporation	900·0	—	—	645·0	645·0	—	—

From April 1951 development expenditure has been charged to the Development Funds. Expenditure on the Development Plan, 1951, which ended at 30 June 1957, was financed from the Development Fund, including the former Special Development Fund; the total spent on projects included in the 1951 Plan prior to April 1951 was £513·8 thousand. Expenditure on the Consolidation Plan, covering the period July 1957 to June 1959, is financed from the Second Development Fund and from balances on uncompleted projects brought forward from the Development Fund.

2 Total expenditure out of Development Funds amounted to £6,667·5 thousand in 1951–2, to £13,765·1 thousand in 1952–3, to £15,469·6 thousand in 1953–4, and to £14,976·9 thousand in 1954–5.

3 Covers the fifteen-month period 1 April 1955 to 30 June 1956.

4 Actual expenditure in 1957–8 also includes expenditure from the Second Development Fund, details of which are not separately available.

5 Expenditure prior to July 1957 represents sums brought forward from this Fund for expenditure on approved projects during the period of the First Plan. For expenditure in 1957–8 see footnote (4) above.

235

INDEX